# CHURCH PLANTING
# **THRESHOLDS**

## A GOSPEL-CENTERED GUIDE

## CLINT CLIFTON

Clint Clifton is a visionary for the modern-day church, especially regarding what God can do through the unique work of church planting. Even better, he's a practitioner: he takes big ideas and makes them practical and imitable for others. I'm grateful he's written down his proven wisdom in this excellent resource. It will be a guide and friend to planters in all stages of planting.

- Christine Hoover, author of *The Church Planting Wife*

This is an excellent, down to earth and practical book on the "how to's" of church planting. There's loads of theoretical stuff being churned out right now, but nothing that helps you really think about the nuts and bolts of this gig. This cheeky little number really deserves a wide audience. I don't know this dude, but I wish he were in the UK because his wisdom and experience would be invaluable here.

- Mez McConnell, author of *Church in Hard Places*, Senior Pastor of Niddrie Community Church, Edinburgh, Scotland & Director of 20schemes

Hardly a conversation in Washington, DC goes by without mentioning the work of Clint Clifton and his church planting network. Clint loves his city and has worked tirelessly to plant churches so more people in the nation's capital can hear the Gospel. This is a book, not written in the ivory tower, but from the trenches of church planting in a difficult region by a man who knows what it takes. This is a book I'd recommend every church planter study and read and then execute.

- Dan Darling, Vice President for Communications for the Ethics and Religious Liberty Commission author of The Original Jesus

My friend Clint Clifton knows church planting. Church planting is not a theoretical exercise for him - it's his life. It's precisely because of this that *Church Planting Thresholds* is such a valuable resource. This book is richly theological and yet intensely practical. It will guide you as you consider your own commitment to church multiplication. I highly recommend that you get this resource!

- Micah Fries, Vice President of LifeWay Research

I wish this book had been available when we planted New Song! We would have gone further, faster, with more joy.

- Hal Seed, Founding Pastor of New Song Church
and author of *The God Questions*

*Church Planting Thresholds* is a fantastic resource. It is comprehensive, specific, applicable, and wise. Clint Clifton has seen everything that a church planter will go through, and has put his experience down on paper for our benefit. I use it to train church planters in my congregation, and I have no doubt it will be useful to any church planter who reads it.

- Mike McKinley, Author of *Church Planting Is for Wimps*
and Sr. Pastor of Sterling Park Baptist Church

What resource is there to help a church planter measure progress and stay on task as he effectively navigates the various stages of church planting? Until recently I would have answered, "There isn't one." But Clint Clifton gives us such a resource. *Thresholds* is a solid work forged through experience, made relevant through personal stories, and able to excite the heart and spirit to embrace one after another after another crucial thresholds in the journey. The genius of this work is that it makes sense. Through ten critical stages, Clifton helps the eager planter chart a course easily measured by simple accomplishments. This tool is not just for the church planter, though. It should be acquired and applied by every church that wants to plant a church again and again and again.

- Randy Ferguson, Director of Church Planter Assessment,
SEND Network, North American Mission Board

You will be hard-pressed to find another man with the vision, drive and passion for the advancement of God's kingdom through church multiplication. Clint has been an incredible gift to the body of Christ In what is arguably the most important city in the world. Already, he has helped plant nearly a dozen churches in the Washington, DC metro area and has quickly become a leading local authority on church revitalization and church planting. What the Lord sent to us, he now also sends to you. *Church Planting Thresholds* is the blueprint that helped our church shift its focus from internal growth to the biblical approach of multiplication. This framework is a biblical model for establishing and sustaining a healthy church plant that is well positioned to reach the world for Christ.

- Lon Solomon, Sr. Pastor of McLean Bible Church

Clint Clifton's voice — full of biblical wisdom and proven in dozens of hardscrabble church plants — comes through loud and clear in this book. This book is practical yet avoids expedient pragmatism. *Thresholds* is for the church planter who yearns for fruit and is willing to pay the price. This book is an easy read, but does not offer an easy ride. Written by a leader with skin in the game, this book will challenge and motivate both new and experienced church planters. Before I finished this book, I began planning how to produce it in other languages. Clint has produced a book that applies to every context.

- Brian Jose, Executive Director of Radstock Ministries

Having had the privilege of watching the life of Clint Clifton from rebellious teenager, to what now is one of the most insightful Gospel-centered church planting leaders in North America, thrills me to no end. I delight to say I was, and in many ways, I still am his pastor. Reading *Church Planting Thresholds* causes me to raise my head to heaven and say one more time, "What a mighty God we serve. " This book should be required reading for every church planter and pastor. It answers so many questions that every planter wonders about, and it compels attention to kingdom work not embraced by most church leaders. It challenges every want-to-be planter to count the cost and every dreamer of personal greatness to consider whose glory is really at stake after all. It is a masterwork, written by one who has paid the price and is leading others to embrace this noble endeavor for Christ.

- Dannie Williams, Sr. Pastor, First Baptist Church of Lyons, GA

Clint Clifton brings both heart and knowledge to the high calling of church planting. As a result of his own experience and through interactions with numerous church planters and church planting teams, Clint has provided a resource that succinctly and strategically speaks to the need in church planting for systematic church development and mission advancement. Just as we take note of our own children's milestones, churches also have key thresholds in their birth, growth, and development. Keep this resource in hand as you pray about God's calling to plant a church, as you are engaged in the early days of church planting, and as you become a part of the movement of churches planting churches.

- Dr. Brian Autry, Executive Director, SBC of Virginia

# CONTENTS

# ACKNOWLEDGMENTS

Jesus saved me. My wife Jennifer gives me courage to attempt things that I don't think I can do. My childhood Pastor, Dannie Williams, and his wife Gwen gave me a passion for the local church. The people that make up Pillar Church of Dumfries are really wonderful – the church was a laboratory for the ideas you'll read about in this book. McLean Bible Church pushed me over the finish line with this project. My amazing kids, Noah, Ruthe, Isaiah and Moses make my life full and fun.

# FOREWORD

*"Son, the resources I've given you aren't just for yourself.
They're not for your church. They're for MY church. And
for MY glory."*

These are the words the Holy Spirit spoke to me as clear as a whistle
during a time of private prayer a year ago.

After serving as the senior pastor of the largest church in the Mid-
Atlantic region for 35 years, I had grown accustomed to doing ministry
on a large-scale. Our church was meeting at five campuses throughout
Maryland and Virginia and boasted an average weekly attendance of
more than 13,000. God had graciously given us an annual budget of $32
million – more than some churches collect in their entire *existence*.

I was proud of all our church had accomplished – not only our size, but
also our impact. By all accounts, we were *thriving*. We had a reputation in
Metro Washington. People knew who we were. We were doing ministry.
Lives were being transformed by the Gospel. Surely, God was pleased.

I was convinced that to continue on this trajectory of growth and
ministry success, we needed to keep our church family expanding. So
when staff approached me with the idea of starting new churches from
our otherwise large and healthy congregation, I was vehemently opposed
to it. In many ways, being the pastor of a large church became part of my
identity, and I was holding on to it for dear life. The last thing I wanted
was for members of our congregation to break off and start new churches.
I only wanted our church to continue to grow.

Looking back, I realize that what I thought was a healthy approach to
church growth, was actually sinful.

Sure, we were a large congregation. Sure, we were doing great things for the Lord, by his grace. But I unknowingly gained the reputation as the "Lone Ranger pastor," because our church, though large and well-resourced, operated in a vacuum. We were completely unaware of all that God was doing in and through other churches in our area.

But like a good father, the Lord lovingly chastened me and exposed my selfish desires as I kneeled that day in prayer. He mercifully brought me face-to-face with my own sin, and for the first time, I saw my arrogance for what it truly was.

There was only one appropriate response – repentance.

That day, I asked God to show me how He wanted to move through *His* church. I promised that if He gave me another chance, I would be a different kind of pastor. I would shepherd our congregation in a way that acknowledged that God was Lord of our church – not me.

Praise God for grace! He heard and answered my prayer! In the months that followed, He revealed His will for our church, and as I sought Him daily, He gave me a new vision to refocus our church around becoming "mighty" in five key areas:

- Mighty in Prayer
- Mighty in Evangelism
- Mighty in Disciple-Building
- Mighty in The Word of God
- Mighty in Serving the Lord

Perhaps most importantly, he showed me that this is not just His vision for *our* church – it is His vision for *THE* church. It struck me suddenly, that The Great Commission is such an enormous burden, that it will take hundreds and thousands of "mighty" churches all across our city, our nation and our world to accomplish it.

This means that when we help revitalize churches with a desire to be faithful to the Gospel, and plant new churches where there is a need for a faithful Gospel witness, we are effectively advancing the Gospel.

This multiplication strategy is not just a good idea. It's also biblical.

In the New Testament, we find the Apostle Paul taking up an offering from the Gentile churches for the church in Jerusalem, which was poor and under-resourced. In 2 Corinthians chapter 8, Paul urged the Corinthian church, in their abundance, to give to help the Jerusalem church. How does he describe it? As a "ministry of service" to the Lord Himself.

Just like the Corinthian church, the Lord has blessed the American church with abundance that many churches throughout the world will never know. Our blessing is not just for us. It is so that His glory may be proclaimed in our cities and among the nations.

I know that my change of heart could have only been the work of the Holy Spirit. All at once, partnering with other churches became imperative, only we didn't know where to start. And so we again sought the Lord in prayer, and He sent us Clint Clifton.

I promise you will be hard-pressed to find another man with the vision, drive and passion for the advancement of God's kingdom through church multiplication. Clint has been an incredible gift to the body of Christ in what is arguably the most important city in the world. Already, he has helped plant nearly a dozen churches in the Washington, DC metro area and has quickly become a leading local authority on church revitalization and church planting.

What the Lord sent to us, he now also sends to you. *Church Planting Thresholds* is the blueprint that helped our church shift its focus from internal growth to the biblical approach of multiplication. This framework is a biblical model for establishing and sustaining a healthy church plant that is well positioned to reach the world for Christ.

I should know. Earlier this year, we used the *Church Planting Thresholds* model at McLean Bible Church to launch the New City Network, our church planting and revitalization collective. By God's grace, we hope to launch 30 churches in our first year of church planting alone, and we owe much of what we have learned to the work of the Holy Spirit and the incredible way God has gifted and wired Clint.

Brothers and sisters, I believe God is ready to spark revival in His church throughout our country. And like all revivals, it will begin with prayer and hearts that are completely surrendered to Him.

My prayer for you as you read this book is that the Holy Spirit will clearly show you your role in the advancement and multiplication of His church. I pray that He will raise up the next generation of godly leaders who desire nothing more than to "make known his deeds among the peoples (Psalm 105:1)." And I eagerly await the day the Scriptures speak of in Ephesians 5:27, when Christ will present "to Himself a glorious church, not having spot or wrinkle or any such thing, but that she should be holy and without blemish." Amen!

For His Fame,
Lon Solomon

# INTRODUCTION

Jesus saved me through the ministry of a moderately-sized, perfectly ordinary church in my hometown. I started going to church for less than pure motives—I was chasing a girl. To my surprise, I ultimately found Jesus more attractive than any girl. After a period of time, Jesus saved me and set my life on a trajectory for gospel ministry.

Looking back on the last twenty years of my Christian life, I can say with sincerity that no institution has had as much lasting and dramatic impact on my life as the church I was a part of when I became a Christian. Peniel Baptist Church in Palatka, Florida, discipled me, loved me, and rebuked me. They hammered me into the rough form of a man I am now.

One of the most significant contributions they made in my life was their modeling a greater concern for the growth of the Kingdom of God than for the growth of their own congregation. The church regularly sent out teams of people to form new congregations in places that were lacking, and they did all they could to see that other churches in their community also thrived. This, I have learned, is an incredibly unique posture for a local church to take.

Almost immediately after I became a Christian, I began serving in various capacities in the churches we were planting. In one I'd play the guitar; for another I'd participate in door-to-door evangelism. The opportunities were endless because there were new congregations forming all the time, and the laborers were few. The message was clear to me: *Churches make disciples and disciples make churches.* I resolved that's how I wanted to spend my life. So, that's what I did. I went to college then seminary, and within a few weeks of graduating from seminary, I began working to plant Pillar Church near Quantico, Virginia, the crossroads of the US Marine Corps, in the suburbs of Washington DC.

From the earliest days of our church, we determined to measure our success by our sending capacity rather than our seating capacity, thus aligning the primary mission of our local church with the primary mission of Jesus' universal church: making disciples of all nations. This emphasis has required us to put a tremendous amount of energy and resources into the founding of other churches. It has also required us to intentionally choose the spread of the Gospel over our own numeric growth. Since our church's first worship service in 2005, we have had a hand in planting more than a dozen new churches, with several more preparing to begin. Many of the men we have sent to plant new churches began as members of our church, laymen working in non-ministerial occupations. About half of these men still have no seminary training, and they had no aspirations to plant a church before joining Pillar. That's not to say that the men are not well-trained or competent for the work. They are faithful and godly men with a love for the Gospel, good character, and an undeniable ability to *"rightly divide the Word of truth"* (2 Timothy 2:15).

I don't say these things to brag about Pillar Church but to emphasize that church planting is not just a sport for megachurches with multimillion-dollar budgets. I'm often asked how large a church should be when it begins to plant another church or how much it costs to start a new church. These questions, as well-intentioned as they might be, are the wrong questions. Here's the right question: At what age and size is a church responsible to begin obeying the Great Commission in Matthew 28:18-20?

The Great Commission is the duty of every church regardless of size, demographic, or budget. The Great Commission does not say, "Go ye therefore and make disciples of all nations, baptizing them in the name of the Father, Son, and Holy Spirit as soon as you have the money" or "as soon as you have more than 500 people." The command stands for every New Testament church, period.

In my observation, only one resource is necessary for a church to begin planting another church, and it has nothing to do with buildings or budgets. That one necessary resource is a ready leader. Churches are planted by missionary-pastors sent by Kingdom-building churches. So, if you've picked up this book looking for the church planting silver bullet, here it is. The only thing you absolutely must have in order to plant a new church is a scripturally qualified, missionary-pastor to send.

In our current environment, the majority of evangelical churches in North America do not attempt to plant other new churches. American churches have been far too busy with ministry to give much thought to mission. Church planting has been about as regularly practiced as foot washing and street preaching, but that seems to be changing. A noticeable surge in church planting has taken place over the past few decades. Many denominations and networks are offering resources and training to those wishing to plant new churches. Colleges and seminaries are developing programs in church planting, and a small library of church planting books and training materials are now in print.

But as denominations, networks, and seminaries get on the bandwagon, let us not forget that church planting is the responsibility of the local church much more than it is the responsibility of any network, denomination, individual, para-church ministry, or educational institution. Our greatest potential for Kingdom growth is found in local churches, whose elders and members dedicate themselves to equipping and sending members to establish new churches in communities that need them. Local churches are better positioned to start new churches than any other organization on the planet. In the same way that a mother would give birth to a child, churches most naturally give birth to churches. Denominations and para-church organizations are tremendous resources for the church planter and should be utilized to the extent that they are helpful, but these organizations should never replace the local church as central figure in church establishment and renewal. That is not to say that denominations and networks are completely unsuccessful in the endeavor to start new churches or that churches planted by such organizations are illegitimate. However, churches are the normal and natural means for starting other new churches.

The aim of this writing is to assist healthy, Christ-centered churches through the process of starting other new churches. The stages proposed in this material were developed through the joyous and sometimes painful experiences I have had leading a small church to reproduce aggressively. They are meant to be a general guide for pastors and churches wishing to prepare leaders for a ministry in church planting.

## Stages in the Church Planting Process

Church planting is extremely difficult and discouraging work. It is the sacred equivalent of starting a small business with only a slightly better success rate. According to the Small Business Administration, about half of all new businesses survive for five years or more, and about one-third survive ten years or more.[1] New churches fare slightly better through the upstart difficulties. The North American Mission Board's Center for Missional Research reports that 99% of church plants survive the first year, 92% the second year, 81% the third year, and 68% the fourth year.[2] With one out of three church planters giving up on their calling before their 5th year, every person entering the field of church planting should do so with an appropriate level of humility and trepidation. Church planting is fraught with difficulties. Remember that your continual prayer, your reliance on God's direction, and your faithful obedience will be crucial at each and every stage in the process.

Church planters are missionaries who face relentless spiritual attacks from Satan and his demons. By its very nature, the church is an organization that Satan hates. Churches help Christians cleave to Christ and resist Satan and his schemes (2 Corinthians 2:11). The church is an organization that teaches the Word of God (1 Timothy 5:17), which is the very thing Christians use to wage war against Satan. Satan's archenemy, Jesus, is the head of the church; so don't think for one minute that your church planting work will go unnoticed by the *"ruler of this present world"* (John 12:31). The very last thing Satan wants is a healthy, faithful, and vibrant new church.

As if that weren't frightening enough, the "goods and services" offered by Jesus' church, apart from the Spirit of God, are not of interest to our world. If given the choice, most communities would choose a new convenience store over a new church. Churches are seen as out of touch, a waste of otherwise taxable land, and a general nuisance to civic authorities. In nearly every vein of modern American life, both in the city and in the suburbs, our nation is spitting in the face of Christianity.

## Tenacity

If you're going to plant a new church or lead your church to plant a new church, you will have to maintain a deep resolve to endure the difficulties ahead. Church planting requires an unwavering commitment to preach, pray, evangelize, and stay. There will be many moments along the way when you will want to quit—I have certainly faced those times—but the best church planters I know are not the guys who started churches that grew to hundreds or thousands in a few short years, but they are those who continued faithfully through adversity. If you are thinking of starting a new church, I encourage you to work through the worksheet in Appendix B.

This book is organized around ten stages in the process of planting a new church. Each stage, especially the first eight, should be accomplished before moving on to the next stage. Skipping a stage or moving on before reaching the "thresholds" of any given stage will weaken the outcome and could endanger the church's sustainability or long-term effectiveness. Think of these stages as a series of doors. Behind each you will find the keys to the next.

Don't allow yourself to grow hasty in the process of building God's church. The work is too important and the stakes are too high. **My experience planting churches and helping others plant churches has convinced me that the majority of problems new churches face stem from a compromise made in the church's formation.** Completing these stages will not ensure that the church you are attempting to plant will survive, but it will increase the odds that you avoid a pitfall along the way.

## Thresholds

Since there are a number of definitions for the word "threshold," I'll explain exactly what I mean. A threshold is "a level, point, or value above which something is true or will take place and below which it is not or will not"[3] For each stage to be considered complete, there is a minimum threshold that must be reached.

Let me use a monetary example to explain. If you're starting a church and plan to meet in a school or other rental facility, you will have to pay rent and insurance costs. Let's say $1,000 per month. If you're planning to earn your living as a church planter, you will have personnel costs. Let's say $2,500 per month. If you're planning to hold Bible studies, you will have curriculum costs—$200 per month. If you're planning to save money for a future church planting effort, you need money for that—$300 per month. All of these needs add up to a particular dollar amount, and in this case it is $4,000. So $4,000 is the minimum amount you will need to accomplish all the things you plan to do. That's the threshold. If your income falls below your threshold, you will be forced to do one of two things: settle for a less expensive and potentially less effective meeting facility, even though you know it's not the best idea; or make a worse compromise by totally scrapping something that you believe will be good for the new church.

Neither abandoning nor adjusting your plan will get you any closer to planting this new church. Therefore, the thresholds are necessary in order to accomplish the aspirations you have for this new church. As you work through this material, you will notice that each stage in the planting process is associated with a number of thresholds. In most cases you, the church planter, in agreement with the elders of your sending church, should set these thresholds. The elders of your sending church, in addition to your mentor, will have the responsibility of holding you accountable to the thresholds when you are tempted to abandon or adjust them. Remember that thresholds are minimum requirements for moving on to the next step of the process. Exceeding the minimum thresholds is advisable when possible. As with most things in life, each stage will likely cost more and take longer than you expect. Having a little extra on hand at each step is prudent stewardship.

In Appendix A you will find a checklist with all of the thresholds listed. You should use this list to keep track of your progress. You will also find the thresholds throughout the chapters. Some of the thresholds are simple tasks that can be completed with relative ease, and others will take a long time and a lot of effort to complete. When you set a threshold, you should write it down in pen and not change it without consulting the leaders of your sending church. This will help you measure progress and stay on task as you work through the stages.

## The Sending Church

I encourage you to fight the temptation to do this work alone. If a healthy church is sending you, seek the guidance of the church's elders as you work through the stages and determine the thresholds. Communicate regularly with them and tell them when you are ready to move from one stage to another.

Keep in mind that the leaders of your sending church are likely occupied with matters related to the health and well-being of their own congregation. It is your responsibility to keep them informed of both the struggles and successes you experience along the way. This is particularly important if you are a young church planter or new to pastoral ministry. Young and inexperienced planters often have an independent rebellious streak, which is almost always sinful.

I know one church planter, "John," who was a well-loved associate pastor at "Community Church" in his city. The ministry at this church had grown rapidly during his tenure, and both the staff and the congregation loved Pastor John. After serving at the church for a few years, Pastor John grew restless and began considering starting a new church. John went to Senior Pastor Bill to share the news of his new calling. Unlike most senior pastors, Bill responded with excitement. He promised to do all he could to lead Community Church to support John's new work. With the endorsement of his senior pastor, John began sharing his dream with the rest of the staff and the congregation of Community Church. Excitement started to brew around the church for John's new ministry. Community Church gave John a "hunting license" telling him he was free to recruit members from within the congregation to join his core team. As if that weren't enough, Community Church promised to support him financially until the church got off the ground. John recruited hard, attempting to gather as much support as possible to launch his new church. When all was said and done, John had a large team from Community Church.

Of course, with all the momentum, the new church grew rapidly. John let all the success go to his head. He honestly believed that the success of the ministry was because of his outstanding leadership and charismatic preaching. It wasn't long before John's team began returning to Community Church. When they returned, they were shocked to find that Community Church was still struggling to recover from the loss of resources and members that left with Pastor John. The members who returned spoke negatively of John's leadership and warned the members of Community Church against planting more churches. A few years later, another man at Community Church felt God's call to plant a church. With memories of Pastor John still fresh in their minds, Community Church opted not to plant again.

A shortsighted church planter sees his job as simply to plant a church. Church planters should work hard to maintain good relationships with their sending and supporting churches so that those churches will endeavor to plant more churches in the future. Plainly speaking, if you're planting a new church with the support of a more established one, you should both submit to and support your sending church as well as you can throughout the process.

## Paul's Example

Consider the example of the Apostle Paul. His ministry was characterized by concern for the churches; he faced *"daily pressure"* and *"anxiety"* for them (2 Corinthians 11:28-29). The churches of Macedonia gave sacrificially so that the Gospel would take root in Corinth. At one point Paul actually says, *"I robbed other churches by accepting support from them in order to serve you"* (2 Corinthians 11:8). Another time Paul writes to urge the Corinthians to take an offering for the saints in Jerusalem—the sending church. Follow Paul's example here as you prepare to plant a new church. Recklessly pillaging your sending church's resources may look like success in the short run, but it will be detrimental to Kingdom growth in the long run.

Maintaining a good relationship with your sending church will have its fair share of challenges, but don't give up on the process. Little else will contribute more to the long-term health of this new church than the advice and wisdom offered by godly men who know you and who share a vested interest in your personal well-being and the success of this new church.

Never lose sight of the fact that churches plant churches. You are an extension of the ministry of your sending church. Church planting is a team sport, not an individual sport. Churches with singular leadership stand vulnerable to the schemes of the devil and are susceptible to innumerable strains of church cancer. If you can't get on the same page with other godly men now, you won't be able to later when you have new, local leaders. Work through difficulties together. And as always, *"mutually submit to one another out of reverence for Christ"* (Ephesians 5:21).

# CONFIRM

Watching church planters get started reminds me of my favorite boyhood pastime: visiting the local public pool. My buddies and I would hike to the pool in our hometown for hours of unsupervised leisure. The best part of going to the pool was watching inexperienced divers rocket from the spring-loaded diving board perched four feet above the water's surface. Some slid gracefully into the water like an Olympic diver, while others delivered belly flops worthy of YouTube.

Although it's impossible to accurately predict which church planters will be effective and which ones will flop, there are factors that contribute to the success or failure of a new church. In my opinion, the most significant factor is the calling of the church planter. If you miss this, the consequences will be traumatic. At a minimum, it will mean years of misery for you and for those who have the misfortune of attending your church. In the 1890s, the great British theologian and preacher, Charles Spurgeon, advised his students:

> Do not enter the ministry if you can help it. …We must feel that woe is unto us if we preach not the gospel; the word of God must be unto us as fire in our bones, otherwise, if we undertake the ministry, we shall be unhappy in it, shall be unable to bear the self-denials incident to it, and shall be of little service to those among whom we minister.[4]

I spent a lot of time thinking about Spurgeon's advice before coming to the conclusion that no other pursuit was an option for me. I had a sincere aspiration to the office of elder (1 Timothy 3:1) and met the biblical qualifications (1 Timothy 3:1-7; Titus 1:5-9; 1 Peter 5:1-4). I was then affirmed and sent out by the leadership of my local church. I could say with confidence that I was called to the ministry of church planting, and more importantly, others could also attest to my calling.

Over the years, I have met and talked with a lot of people interested in starting new churches, many already serving in some form of ministry. In these conversations, I have encountered pastors who see church planting as the solution to all of their ministry problems. Sometimes it is a restless youth pastor who is sick of "babysitting teenage reprobates" or an associate pastor who is hoping to take the next step up in the ministry ladder or even a senior pastor ready to hand his sheep over to the neighborhood wolf because of their waywardness. Other times, desperate for a more sacred occupation, a potential church planter will rise from the secular labor pool with a vision of ministry as the nearest off ramp from a job headed nowhere. The prospect of planting a new church can be enticing to those wearied from their current work, but neither restlessness, passion, nor frustration constitute a calling.

In Appendix B you'll find an Abandonment Worksheet that will help you consider what circumstances might cause you to abandon the work of church planting. Work through this with your spouse and share your findings with the leaders of your sending church.

> I have completed the Abandonment Worksheet.

If you believe God has called you to plant a new church or to revitalize an old one, the calling must go deeper than a restlessness and frustration with your current circumstances. If you find yourself contemplating a public ministry, confirm your calling by making sure you have genuine aspiration, scriptural adequacy, and the affirmation of a healthy church.

## Aspiration

In 1 Timothy 3:1, the Apostle Paul prefaces his list of qualifications for an elder with this statement: *"If anyone aspires to the office of overseer, he desires a noble task."* The Greek word translated as "aspire" means "to stretch one's self out in order to touch or to grasp for something."[5] The word "desire" means to "long for" or "lust after."[6] Paul is saying that to be fit for the job of elder, one must stretch for it and lust after it. God is a master at producing desire where there once was apathy. The same God who wired men to desire women, and sharks to long for blood, will grant you a voracious appetite for the spread of the Gospel. The psalmist felt this passion when he said, *"I would rather be a doorkeeper in the house of my God than dwell in the tents of wickedness"* (Psalm 84:10). Peter and John felt it when they said to their captors, *"We cannot stop speaking of what we have seen and heard"* (Acts 4:20). This is the kind of gut-level drive you will need to plant a new church.

We need more soldier-like, brave, faith-filled, "whatever-it-takes," missionary type of pastors like those in the book of Acts. Such mighty men of God are rare today. Instead, a milder, more professional counterpart has emerged. "Professionalism," John Piper writes, "has nothing to do with the essence and heart of the Christian ministry. The more professional we long to be, the more spiritual death we will leave in our wake. For there is no professional child-likeness, there is no professional tender-heartedness. There is no professional panting after God."[7] As one entering this line of work, you must ask yourself whether your aspiration is to make Christ known or to make yourself known.

The life of a churchman is a life of service and sacrifice. In order to properly put Jesus on display, we must be willing to remain unseen. No biblical figure gives us a clearer picture of this kind of worship than Jesus' forerunner, John the Baptist. John's life was marked out for a single, simple, self-proclaimed purpose: *"to prepare the way of the Lord"* (Matthew 3:3). John dedicated his entire ministry to the unveiling of Jesus. When asked whether he were Elijah or the prophet, John replied, *"I am the voice of one crying out in the wilderness, 'Make straight the way of the Lord'"* (John 1:23). Though he had plenty of opportunity to gain glory for himself, John understood the beauty and glory of Christ and considered himself unworthy to even unstrap the sandals from Jesus' feet (John 1:27). When Jesus arrived, all attention turned from John; John was no longer the focus of the spotlight. At the moment when he was completely upstaged by Jesus, John proclaims in utter delight, *"This joy of mine is now complete"* (John 3:29).

Have you ever seen the man who draws the curtain for a theater performance? Probably not. He hides away in the darkness so he doesn't distract your attention from the stage. If he has done his job properly, he presents the stage while staying out of the spotlight. Likewise, if your ministry is fruitful, Jesus will stand center stage while you are hidden in the shadows. If this is the life that you long for, then there's a good chance you have a true aspiration for ministry.

Since you're the only one who can explore your own motives, only you can approve this threshold. Spend some time testing your motives, and ask for the honest opinion of others who know you well. Ask yourself lots of questions. What are your true motivations for planting a church? What if God calls you somewhere you don't want to go? Will you continue to work for Christ even if your ministry isn't successful in human terms?

## Adequacy

At first glance, the qualifications of a church planter may seem different from an elder in a more established church. But since the church planter will be in a role of shepherding and giving oversight, the same qualifications for an elder laid out in 1 Timothy 3 and Titus 1 apply. The Bible cites more than 25 qualifications for the elder. Scripture is emphatic that these are essential qualities for the man of God who will lead a local congregation.

In Appendix C you will find a Scriptural Adequacy Worksheet designed to help you assess whether you meet the qualifications found in Scripture. Rate yourself; if married have your spouse rate you; then ask a mentor to rate you. Encourage them to answer honestly, and then compare the ratings to help you determine if you are, in fact, scripturally qualified for pastoral ministry.

> I have completed the Scriptural Adequacy Worksheet.

In addition to the scriptural qualifications given in God's Word, there are some secondary qualities commonly found in fruitful church planters. Scripture does not mandate these qualities, thus you shouldn't consider them mandatory either. However, it is wise for aspiring church planters who lack these qualities to work diligently to develop these areas and seek the help of those who obviously posses these qualities.

- **Evangelistic Fervor** – All Christians should evangelize because Scripture commands us to do so. With that said, we all know that there are some Christians who share their faith more readily than others. Since the ministry of church planting is so tightly connected to winning lost people to Christ, a church planter who struggles in the area of personal evangelism will find church planting particularly difficult and frustrating. If you struggle with boldness, clarity, or consistency in sharing the Gospel with non-Christians, this is an area where you will need to strive to grow before you plant a church.

- **Initiative** – Church planting requires a great deal of initiative. If you're a person who needs clear directives from a supervisor in order to make progress in your work, church planting will prove to be challenging for you. A church planter must be a blend of missionary and pastor. To successfully plant a new church you will have to initiate many conversations, relationships, and partnerships.

- **Tenacity** – As I've already mentioned a few times, church planting is difficult. If you give up easily or grow discouraged quickly, church planting will be nearly impossible. Starting a new church in a community that doesn't want one is an uphill battle. Some of the most effective church planters I know are also some of the most stubborn people I know. They have the unique ability to press through problems rather than retreating from them. They don't easily take "no" for an answer, and, even when they do, they often find another way to get the job done. It's a delicate balance to possess these qualities and still be winsome, humble, and holy. If you are not comfortable with confrontation or challenging interpersonal situations, you won't like church planting at all; it's full of them.

- **Vision** – The church you are planting doesn't yet exist; therefore, much of your early progress will rest on your ability to describe your prospective church to those willing to listen. This is particularly important for stages two through four of the church planting process. A friend once advised me that no one wants to be the last person to write a check to a dying organization. If people don't believe that your church will actually come to fruition, they are extremely unlikely to support it or participate in it. Visionary leadership is especially important in recruiting Christians to serve on your core team and for soliciting support from churches, individuals, and other organizations. In order to stay motivated, these people require consistent reminders about the gospel work this new church is accomplishing. Without those reminders, they are likely to lose interest and abandon the work.

Consider Charles Spurgeon's pointed words to his students:

I have met ten, twenty, a hundred brethren, who have pleaded that they were sure, quite sure that they were called to the ministry—they were quite certain of it, because thy had failed in everything else…. The ministry needs the very best of men, and not those who cannot do anything else. A man who would succeed as a preacher would probably do right well either as a grocer or a lawyer or anything else. A really valuable minister would have excelled at anything. There is scarcely anything impossible to a man who can keep a congregation together for years, and be the means of edifying them for hundreds of consecutive Sabbaths; he must be possessed of some abilities, and be by no means a fool or ne'er-do-well. Jesus Christ deserves the best men to preach his cross, and not the empty-headed and the shiftless…. If we can endure all these (browbeating, weariness, slander, jeering, and hardship, being made the offscouring of all things and being treated as nothing for Christ's sake), we have some of those points, which indicate the possession of the rare qualities, which should meet in a true servant of the Lord Jesus Christ.[8]

Spurgeon knew from experience the hardships and challenges that ministry brings. He did not want his students entering ministry lightly. You should not enter it lightly either.

In summary, I advise you to carefully and prayerfully study 1 Timothy 3:1-7, Titus 1:5-9 and 1 Peter 5:1-4 regarding the biblical qualifications of an elder. After you study, take some time to compare the biblical qualifications to your life. Next, consider whether God has naturally endowed you with an apostolic gift. Your fitness for this job will depend both on your adherence to the biblical qualifications of a pastor and the initiative you employ as an apostle. This is true for both those who plant and for those who revitalize churches. Revitalization requires an equal level of initiative. Until you have properly equipped the saints for the work of the ministry (Ephesians 4:12), you must do the work of the ministry. As the size of your congregation grows, so does your responsibility to equip those under your care. The wise churchman will pay close attention to this shift and manage his time accordingly. If you meet the biblical qualifications of an elder and possess an apostolic gift, you are likely to have a good experience with church planting.

> I, as well as others who know me well, believe that I have the evangelistic fervor, initiative, tenacity, and vision to plant a church.

## Missionary + Pastor = Church Planter

Most jobs have a static job description; the job is the same in the first year as it is in the fifth year. Church planting is not one of these jobs! When you start planting a church, you are a missionary, or at least you should be. Missionaries baptize, teach, and make disciples (Matthew 28:19-20). Pastors, on the other hand, work to equip Christians for the day-to-day work of ministry (Ephesians 4:12). Both of these jobs are important. If you perform only the duties of a pastor in the first year of your church planting and avoid missionary activities, you're likely to find that you're new church won't grow very much.

The bottom line is that the needs of a church change as the church matures. The church planter must also change. The chart below depicts the gradual shift a founding pastor should make over the first few years of a church's life.

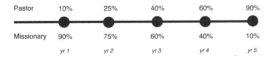

Church planters with a strong missionary gifting will be right at home with evangelism and leadership development but struggle with daily pastoral work such as discipleship, sermon preparation, administration, and counseling. On the other hand, church planters with a strong pastoral gifting will likely be inclined to spend all their time caring for the concerns of core team members, leaving little time for building relationships with those far from God. It will help to do some self-evaluation to get a good handle on how you are inclined. In the early stages of a new church, missionary engagement is essential. As you win people to Christ, the church's pastoral needs will require more of your attention.

## Affirmation

Finally, affirmation of the church itself is the indispensable third confirmation you should seek. Though you may believe God is calling you to plant a new church, if the elders and members of your current church don't agree, this is a major red flag and should result in slowing down the church planting process, if not ending it all together. The local church is the means by which God will expand His Kingdom. Denominations and para-church organizations are tremendous resources for the church planter and should be utilized to the extent that they are helpful, but these organizations cannot replace the local church as the central authority in the establishment and renewal of the local church. Seek help from godly individuals who know you well, and employ them to give you an honest assessment of your weaknesses. Ask them difficult questions. Do you consider me to be self-controlled? Do you think I am a good manager of my household? Listen to the answers they give, and take their suggestions and evaluations to heart.

Many planters worry that a close relationship with their sending church will somehow stifle what God has called them to accomplish. In fact, the opposite is true. A church planter needs the guidance, wisdom, and assistance of a mature congregation and a faithful body of leaders to help make difficult decisions and to guide the wild heart of a church planter. It has become increasingly popular for planters to gather monetary support from many local churches but accept instruction from none of them. The church planter should only consider planting when the leadership and congregation of his local church commission him to do so. In Appendix D you will find Sample Church Planter Commitments, designed to begin clarifying expectations between the church planter and his sending church. Use this document as a guide to create clear expectations between you and the leaders of your sending church.

> I have reviewed the Sample Church Planter Commitments and have agreed on something similar with my sending church's elders.

## Is My Church Healthy?

If you are not part of a healthy local church, it is especially important for you to be part of one before attempting to plant one. Many planters confuse the call to plant a new church with the restlessness they feel while being a part of an unhealthy one. If you find yourself in this situation, join a healthier congregation.

Perhaps you're not sure how healthy your current church is. Consider these diagnostic questions to help you consider the health of your current congregation.

- Does my church teach biblical doctrine?
- Does my church have godly leaders?
- Does my church communicate the Gospel clearly?
- Does my church view other churches as competitors or allies?
- Do the elders and pastors of my church make themselves available to me for mentorship and discipleship?

- Would my church attempt to rescue me if I fell into grievous sin?
- Are the members of my church generally maturing in their relationship with Christ?

If you can't answer these questions affirmatively, you are not part of a healthy church. You should realign yourself with a healthy church, and seek to live out this passion through the ministry of that church. Then, at a pace the leaders of that congregation are comfortable with, work with them to plant a new church.

My home church has developed a Prospective Church Planter Questionnaire that we use to get to know those who are interested in entering pastoral ministry. You can find this resource in Appendix E. If your church doesn't already have something similar, use it as a guide to share with them details about your aspirations, experiences, and theological positions.

> I have completed the Prospective Church Planter Questionnaire and given it to the leaders of my sending church.

## Spousal Affirmation

Your spouse can also be of great help to you as you seek to affirm your calling. Once I gave my wife a description of four types of Christian men: the Slug, the Ant, the Bear, and the Dog. I described each of them in great detail so that she could easily identify me. I asked her to be honest and tell me which one I most resembled. I was shocked when she described me as an Ant, whose good deeds and religious piety monopolize his life, leaving no room for his ministry in the home. (Ouch!) My perception of myself and my wife's perception of me were worlds apart. Because she is part of the church and one who knows you well, allow your wife the freedom to confirm or deny your fitness to the office, and don't be frustrated with her if she questions your calling.

> My wife has affirmed my desire to plant a new church and is prepared to join me in the work of church planting.

## Make it Public

Once the leaders of your church have agreed to send you to plant a new church, it is important that they communicate this decision to the congregation. Our church accomplishes this by holding a public ordination service. The service is preceded by a public defense of the planter's doctrinal positions, philosophy of ministry, and position on marriage and family. For more information about the ordination process, refer to the Ordination Process in Appendix F.

Ask your sending church to publicly affirm your church planting plans. This will change the relationship between you and the congregation and catalyze many good conversations with other members in the future. I have found that nothing promotes missional zeal in my congregation more than ordinary members being called, prepared, and commissioned for a life of ministry.

Once you have confirmed your aspiration to ministry and your scriptural qualification and have received affirmation from your sending church, you can begin the work of church planting.

> My church has formally and publicly committed
> to send me to plant a new church.

## Pastoral Ministry is an Honor

As you prepare, regularly remind yourself that there is no greater honor in this life than to serve King Jesus by building His church on earth.

At times we can delude ourselves into thinking that we earned our position or that we deserve it. This is a satanic lie. You belong wholly to King Jesus. He created you and then bought you with His own blood. He may send you any place He wishes any time He wishes, and, when He does, you should joyfully obey Him. When you arrive wherever He sends you, work hard for Him and obey every command He gives you. Do not abandon His call, no matter how difficult the conditions may be or how discouraged you may become. God will accomplish His purposes through you and in you, and He is not obligated to reveal them to you beforehand. Serving others is the privilege of every good pastor. Do it joyfully. Remember that when you serve sinful people, you are imitating your Savior who served joyfully and suffered along the way.

Beware, your vain heart will tell you that your flock is too small and your potential underutilized. This too is a lie. If you'd gotten what you deserved, you'd be doing something far less meaningful in someplace far less pleasant. Every person God sends you has a soul and was entrusted to you by Christ. When you stand before Him on that great day, you will give account for your treatment of each and every one of them, so care for them as children. If, by chance, for this excellent work you ever receive a wage or an honor, it will be a wage and an honor you were afforded only because of Christ. Wake every morning and breathe a grateful prayer to God, for He knit you together (Psalm 139:13), resurrected your lifeless heart (Ezekiel 36:26), and *"judged you faithful, appointing you to his service"* (1 Timothy 1:12).

# PREPARE

braham Lincoln famously said, "Give me six hours to chop down a tree, and I will spend the first four sharpening the axe." That quote is a good summary of the advice that I'm going to give you in this chapter. Your family and your faithfulness will be severely tested as you attempt to plant a new church. Withstanding those trials will depend largely on how prepared you are for them before they come. Soon you'll be busy writing sermons and planning outreach events, but before you turn your attention to those things, I advise you to take a hard look at the health of your family and your inner life.

Church planting is difficult. It's difficult because resources are scarce, discouragement creeps in, and we live in a day and age when churches are not generally viewed as relevant or meaningful. Telling someone you are planting a new church sounds to most people about like telling them you've come to open an apothecary or a soda stand. People don't generally believe that churches do anything meaningful or offer anything good to society. Most North Americans feel like there are already too many churches. In addition, Satan is actively working to sabotage your efforts. Ultimately, we know that he will not prevail, but it sure seems like he has the upper hand at times along the way.

Satan knows that your church's purity, effectiveness, and vision will be directly related to your personal spiritual health, your inner life. This fact alone puts you in the crosshairs of satanic attack. In this section, we're going to explore some very practical ways for you to protect yourself, your church, and your family from falling victim to the schemes of the evil one.

I don't mean to alarm you with all this talk about Satan. We know that God is *"with you always"* as you seek to make disciples of all nations (Matt 28:20) and that *"He who is in you is greater than the one who is in the world"* (1 John 4:4). So there is no reason for us to be fearful or timid, but there is reason for us to be careful.

For this reason, let me strongly encourage you to make your sending church's leaders aware of all the areas of temptation to which you are particularly susceptible. Knowing these "soft spots" will help them provide appropriate accountability and oversight. In Appendix E you'll find the Prospective Church Planter Questionnaire. Before beginning a partnership with a church planter, our church asks each planter to complete and submit this document to help identify some of these areas of weakness.

## Family and Flock

Your family is your proving ground as a pastor. If you are a good pastor to your wife and kids, you'll probably be a good pastor to more people as well. On the other hand, if you don't care for the souls of those under your own roof, you're not likely to care well for your neighbor's soul. Paul seems to share this belief when he asks, *"If someone does not know how to manage his own household, how can he care for God's church?"* (1 Timothy 3:5). Becoming a pastor to your family is the ultimate test of your suitability for pastoring a church. As a pastor, your family is the most visible display of the Gospel that you have.

No matter how strong of a Christian you consider yourself to be, you are only as faithful as you are in the home. Home is the hardest place to consistently live a life that pleases God and displays the good fruits given by the Holy Spirit. Our deepest relationships are with members of our own household. Family relationships produce stress, pain, joy, and emotion unmatched in any other arena of life. For the Christian, marriage and child-rearing are spiritual disciplines designed not to make us happy, as we commonly think, but to make us holy. Every aspect of marriage—the good, the bad, and the ugly—is given by God to help us understand and love Him more. A man who can consistently love, protect, and teach those who regularly sin against him is well-suited for the position of pastor.

If I had a dollar for every time someone has advised me not to "sacrifice my family on the altar of ministry," I could buy all the materials necessary to build such an altar. I know those who advise me this way mean well, but ministry and family are not in competition with one another. I could stack the benefits of ministering alongside my family far above the advantages of shielding my family from the work and pain of ministering to others.

It's ironic that we celebrate Hannah and Abraham for their willingness to lay their offspring down on the altar, yet we advise our ministers to do the opposite. Hannah carried Samuel to the temple with the rest of her offerings as soon as he was weaned (1 Samuel 1:24). We exalt her faith and figuratively join her in our commitment to give our children to the Lord. Yet, in our own homes, we strive for a balance between ministry and family. What about Abraham? He actually led his son up a mountain to sacrifice him in obedience to God (Genesis 22). How many times have we celebrated Abraham's faith from the pulpit but neglected his example in the home?

Living a life of familial sacrifice yields long-term benefits to your church and your children. Some parents believe that the more education and extracurricular activity provide for their children, the happier and healthier they will be. They wrongly assume that simply involving them in student government and making sure they are well socialized will insure success as an adult. Please remember that Christian parents are on earth not to raise upstanding citizens, but eternal citizens. Since we long for our children to grow up with a great love for Christ and affection for His church, we should expose them to the joys and sorrows of living in Christian community.

The Bible describes the church as the household of God (Ephesians 2:19), it describes God as the Father to all Christians (Gal. 4:7), and it commands Christians to be devoted to one another in brotherly love (Romans 12:10). There is no end to the biblical connection between church and home. Problems that arise in the home are likely to arise in the church also. The husband who applies the Gospel to every problem in the home is likely to do so in the church as well. A man's capacity to manage the affairs of his home is a helpful measure of his fitness for the pastorate.

## Priorities for Church Planting Families

It's easy to allow the stress of planting churches to distract us from the primary task of being a good pastor at home. Church planting is filled with problems, unmet expectations, exhausting schedules, failed projects, spiritual warfare, difficult people, and the uphill battle of building a gospel witness in a community that doesn't want one. But there are a few priorities that can help you remain a good shepherd to your family.

**Choose blend over balance.** There seems to be an agreement that pastors must keep a healthy balance between family and ministry in order to be successful at both. The problem is that two items as weighty as family and ministry cannot be properly balanced without breaking the scale that's balancing them. Any time I am forced to choose between the sheep in my church and the sheep in my home, one of them will go untended. Imagine a real shepherd managing two flocks. The further away those two flocks graze from one another, the more difficult the task of caring for both. Picture the busy shepherd running back and forth to get a quick head count at one flock while feeling the need to return to the other. What if one of his flocks needs something special, a wolf to be chased off, or a wound to be nursed? His work will be hurried and some of his sheep will always be vulnerable to attack.

No one is forcing you to choose between family and ministry. What would happen if we stopped trying to balance the two and started trying to blend them? The more we are able to blend family and ministry, the less we will be forced to choose between them. Think about the way God directed the people of Israel on the matter of raising children:

> *Love the LORD your God with all your heart, with all your soul, and with all your strength. These words that I am giving you today are to be in your heart. Repeat them to your children. Talk about them when you sit in your house and when you walk along the road, when you lie down and when you get up. Bind them as a sign on your hand and let them be a symbol on your forehead. Write them on the doorposts of your house and on your gates (Deuteronomy 6:5-9).*

Notice that God doesn't ask them to stop their regular work in order to instruct children on spiritual matters. Instead, He tells them to give instruction in the normal course of their lives along the way. This is how we blend family and ministry. Imagine family and ministry as two very important spheres in the life of a pastor. The more the spheres overlap, the less tension will exist between them. If you view these spheres as completely separate, then you will find there is not enough time in the day to do both jobs well. If you can find ways to involve your family in ministry and involve ministry in your family, you will enjoy time with both.

**Give your family priority on your schedule.** One of the unique privileges you have as a church planter is the ability to leverage your schedule for the benefit of your family. You can align your ministry and family calendars and still be able to accomplish all of the important tasks in ministry during the week. Sometimes this means studying at home or bringing your family on a ministry outing. As a missionary pastor, you work when people are off of work. When everyone is working, you should dedicate time to your family. When it comes to your calendar, there are real advantages to being a church planter. For the first five years of my church's life, I organized the church calendar around our family's personal calendar! That luxury will not be available to you for long, so enjoy it while you can.

> I have placed important family events on my calendar before creating a ministry calendar.

**Spend one-on-one time with family members.** It is common for ministry families to feel as if their dad/husband cares more about the members of his church than he does about the members of his family. One way to avoid this feeling is to spend one-on-one time with each member of your family. It doesn't have to be weekly, but it should be regularly. On every occasion when you spend one-on-one time with your wife or children, you communicate the value they hold in your life. It would be tragic if your family watched you leave the house time after time to attend meetings with other people but never made time to meet with them.

> My weekly schedule includes an appropriate amount of family time.

**Don't do for your church what you are unwilling to do for your family.** The sad truth is that many pastors view their home life as a place to decompress from the stress of ministry, a place where they don't have to be the pastor. These pastors exhaust themselves in service to others, yet are unwilling to serve their family with the same zeal. If you meet with members of your church for prayer when they are sick, make sure you do the same with members of your family when they aren't feeling well. If you teach the Bible to members of your church, be sure to teach the Bible to the members of your family too. If you are patient with those who disagree with you in the church, be sure to show the same grace toward the members of your own household.

**Use the benefits of ministry for the joy of your family.** Planting a new church will tax your family in unexpected ways. Your wife and children will experience the ups and downs of church planting as much as you will. Because of this shared experience, you should search for every opportunity to use the benefits of ministry for the joy of your family. A few years ago our church ordered a new portable baptistery to use for an upcoming baptism service. Knowing everything always goes wrong on Sunday mornings, I decided it would be wise to give the baptistery a test run in my garage. It took my family a few hours to figure out how to get the thing together, but once it was up and running, we had an impromptu pool party in our garage. My kids will never forget the fun we had that day, and neither will I! Maybe your flexible schedule will allow you to be a frequent visitor at school lunches, or your access to an LCD projector will allow for a memorable family movie night. Perhaps a church member will let you use their vacation home for a weekend getaway, or maybe the leftovers from a church ice cream social will make the biggest banana split your kids have ever seen. If you keep your eyes open, you will find small ways to bless your family and a make ministry enjoyable to them.

## The Story of One Church Planting Family

I know a church planter who has done a particularly good job combining ministry and family. Over his 35 years in ministry, Dave Proffitt purposed to involve his son Aaron in his work. When Aaron reached adulthood, he and his dad moved across the country and planted Aletheia Church on the campus of James Madison University in Harrisonburg, Virginia. Now, Aaron is leading the Aletheia Network, planting churches at university campuses. I once asked Aaron what his dad did to make him want to go into ministry. Here is Aaron's response:

> From as far back as I can remember, my father included me in his work, his passion, and his life. There was never a separation. In everything he did, he lived out the Gospel; therefore, I was never confused about how I could be included in it. My dad went above and beyond to make ministry appealing to me—he made it fun. I remember countless trips to Spain to do church planting, beginning at the age of eight. The work of those trips never seemed taxing. It was full of basketball, swimming, ice cream, candy, midnight bullfights, and train trips all over the country. I remember cross-continental Europe trips with hostel stays, great food, sightseeing, and lots of laughs. But he never sugarcoated anything; rather he used the ugly ministry moments as a time of instruction. I was able to see the good, the bad, and the ugly of ministry, which at times made me despise it, but in the end, I had a healthy perspective and I learned a lot. The focus was always on seeing people reached rather than building megachurches, tackling church logistics, or climbing the ladder to the highest denominational position. My father never cared about any of that stuff. He just cared about winning the lost, including me in the process, and making it as fun as possible. I had an awesome childhood!

The Proffitt family's experience demonstrates how building church plants can also build your family.

## Blending My Family and Ministry

The way I see it, the church-planting pastor has two options regarding the balance between family and ministry: he does ministry work for 40-50 hours a week, giving the remaining time to his family, or he searches for ways to make ministry the lifestyle of his family. I have chosen the latter. I began working in ministry soon after becoming a Christian. When I began a relationship with Jennifer (now my wife), she joined me in the work. When our first son was born, he joined the work as well. Every time God gave us another child, our team was expanded. As a family, we pray together for the needs of our congregation. I test illustrations and sermon ideas on them, and I talk with them about issues of direction for our church. When someone is hurting or in need, I take my family along to assist in the ministry. Just as a real shepherd might take his child out to tend sheep with him, when possible, I take mine to tend sheep with me. I want them to learn what I do, and I want to spend time with them. It only makes sense to bring them with me.

Sure, it may not seem professional to some, but professionalism is not the goal of a pastor or a dad. There have been times when my children have done more to minister in hospital rooms and on front porches than I was able to do. This doesn't mean that everything we do as a family is centered on the work of ministry, but it does mean that much of what we do is aimed at serving our local congregation or reaching the lost around us. It also means that there are fewer hours in the day for the activities that do not benefit the church. Please don't feel sorry for my children or my wife. They are not slaves begging for more time on the baseball field or at the local park. Trust me, my children are well-acquainted with the inside of a Chuck E. Cheese's. But they also recognize that, even in Chuck E Cheese's, we are ministers of the Gospel.

## Your Wife's Experience

There is no chance I can write something meaningful to you under this heading, so I'm not even going to try. Instead, I've invited a church planting wife to help. I asked Christine Hoover what she thinks church planters should know about how their wives will experience the first few years of church planting. Here's what Christine said:

> "Words of encouragement to a wife are like water to a plant." When I read that quote recently, I thought about how true that statement is; every wife needs and craves encouragement from her husband. My husband

is masterful at showing me love: he plans date nights, he gifts me with a box of Junior Mints just when I'm withdrawing, he lovingly engages our children, and he leads our home well. But there is nothing like a well-timed word of encouragement from him! Hearing Kyle say that I'm a good mom, that he appreciates my cooking, that I'm beautiful, that he sees God using me—those words reenergize me for days.

There is another reason why his words of encouragement are necessary: my husband is a church planting pastor. For the past three years, God has used us to build a church from the ground up, work that has been both grueling and rewarding. The first year of church planting was especially difficult for me because of the uncertainty, the instability, and the magnitude of the work. Without my husband's verbal encouragement and attentiveness, I could not have made it through.

Your wife, too, will face unique challenges in your first year of church planting. At times she will feel discouraged, overwhelmed, and even resentful of the time and energy your job requires of you. As you seek to nurture your wife, there are many things you can do: draw clear boundaries between ministry and home life from the very beginning, protect her from essentially becoming a second staff member, and strive to ease your own worry and distraction so you can give her your undivided attention. But there is nothing you can do that equals the effect of your encouragement.

After a sermon or a church outreach event, my husband receives a pat on the back or words of affirmation about how God has used him. But who encourages me in my role as the pastor's wife—focusing on the needs of the pastor? That opportunity primarily belongs to my husband.

When he acknowledges and affirms my ministry to him and to others around me, he waters my soul, helping me grow and blossom in my role.

This need that pastors' wives have isn't irrational or the result of a wrong focus. Proverbs 31 describes a husband who is well-known in the community, sitting among the elders of the land. At the gates of the city, he receives respect and affirmation. His wife also offers her admiration and honors him by how she lives. But where does the godly wife receive encouragement? *"Her children rise up and call her blessed; her husband also, and he praises her: 'Many women have done excellently, but you surpass them all'"* (vv. 28-29). Just like the Proverbs 31 husband, water your wife through specific praise:

- "I was feeling discouraged, but your words helped me persevere."
- "You and your gifts are vital to our ministry."
- "You are more important to me than the church."
- "Thank you for the sacrifices you make that allow me to do my job well."

Like you, church planters, your wife continually gives to others. Many people don't think about or understand her needs or the demands on her life. You may be the only source of encouragement your wife receives on a continual basis, and her well-being will have a profound influence on your success. Through your words of blessing, you have an opportunity to minister to your wife in a way that no one else can, especially through the first grueling year.

Christine Hoover is the wife of a church planting pastor in Charlottesville, Virginia, a mom to three boys, and an author of several good books including, *The Church Planting Wife: Help and Hope for Her Heart* (Moody 2013).

## Your Inner Life

Your family life is not the only aspect of your life likely to come under attack as you begin church planting. Your inner spiritual life will also be under siege. Allow me some creative liberty to explain what I mean.

Imagine that your family moved into a new home situated on a major highway. Traffic on the highway is steady at 55 miles per hour for most of the day. When you meet your neighbors for the first time, they warn you that that many accidents have happened on the road and that dozens of family pets have fallen victim to the dangerous highway. One neighbor even tells you the tragic story of a boy who was hit by a car while he was riding his bike near the road. Your previous house was safe, and you were in the habit of sending your kids out to play without supervision and your dog out to run without concern. How would you protect your family at this new home? Would you make adjustments to your lifestyle? Would you build a fence in the front yard? Would you stop sending the kids out to play unsupervised? Would you get a leash for the dog? Of course you would! The heightened danger would cause you to be extra cautious.

Becoming a church planter is like moving into this new home. The highway is sin and temptation, the fence and leash are measures of accountability, and I come to you as a concerned neighbor with a sobering warning.

As a church planter, the temptation to sin is great and so is the wake of damage left behind by sinful choices. It's not uncommon to hear of a pastor or church planter who has fallen prey to sin. You may think that will never happen to you, but no pastor who falls into the trap of sin started his ministry intending to do so. Instead, Satan outwits them because they are ignorant of his schemes (2 Corinthians 2:11). As a result, churches are destroyed, families are devastated, and the name of Christ is dragged through the mud.

How do you guard yourself from the schemes of Satan and protect yourself from "the lust of the flesh, the lust of the eyes, and the pride in one's lifestyle" (1 John 2:16)? The following suggestions may help you guard your heart against the schemes of Satan.

**Clothe Yourself with Humility.** Many pastors talk as if they are experts on the Christian life. They don't speak honestly about their own struggles with sin and pride. They don't ask others to pray for them, and they don't ask for advice or counsel from members of their congregation. This type of relationship with the church is harmful. Here are some practical ways you can practice humility in your ministry:

- Don't be concerned with only the questions other people have about God. Be sure to ask your own questions, and be willing to learn from others.
- Don't only speak to others about areas of sin and pride in their lives, but be willing to speak honestly about your own issues and seek wise counsel from other Christians.
- Don't speak to your congregation as if you are not a member of it. Don't seek to be viewed as a "professional Christian." Since we are all priests to one another (1 Peter 2:9), and we are to be *"submitting to one another out of reverence for Christ"* (Ephesians 5:21), it is necessary for us to clothe ourselves in humility (1 Peter 5:5), especially before our congregations.

**Redefine Success.** As visionaries, church planters tend to speak in abstract, immeasurable terms. For example, one might say, "I want to make an impact on my community" or "I want to see people far from God come to new life in Christ." These phrases, and others like them, are fine for our church signs but are unhelpful as gauges for our effectiveness in ministry. Deep down, there is a set of measurable expectations that you have never voiced. If you're not aware of them, they will wreak havoc on your self-worth in the years to come. If you were to close your eyes and imagine your church's worship service five years from now, what would it look like?

- How many people are there?
- How does the band sound?
- Where are you meeting?
- How many people respond to your sermon?
- How many staff members do you have?
- How much was the offering?
- What is your wife doing?
- How many people were baptized?
- Are all the seats filled?
- Do people express thanks and appreciation for the work you do?

If you're not careful, you will determine the success of your ministry by the answers to these questions. The Bible warns us against this type of presumption (James 4:13-17) and reminds us: *"Many plans are in the mind of a man, but it is the purpose of the Lord that will stand"* (Proverbs 19:21). Don't allow your zeal to accomplish great things in the name of God cause you to forget that you lead a church that belongs to God.

**Limit Comparisons.** New churches that experience explosive growth are featured in books, blogs, and popular conferences, leaving the average church planter feeling inadequate. For the good of your soul, limit your exposure to the success stories of other churches. Instead, focus your attention on the story that God is writing about your church. In Appendix G you will find an Expectations Worksheet designed to help you identify your ungodly church planting expectations.

> I have completed the Expectations Worksheet and have shared the outcome with the leaders of my sending church.

**Pursue Piety.** This might seem obvious, but pastors should pray and read their Bibles regularly. A church is like a distribution center for the Gospel. You are distributing the Gospel to the congregation, and hopefully they are distributing it to the world. But you cannot distribute what you do not have. If you're not growing in your prayer life, your understanding of God's Word, and your reliance on the Holy Spirit, you will have little to dispense. If the flow of the Gospel into your life is slow, so will be the outflow. Dedicate time each day to prayer and study. This will bring immeasurable value to you and your congregation.

**Observe a Sabbath.** Church planters generally swing to one of two extremes when it comes to the scriptural mandate to rest (Exodus 20:8). Some ignore the command altogether, unable to find any self-worth apart from their work. These types are unable to detach themselves from ministry for any length of time. They are checking email on vacation, thinking about church government at the dinner table, and looking for sermon illustrations in every conversation. Others don't work nearly hard enough. Church planting takes a lot of initiative, and this can be overwhelming for some. These types prefer to look busy, yet are accomplishing little. Neither of these extremes is good for the planter, the church, or his family.

God's design for all people is to choose one day each week to be free from work, even if your work is planting a church. It should be a day other than Sunday. Spend time in rest and worship. It might be helpful to choose a faithful person in your church to handle problems that arise on that day so you are not forced to choose between helping someone in need and getting the rest you require.

> I have chosen a day of the week for rest.

**Surround Yourself with Accountability.** Surround yourself with trusted advisors who are faithful to the Lord and committed to your well-being and the well-being of your congregation. Seek men who know you well, understand your weaknesses, and are confident enough to confront you when they see unhealthy patterns forming in your personal life or your pastoral ministry.

**Serve in Partnership.** For the protection of the church, it is wise to begin with a team of competent and qualified leaders. If this isn't possible, be sure to find at least one partner to join you, assist you in wise decision-making, share the workload, and validate your work. Unless your sponsoring church is helping you with oversight, you are left to make all of the formative decisions about your church alone. This is unwise. Scripture teaches: *"Without counsel plans fail, but with many advisers they succeed"* (Proverbs 15:22). This is where a partner can be a tremendous asset. When searching for a partner, make sure it's someone who is willing to make the same personal sacrifices that you are in order to participate in the ministry. Seek someone whose gifts complement yours, and consider whether he is a candidate for leading a future church planting endeavor.

As a church planting pastor, you will spend countless hours investing in other people. Be sure to spend ample time nurturing your own relationship with Christ so that you have valuable wisdom to dispense to others. These measures of accountability will not ensure your survival as a church planter, but they will certainly increase the odds that you and your family remain healthy through the process of starting a new church.

# ENLIST

In my early stages of planting, there were two individuals who influenced me significantly as I prepared for the church plant. These men were Dale Marks and Naethan Hendrix. At the time, Dale was an injured Lt. Colonel in the Air National Guard, who was providentially healing from knee surgery for a few months at the precise time when I was preparing to start a new church. Dale was a member of my sending church and a gifted leader with a genuine love for Christ. He had assisted in the planting of several churches throughout his military career, and, as a strategic planner for the armed forces, Dale was accustomed to taking a big vision and breaking it down into manageable pieces. He helped me to think through every aspect of this new church and was a sounding board for the decisions I was making. He prayed for me and spoke honestly to me about areas of pride and weakness that he noticed in my life.

To prepare for my church planting, Dale advised me to seek a pastoral partner to share the ministry. He pointed out that having a partner was both biblical (Mark 6:7) and practical. After considering various mutual friends for the job, but not finding a good fit, Dale suggested that we pray. Day after day we prayed that God would provide a partner. One day I told Dale that I had someone in mind, an acquaintance from college named Naethan, who I hadn't spoken to in several years. Dale urged me to call Naethan and invite him to partner with me in planting the church. Naethan accepted the invitation and was willing to make the sacrifice of leaving his current job to come on board. Naethan moved at his own expense and took up residence in Dale's basement. He delivered pizza and dedicated all of his extra time to the work of the ministry. Not long after the church began, Naethan became our first church planter and led a small team from our young congregation to begin a new church just a few miles away. His sacrificial example set a precedent for our church that remains to this day. Dale and Naethan have both moved on to other pursuits, but remain trusted friends and advisors.

As I look back on the developmental stages of Pillar Church, I can honestly say that no two individuals were more significant to the church's foundation than Dale and Naethan. My experience has convinced me that every church planter needs a partner and a mentor to share in the joys and hardships of pastoral ministry.

## Choosing a Pastoral Partner

There are a many advantages to having a pastoral partner when you plant a new church, but those advantages are not the only reason we require our church planters to have a ministry partner. Our motivation is a biblical one. As churches are being established throughout the New Testament, the pattern for pastoral partnership is clear. It started when Jesus sent His disciples out in twos (Mark 6:7; Luke 10:1), and it continued as the church at Antioch commissioned their first pair of missionaries (Acts 13:2). Even the Apostle Paul, history's most famous church planter, took partners on his missionary journeys. Barnabas (Acts 15:36-41), Aristarchus (Acts 19:29, 20:4, 27:2), John Mark (Acts 13:13), and Tychicus and Onesimus (Colossians 4:7-9) were all mentioned in the New Testament as Paul's companions during his church planting endeavors. Pastoral partners were so vital to the ministry of church planting that New Testament planters were instructed to continue working in teams even after the church was established (Titus 1:5-9).

As I already mentioned, my first pastoral partner's name is Naethan. When we began, I was working in the ministry full time and living in my own house. Naethan, on the other hand, was living in Dale's basement and staying up until 1:00 a.m. delivering pizza. That reality made it very difficult for me to whine or wallow in any measure of self-pity about the difficulty of my work. He was just as qualified as I was for the task, was just as dedicated as I was, and was every bit as loved by our people. With no notable rewards, Naethan was working selflessly to help the church grow roots. The experience of working with Naethan to plant Pillar Church and the clear precedent for pastoral partnership in the New Testament have caused me to urge church planters to work in pastoral teams. Allow me to close my commendation on this subject by listing four other practical advantages to pastoral partnerships.

- **Rapid Reproduction** – Maybe the most obvious advantage to planting with a pastoral partner is that you don't have to spend years preparing a member from your congregation to plant a new church. If the partner you choose is qualified and already aspires to plant a new church himself, you will likely be ready to plant again within the first few years of your church's ministry. In many of our church planting endeavors, the pastoral partner has agreed to serve as a future church planter before even joining the team. We call this "planting pregnant," and we'll talk about it more in stage nine.

- **Burden Sharing** – Church planting is hard. It is hard on your family, hard on your schedule, and hard on your budget, and it is even harder if you have to do it alone. Sharing the burden with someone else actually does make it lighter. One of the elders in my church frequently says, "Working together multiplies our joy and divides our burdens." There will be days when you will not want to work. There will be days when you will wake up, look out the window of your small apartment at the community you're there to reach, and you will want to go back to bed. And if you are working alone, you just might.

- **Work Volume** – It's funny that when you start talking to people about their spiritual lives, you quickly realize that people don't like to talk about their spiritual lives. You may volunteer in the community, meet people in a coffee shop, or visit patients in the hospital, and for every twenty people you talk to, typically only one or two of them show any interest in what you have to say. In order to make any progress, you will have to talk to a tremendous number of people. With two people, that work goes much faster.

- **Accountability** – Planting a church opens up the floodgates for spiritual warfare. Satan will try to attack you and your family at every vulnerable point. A good pastoral partner will shield you from many of the enemy's darts. Satan usually attacks when you're alone and without accountability. Keeping someone by your side in the work of ministry will shield you from many of the temptations you will face as a church planter. When working alone, it is much easier to compromise, cut corners, and skip important steps. Having a pastoral partner helps you stay on track. You and your partner will work together to make plans for every aspect of this new church's ministry. Since both of you know the plan, he will know when you're compromising it.

## A Pastoral Partner IS...

A pastoral partner is a capable and qualified man eager to join you in the day-to-day work of church planting. He should be as capable for the work as you are and wholly dedicated to the establishment of this new church. The right pastoral partner is someone who shares your philosophy of ministry and your theological positions. If you are not careful in the selection process, you may find yourself in regular conflict over issues of practice and policy in the new church. Choosing someone you know well or have worked with in the past is generally a good idea. Since your pastoral partner will be a close comrade in the work, you should first consider individuals you have successfully worked with in the past. Your pastoral partner will work with you in making decisions regarding the church; so take your time with this very important selection.

## A Pastoral Partner IS NOT...

A pastoral partner is not an intern, apprentice, assistant, or caddie. He is not someone you are training for future ministry, and you are not his boss or mentor. Seeing your partner as a minion will not help you receive the type of accountability and decision-making help a pastoral partner is intended to provide. To be clear, I'm not against the idea of having interns or assistants in the work of church planting, but those who act in these positions serve a distinct role from that of your partner.

## Finding a Pastoral Partner

Assume that since God has called you to this work, He is also calling others to this work. If God has called you to plant a church, He also intends to give you all of the people and resources you need to accomplish it. Be looking for evidence that God is calling someone else to partner with you. It may be someone you wouldn't expect. Ask yourself whether this man has the character required to take your place if you were no longer available to lead this church. Many church planting teams make the distinction of "Lead Pastor" and "Associate Pastor," but I believe it is more helpful to think in terms of "Long Term Pastor" and "Short Term Pastor."

Since you will work so closely with your pastoral partner, you should thoroughly explore his views on life, family, and ministry before offering him the role. It will be very difficult to make progress in church planting if you disagree over foundational principles. Refrain from committing the position to him until you are very confident that God is calling him to the work as well and that you are both on the same page regarding views on theology, family, and ministry. This relationship will likely last a long time. Aside from you, no one will have as much influence and leadership in this new church as your pastoral partner, so be sure to give ample thought and consideration to this decision. Below you will find some advice for finding your pastoral partner.

- Look for someone who is willing to make personal sacrifices in order to participate. Generally speaking, you don't want to have to talk someone into being your partner. If you are dragging him along in the initial stages, you may find yourself dragging him through the work as it progresses. You want a partner who feels as called to this work as you do.
- Look for someone whose gifts complement your own. If you are a dreamer but have difficulty with practical matters, look for someone who is intensely practical. If you are an introvert and

given to much study and preparation, look for someone who is an extrovert and given to relationships and community.

- Look for someone who may serve as a future church planter. Since you desire to plant a church that will multiply, consider a person who has aspirations to become a church planter.
- Look first within your sending church. Assuming you have strong relationships there, you will find that your current church provides a rich pool of candidates for the job.

Once you have identified a pastoral partner candidate, get affirmation from your sending church before offering him the role. Your sending church may have a different or better vantage point on your potential partner's fitness than you have, so seek their advice before making a final decision.

I have enlisted a pastoral partner.

## Choosing a Church Planting Mentor

A church planting mentor is equally as important as a pastoral partner. The mentor's primary role is to keep you on track as you attempt to reach your church planting thresholds. This person should have a proven track record of effectiveness in ministry and be willing to make himself available for mentorship throughout the first year of your new church's ministry. Your mentor serves as an objective third party in the creation of your church planting prospectus and will help you determine appropriate thresholds for the stages of the church planting process that lies ahead of you.

- Look for someone who has some experience in church planting. The business world and the world of pastoral ministry don't share many similarities. For this reason, it is wise to find someone who understands the nuances of church planting and pastoral ministry.
- Look for someone with an obvious gift for leadership. This is not a position peers should fill. You are looking for someone who is several steps ahead of you in competency and experience.

- Look for someone whose love for God and whose leadership you respect. Because effective pastors and church planters are generally very busy and have a lot of responsibilities requiring their time and attention, you may find it difficult to get them to commit to spend the time with you, but it will be well worth the effort to secure someone you know is effective and worthy of respect. If you don't respect or agree with him, you will have a difficult time taking his advice.

- Look for someone who is willing to make himself available to you. At a minimum, you should be meeting with your mentor at least once a month—if possible, twice a month. The meetings don't always have to be face-to-face, as phone or videoconference will work too. The mentor needs to have the availability and willingness to make the time investment to meet with you.

- Look for someone who understands and respects your sending church's authority. Your mentor is not an authority, but rather is more of an advisor. It is important that he acknowledges and supports your sending church's authoritative role in your church planting process and that he encourages you in your relationship with your sending church.

A church planting mentor will be a tremendous blessing to you as you plan and execute the tasks associated with church planting. As always, be sure to consult your sending church before choosing a church planting mentor.

I have observed that church planters who work on pastoral teams and have mentors seem to weather the storms of church planting much better than those who work alone. Youthful confidence can deceive you into believing that the help of a partner and mentor are not necessary as you plant a church. Solomon's wisdom is helpful to us on this subject:

> *Two are better than one, because they have a good reward for their toil. For if they fall, one will lift up his fellow. But woe to him who is alone when he falls and has not another to lift him up! Again, if two lie together, they keep warm, but how can one keep warm alone? And though a man might*

*prevail against one who is alone, two will withstand him—a threefold cord is not quickly broken* (Ecclesiastes 4:9-12).

The majority of my church planting work has been in the greater Washington DC area. We have seen as many failed church plants in our area as successful ones. Without exception, those who failed were working alone. Our church insists that each church planter has a pastoral partner and a mentor. This doesn't necessarily ensure success, but it definitely increases the odds. In spiritual terms, you are going into battle for the souls of men and women in your community. No good soldier goes into battle without backup, so choose strong men to accompany you to the battlefield and keep your communication line open to base camp.

## Four Stages of Competency

It's impossible to see how difficult the church planting endeavor will be before you actually begin. Those who have experienced unusual success produce most of what we see and read about church planting. Rarely, if ever, will a church planter who failed or experienced significant struggles be invited to a conference to speak about their failures. Without a firm grip on expected difficulties, it is easy to develop a naive confidence that will leave you unprepared for the realities ahead.

In the 1970s Noel Burch developed a learning model he called the "Four Stages of Competence." I stumbled upon it a few years ago and realized his model described exactly what I experienced in church planting. Burch observed that there are four stages in learning any new skill.

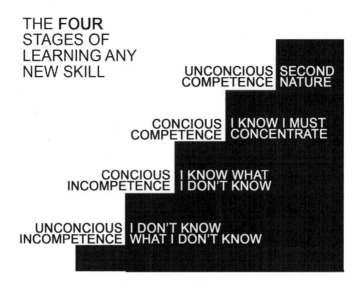

THE **FOUR** STAGES OF LEARNING ANY NEW SKILL

UNCONCIOUS COMPETENCE — SECOND NATURE

CONCIOUS COMPETENCE — I KNOW I MUST CONCENTRATE

CONCIOUS INCOMPETENCE — I KNOW WHAT I DON'T KNOW

UNCONCIOUS INCOMPETENCE — I DON'T KNOW WHAT I DON'T KNOW

- **Unconscious incompetence** – At this stage you don't know what you don't know, and, because you are ignorant of the deficit in your competence, you are optimistic about the outcome.
- **Conscious incompetence** – At this stage you know what you do not know. You still do not know what you are doing, but at least you recognize the deficit, as well as the value of a new skill in addressing the deficit. You will make a lot of rookie mistakes in this stage, but each one of them will be an important lesson you will carry into your future work.
- **Conscious Competence** – At this stage you understand how to do something and have learned the major skills associated with the task, but demonstrating the skill or knowledge requires concentration.
- **Unconscious competence** – At this stage your skill has become second nature. The tasks associated with the skill can be performed easily even while executing another task. At this point you understand the subject thoroughly and can teach it to others.[9]

Right now, you are most likely in the first stage of this process. You are optimistic about the work ahead of you because you've not yet experienced the challenges that come with the work you're about to start. You don't know what you don't know about church planting. Much of what you'll learn over the next few years you will learn through experience. You'll have a few successes and a lot of failures, and over time you'll become skilled at the work of church planting. This, however, is not the only way to learn church planting! You can effectively skip stage one and move to stage two by seeking counsel from experienced and godly church planters. You can avoid many common mistakes in church planting just by spending time with experienced church planters and asking them to advise you through the early stages of your church planting journey.

> I have enlisted a church planting mentor.

## Never Work Alone

Throughout college and seminary, I taught guitar lessons to prepubescent, wannabe rockers from the local middle school. Without fail, the kids who excelled were those who listened to my guidance and had other friends or siblings to "jam" with them. The kids who were trying to learn alone usually did not succeed. As a new church planter, you are about to enter the first stage of competency. It will be difficult, and it will be discouraging. Take a teammate and a guide along on the journey, and you'll be much more likely to succeed. If you've ever experienced the frustration of learning a new skill, you know that the odds of your success depend heavily on who is with you while you are learning.

Recently a church planter sent me an email explaining that he was giving up on his church planting endeavor. He cited a number of reasons for the decision, but the one that stood out to me was his sense of loneliness in the work. Despite his good intentions, he felt like he had been "parachute dropped" into his church plant. I urge you not to work alone. If God has called you to this task, He is calling others to join you in it. You should assume that God is preparing others to work along with you, and your job is to discover them before beginning your work.

# PLAN

N ow that your pastoral partner and church planting mentor are on board, it is time for the three of you to begin prayerfully planning. If you're like me, you'll have no problem getting busy planning, but prayer—real honest prayer—is harder.

Early 18th century commentator, Matthew Henry, writes, "How apt worldly and projecting men are to leave God out of their schemes."[10] They make plans and then set them into motion without consulting God. Proverbs 19:21 teaches, *"Many are the plans in the mind of a man, but it is the purpose of the Lord that will stand."* It is worldly and foolish to make plans to plant a new church without seeking confirmation from God.

Don't allow your zeal to accomplish great things in the name of God cause you to forget that you lead a church that belongs to God. It is necessary for you to get in the habit of consulting God before setting any plan into motion. Most church planters are dreamers, easily intoxicated by notions that unexpectedly burst into consciousness. These idea bursts are easily mistaken for direction from the Holy Spirit, so they should be tested before they are acted upon.

The book of 2 Samuel includes a story about King David making plans for God without God's agreement. David was living in an extravagant palace built with fine materials and experiencing unusual peace from his enemies. Out of gratefulness to God, David decides that it's not right for him to live in such luxury while the God who is responsible for all of the peace and prosperity lives in a tent (the tabernacle). David calls his trusted advisor, Nathan, to share his plans to build a temple for God:

> *The king said to Nathan the prophet, "See now, I dwell in a house of cedar, but the ark of God dwells in a tent." And Nathan said to the king, "Go, do all that is in your heart, for the Lord is with you." Initially Nathan's response was positive, but later that same night the word of the Lord came to Nathan, "Go and tell my servant David, 'Thus says the Lord: Would you build me a house to dwell in? I have not lived in a house since the day I brought up the people of Israel from Egypt to this day, but I have been moving about in a tent for my dwelling. In all places where I have moved with all the people of Israel, did I speak a word with any of the judges of Israel, whom I commanded to shepherd my people Israel, saying, "Why have you not built me a house of cedar?"'"* (2 Samuel 7:2-7).

The thing that troubles me when I read this passage is that David's motives are no different from my own. I love God, I am thankful for all that He has done for me, and in gratefulness I want to offer gifts of sacrifice to Him. Apparently, in God's economy, the extravagance of our gifts and the motives with which we give them are not nearly as significant as the purposes of the Lord. Since we aren't privy to His purposes, it is necessary that we confirm with God before setting our plans into motion. David even went the extra mile and consulted Nathan about his decision. But none of this changes the fact that God didn't want a temple, and God didn't ask for a temple.

My experience has taught me that not all of my plans are divine. As I look back over the projects and plans I have brought before my young congregation, I am ashamed of how little I have looked to Scripture for concurrence. In vain pursuit of my plans, I have wasted resources, compromised my own credibility as a spiritual leader, and been distracted from paying close attention to the purposes of the Lord. Matthew Henry encourages the man of God to consider, "How vain a thing it is to look for any thing good in futurity, without the concurrence of Providence."[11]

Thankfully, the Lord was gracious to me—and our church. In many ways this problem corrected itself in the third year of our church. After a few years of operating our church as the only elder, I appointed a few other men to assist me with congregational oversight. These men urged me to carry my plans before the Lord in search of His approval before setting any plan into motion. If I had known earlier how significant this change would be, I would have appointed elders as soon as qualified men were available. If you are a new pastor or planter, I encourage you to refrain from implementing a plan that is not tested and proven by God and those who love Him.

Matthew Henry warns, "How much of worldly happiness lies in the promises men make to themselves beforehand. Their heads are full of fine visions, as to what they shall do, and be, and enjoy, in some future time, when they can neither be sure of time nor of any of the advantages they promise themselves."[12] This warning brings to mind a flood of personal peaks and valleys in my church planting experience. I have made plans without God, I have wagered my happiness on the success of those plans, and I have consistently been disappointed that those plans didn't produce the success I expected. On the other hand, when Scripture has been my inspiration for a project or a strategy, I have seen results beyond my imagination. Pray for God to use His Word and the church to confirm all aspects of your plan.

## Begin with the End in Mind

Build into the beginning what you want in the end. If you want to plant a church that values the faithful expository preaching of God's Word, preach faithful expository messages from the beginning. If you want a significant ministry to the nearby military base, minister to soldiers from the start. If you want to plant many churches, make plans to plant one as soon as possible. Pastors seem to think that there will come a time in the future when it will be easier to become the church they wish to lead—when the budget is bigger or when they have more volunteers or greater influence. In my experience, change only becomes more difficult with time. If you act in infancy as you wish to act in maturity, you will find that the church will grow around the priorities you set forth.

The strength of this approach is that the priorities of your church will be so interwoven with the structure of your church, that it is unlikely to abandon those priorities easily. If, during development, your church overlooks the immigrants and foreigners living in your community, and you later try to lead the church to embrace ministry to those people, you may meet with resistance. On the other hand, if your teaching and actions show a love for sojourners from the earliest stages, your congregation will be eager to embrace the needs of those far from home.

Our church "planted pregnant." When we held our first meeting, I already had a plan and a man in place to plant another church. As I was dreaming of planting a new church in the suburbs of Washington DC, I realized that one new church alone was never going to impact the millions of people who lived within driving distance of my church. I determined early on to make church planting a part of our daily operations as a church.

When I was searching for a partner to join me in the ministry, I sought a man who aspired to plant and pastor a church himself. I helped our church understand that the partner would soon leave us to plant another church. We prayed for him, we supported him, and we advocated for him every step of the planting process. In fact, our church has never stopped endeavoring to plant churches.

## Writing a Prospectus

Once you have a plan that you're sure is in accordance with God's Word, you should capture the plan in a clear and concise church planting prospectus.

A prospectus is a written presentation of your church planting plan that's designed to present concisely and uniformly all of the important details related to the planting of your new church. It is created for the benefit of your sending church, potential supporting churches, individual financial supporters, potential prayer partners, and potential core team members. The details you compile in this document will become the basis for all of the presentations you create to solicit support for your church planting initiative. Your prospectus will take several weeks if not several months to create. Since the content of this document will serve as the foundation for other types of presentations, it is important that the data and wording you include in your prospectus be thorough and accurate.

I suspect that some who read this will think that a church planting prospectus sounds a lot like a business plan. Since you may initially recoil at the idea and be tempted to think that approaching such an endeavor of faith by such worldly means is ungodly, I'll begin my argument for the importance of creating a prospectus with some scriptural principles that will help you recognize the importance of careful planning.

## Scriptural Encouragement for Thoughtful Planning

In the parable of the wise and foolish builder, Jesus teaches plainly that those who are wise will carefully *"count the costs"* before building a tower because, if they don't, they may find that they don't have enough materials to complete the project (Luke 24:28). This is very practical advice from Jesus Himself, and it should not be disregarded. As a church planter, you'll be endeavoring to build a house for God. This house is made up of *"living stones"* (1 Peter 2:5), and these living stones are souls who will be entrusted to you by God. Not only that, but most of the resources you use to build this spiritual house will be provided to you by other Christians who entrust you to steward with care the resources they provide.

## Another Perspective

For just a moment, imagine yourself as a pastor of an existing church. Imagine an aspiring church planter has requested a meeting with you. As you sit down with this young man, he begins describing his need for your support. You see quickly that his heart is in the right place, but his head is not. He explains how he's rearranging his life to plant a new church. He tells you about the new city he's planning to move to, the job he's quitting, and the friends and family he'll be leaving behind. You honestly admire him for his act of courageous faith, but his presentation includes very little about how he plans to accomplish this work. After his presentation is over, you ask him some questions:

"What kinds of people live in this community?"

"All kinds of different people."

"How much will it cost to rent a house there?"

41

"Oh, it shouldn't be too much."

"How will you go about meeting people in this new city?"

"Just go out and talk to people like Jesus did!"

Again, his faith is admirable, but he seems to have put little to no thought into the details of his plan. Furthermore, he is a recent seminary graduate with very little pastoral ministry experience. The more this young man talks, the less confident you are that he has any idea what he's getting into. He doesn't know the community or the costs. He has no timetable or potential meeting locations. On top of all of this, he's asking you to entrust him with the resources of your church.

After the young man leaves your office, you are faced with the decision of whether you will lead your church to support him. He is very nice and obviously loves God, but you have been entrusted with the responsibility to be a good steward of the resources of your church. Would supporting this young man be good stewardship? Will you lead your church to support his ministry? I venture to say that most of us would not.

The old adage is true: "Those who fail to plan, plan to fail." It's important that you understand that any pastor you're seeking support from has a heavy responsibility to be a good steward of his church's resources.

I've heard many church planters whine and moan about how "selfish" and "inwardly focused" established churches are, yet I have found just the opposite to be true. Many churches are incredibly generous and sacrificial when presented with a clear and compelling plan by a man who seems to have the faith and aptitude to accomplish it. No church has any obligation to support you and your church planting endeavor, especially if you give them no reason to trust your plan or your credibility. You must approach churches with the respect and honor they deserve.

## Choosing a Location

Often the decision to plant a new church is fueled (at least in part) by a burden for the Gospel to become more widely known in a particular community. In this case the question of location isn't that complex. If you find yourself in this situation here are a few things to consider.

**Does this community really need a new church?** On some level every community needs more faithful churches. No community in North America (or anywhere else for that matter) is fully reached, and no community even comes close to having an adequate number of faithful churches. With that said, there are some communities where the Gospel is taking root more notably than others. Paul noticed this when he was starting churches and opted to move to communities without a gospel presence. Paul says,

> ... *from Jerusalem and all the way around to Illyricum I have fulfilled the ministry of the gospel of Christ; and thus I make it my ambition to preach the gospel, not where Christ has already been named, lest I build on someone else's foundation* (Romans 15:19-20).

Many church planters I meet are ready to be sent, but simply don't know where to go plant. For those who don't know where to go, I want to share a few things that might help as you select a ministry field.

**Don't overthink it.** There are a lot of factors at play in the decision about where to plant a new church: the need, the schools, the home prices, the weather, how much you like the community, etc. So many factors can paralyze you from making a decision. No place will meet all of your criteria. Remember that God commonly does extraordinary things in unexpected places.

**Don't be too spiritual.** Some planters want to be in the most challenging place they can possibly find. This is admirable but not always advisable, particularly for those with families. Make sure the place you land is a place your wife and kids can live for a long time.

**Don't be too specific.** Be open-minded as you choose your ministry field. Don't be too specific about the exact neighborhood or community for your church. The truth is, the church is made of people, and you don't yet know where the people are that God will draw into this new congregation.

**Don't decide in isolation.** Be sure to spend plenty of time talking to local pastors and getting to know the community from their point of view. Even clergymen of other faiths and denominations can relay meaningful information about the community that will serve you well in the process of choosing a location to serve.

> I have chosen a location for this new church.

## Choosing a Name

The name of your new church will be its primary identity well into the future, so it should be thought out carefully. It's common for church planters to choose the name of their new church simply because they like it. It's shortsighted to name the church without considering the identities of nearby churches, the public's perception of the name, and the name's endurance. Church names fall into some common categories:

- **Geographic Name:** Springfield Community Church, 1ˢᵗ Street Church
- **Scriptural Name:** Grace Church, Koinonia Church
- **Illustrative Name:** Mosaic Church, Impact Church
- **Denominational Name:** First Baptist Church, Calvary Assembly
- **Trendy Church Name:** The Edge Church, $H_2O$ Church
- **Non-Church Names:** The Spring, Access Fellowship

Of course there are variations and combinations of these approaches, such as Grace Baptist Church or Mosaic Fellowship, but basically all modern church names fall into one or more of these categories. Since the name of your church will be it's primary identity for the foreseeable future, here is some advice to consider as you choose a name.

**Don't make the decision too quickly.** The name is not a decision to be made overnight or even in a week. Take time to field test potential names. Allow some time for your first choice to simmer before making a final decision.

44

**Don't make the decision alone.** Talk to your spouse, your friends, and your ministry partners about the name before making a decision. Some of the worst church names could have been avoided if the church planter had spent a little time consulting others. Other pastors in the community may also be good sounding boards. Seek their advice and consider their opinions in your decision.

**Don't make a shortsighted decision.** Many churches have used a geographical name based on their original location, but then move to a different location, which no longer fits the description. Two megachurches in Virginia come to mind: McLean Bible Church now in Vienna and Lynchburg's Thomas Road Baptist Church now on Mt. View Road. When these churches chose their names years ago, they probably never considered that they might change physical locations. Shortsightedness can also apply to names that are trendy or popular now but become stale over time. Think about your church name like your outfit. Buying the newest, trendiest thing may seem like a good idea right now, but if you had to choose an outfit to wear for the next 50 years, you'd probably choose something a bit more classic. Take the same approach with your church's name. Choose one that will endure the test of time.

> I have chosen a name for this new church.

## Available Resources for Research

As you collect data for your prospectus, a tremendous amount of resources are available to you. Many denominations offer excellent demographic information including the number of churches, people, households, educational institutions, and housing opportunities in your city. This data is sortable and can be delivered to you with the geographic parameters you request. Additionally, detailed data such as people groups, median ages, and income levels are available for most metropolitan areas in the United States. Obtaining this information is easy and relatively inexpensive. In Appendix H you will find a list of many available research resources to assist you. This information will not only help you create a compelling presentation, but will also arm you with important data that will serve you as you consider ways to minister to those living in your mission field.

> I have researched the demographics of my ministry field and have an accurate picture of the types of people who live there.

## Key Components of a Good Prospectus

There are at least ten components that should be included in every church planting prospectus. These components will answer the majority of questions that potential partners will have about your ministry field, your qualifications, and your resourcing needs. Other sections can and should be included as you see fit. Keep in mind that pastors are generally very busy; therefore, it is important that you keep your presentation concise. I recommend that the entire document be short enough to read in one ten-minute sitting. Following are the ten most important components to your prospectus.

**Personal Introduction** – Introduce yourself and your family by including a brief biography and a large picture of your family. This section may also include your educational achievements and other unique qualifications you have for this particular ministry. Include a similar feature for your pastoral partner and any other key committed leaders.

**Overview of Context** – Explain the unique features of the ministry context. If you are planting near a college, military base, or any other interesting location, explain the special opportunities that exist in this location. If your new church is part of a larger church planting initiative, this is also a time to explain that relationship.

**City Profile** – Bullet point the features of your city: population, demographic makeup, number of churches, need for new churches, culture, socio-economic makeup, statistics, etc. Highlight unique ministry challenges in this section. This is also a good place for a city map or photograph of an important landmark in your city.

**Strategy** – Address the information in the city profile section by explaining how you plan to meet the unique ministry challenges that you mentioned in the previous section. Explain how you will go about ministering to the people in your particular city.

**Ministry Overview** – Provide an overview of the services and ministries you plan to provide to the community through this new church's ministry. Include basic logistical details as well as broader information about what people should expect from those services and ministries.

**Doctrine** – Include your theological and doctrinal positions, preferably in summary form. You may also wish to include a church covenant or a statement of faith and a summary of your philosophy of ministry.

**Timeline** – Starting with your calling and preparation for church planting, make a simple timeline showing when and how you expect your church planting endeavor to unfold.

**Budget** – Because it will probably generate the most interest and questions, take great care in preparing this section. More detailed instructions about your personal and church budgets appear later in this chapter.

- **Partnerships** – List the denominations, networks and organizations you will be partnering with in this church planting effort. Briefly summarize each organization's role in the work.

- **Action Steps** – Finish the prospectus with a clear call to action. Tell potential supporters exactly what to do in order to sign up for your prayer list, to contribute monthly and to give a one-time gift to your effort. Be sure to include both online and snail mail giving options.

## Presentation of Data

Once you have compiled your prospectus data it is important that the graphic presentation be done by a professional. Think of the prospectus more like a magazine than a book. Using pictures, graphs and diagrams with a consistent color scheme will add to the professionalism of the presentation and subtly give your potential sponsor the impression that you intend to approach this project with excellence. Getting this document professionally designed and printed may cost a few hundred dollars but the investment will be worth it.

Once the prospectus is complete, the images, graphics and body of the presentation can serve as the foundation for all of your promotional media. For example, you can create a PowerPoint version of the presentation for use in churches or other live settings. Most professionally designed presentations can be easily integrated into other forms of media such as response cards, PowerPoint slides, and videos.

## Add Creative Elements

One simple way to significantly increase the chances that your audience will remember your presentation is to add a few creative elements. Find a way to highlight the unique characteristics of the church you will plant, and communicate them to your audience. I once spoke to a group about the need to plant churches in and around Washington DC. I explained that I was in need of hundreds of new churches to reach the hundreds of different people groups in and around the city. I sent home with each person one piece to a 500-piece puzzle of the Capitol and asked them to place it where they would see it often as a reminder to pray for us. After a worship service years later, a woman holding her puzzle piece approached me and told me that she was still praying for us as we planted churches in and around Washington DC.

On another occasion, for a church plant in Reykjavik, Iceland, I filled tiny bottles with black Icelandic beach sand as a memento and prayer reminder for each person who committed to pray for us. Nearly ten years later, individuals will periodically remind me that they still have the sand and are still praying for the people of Iceland.

## Memorize Highlights

You will find that many of the best opportunities to share about your church planting endeavor will come when you least expect them. It may be a chance encounter with an old friend or an unexpected audience with a pastor at a conference or event. It is helpful to memorize a few important elements of your prospectus so that you are prepared to share them at any time.

Years ago, I received a text message from a high school friend telling me that a pastor from a large church in Missouri was in Washington DC for the day. My friend shared the pastor's contact information with me, and I quickly contacted him to see if we could meet. Within just a few hours, I was sitting down with Pastor Vince and sharing about our plans to plant a new church at every Marine Corps base in the world. He asked about our strategy, our training methodology, and the locations we were planning to plant new churches. Though I didn't have any material on hand or any way to give him a formal presentation, I did know the answers to all of the questions he asked me. About a week later, Pastor Vince called to let me know that his church was going to give us a large monetary gift to help with our effort. As the project grew and gained more momentum, Pastor Vince led his church to continue supporting our efforts. Now Pastor Vince is a trusted friend and is deeply invested in our work both as a financial supporter and as an advisor.

Opportunity can come quickly and unexpectedly, so be ready! You never know when you'll be given a chance to share with a potential supporter or team member.

## Empower Others

Another huge benefit to creating a church planting prospectus is that it will help other individuals serve as advocates for the endeavor. Like a church planting street team, your supporters can fan out and cover their personal spheres of influence. Team members, family members, and friends will have the power to answer questions and share about the new church with confidence.

## Prepare a Clear Presentation

When you do finally get the opportunity to address potential sponsors, you will likely have only one shot at convincing them to invest in your new work. Using the prospectus as a foundation, spend some time preparing a compelling presentation for potential supporters. In general, potential supporters are more likely to become investors in your new ministry if they are impressed with you as an individual and are convinced that you have a viable plan for starting a new church.

As a pastor strongly committed to church planting, there are three characteristics that I typically look for in a church planter before I will lead my church to invest in a new ministry: (1) appropriate character for pastoral ministry; (2) similar doctrinal convictions; and (3) spiritual maturity sufficient to endure the roller coaster ride of church planting. It's essential that you approach potential sponsors with a complete and compelling plan. Following are a few tips.

**Meet face-to-face.** Presentations generally go better in person. A videoconference, phone call, or letter doesn't require an immediate response, so do everything you can to meet potential supporters face-to-face.

**Include the "big picture."** Is this an investment in one church plant, or do you plan to plant multiple churches? Where, when, and how do you plan to accomplish this? I have found that the use of imagery can be helpful in this part of the presentation. For example, I have said before that my approach to church planting is an attempt to plant an orchard, not just a tree. This imagery helped me explain that I had something bigger in mind than planting one church in one community.

**Never use guilt.** Any attempt to tell a sob story or evoke sympathy should be excluded from your presentation. Laying a guilt trip on a potential supporter will get you nowhere long term.

**Respect their time.** Set up the meeting in a location and at a time that is most convenient for your potential supporter. Show up a bit early, dress respectfully, and come prepared to get right to the point.

**Ask boldly and specifically.** After your presentation, be specific and direct about your request: "Would it be possible for your church to contribute $500 per month for the next two years to help me plant this new church?" or "Would you consider allowing me to share this with your congregation and ask your members to pray about joining our team for a period of 6-12 months?" Avoid open-ended questions such as, "Do you think you could contribute anything?" Busy people appreciate direct questions. Beating around the bush will not endear you to them. Even if the potential supporter does not agree to support you, they will respect your forthrightness.

**Be persistent but not annoying.** Suggest potential follow up options: "I plan to attend your worship service next weekend. Would you be willing to allow me to treat you to lunch after the service that day?" or "I don't have much experience with sermon preparation; would you be willing to meet with me once or twice to teach me how to prepare a sermon?" After the meeting, send a handwritten thank you note or a personal email expressing your appreciation for the meeting. In the event that the potential supporter is unresponsive to your follow up requests, be sure not to make them feel bad about their lack of interest. Thank them for their time and do all you can to leave the meeting on a positive note.

**Be direct and specific when people ask how they can help.** If there are specific financial, volunteer, or prayer needs, express them to those interested in helping you. You may ask them to buy a few chairs at $40 each or to buy you a roll of stamps for postage. A useful tool in establishing partnerships with individuals is a "Wish List," a simple list of items you'd like to have for the new church. Keep this list handy so you can email it from your smartphone or pass it out on the spot. You should also determine if there are any items you are NOT willing to accept. Some well-meaning people will hear you mention that you need nursery equipment and want to donate their grandmother's rocking chair or the old guidepost magazines they've been collecting for the past ten years. Be sure to graciously let people know that you don't need these kinds of items. When Pillar Church began, we received a lot of donated items. Unfortunately, I forgot to specify what items we were willing to accept and which ones we didn't want. As a result, were given a 50-year-old baby grand piano, a 1970s 30-foot RV, and a 25-year-old Chevy Suburban, all of which proved difficult to liquidate and yielded very little return.

You should be getting positive responses from at least 50% of the people you ask directly. If your positive responses are less than 50%, go back through your presentation to honestly assess whether your presentation is set to accomplish its goal. If not, make the adjustments necessary to more effectively reach potential sponsors.

## Make a Plan and Expect It to Change

I once worked with a church planter, Jamie, who filled his Moleskin notebook with information about the church he wanted to plant, sketching out every aspect of the ministry in great detail. He spent hundreds of hours planning, praying, and dreaming. One day, Jamie threw away his notebook and explained, "Those were my dreams not God's." Years later, the church Jamie planted only slightly resembles those sketches in his Moleskin.

I have created a similar plan for every church I have ever helped start. None of those churches turned out exactly like the plan I created. If God is gracious to you, as he has been to me, somewhere in the midst of all our thwarted plans, God introduces His plans for the new church. God has a way of doing what you would never dream of or write down. He will call you to minister to people in places that you could never have imagined. I assure you, when God begins to reveal how He will use your new church for His glory, you will find yourself very thankful that God chose to accomplish His plan instead of yours.

Even so, planning and preparation remain important parts of the process, so dedicate yourself to prayer and subject yourself to trusted advisors throughout the process. At a minimum, the creation of the prospectus should be a team effort with your mentor and your partner. Creating a prospectus will cause you to think through aspects of the church's ministry that you are otherwise likely to overlook. Most importantly, as you make plans, keep in mind that your plans must always defer to God's plans: *"The heart of man plans his way, but the Lord establishes his steps"* (Proverbs 16:9).

## Budget Warnings

The budget section of the prospectus is typically the most challenging. Many church planters have the idea that if they shoot for the moon, they will land among the stars. It can be dangerous to throw out a ridiculously high goal amount and think that landing anywhere near that number is sufficient. The problem with this approach is that it's misleading. The last thing you want to do is give false information to potential supporters.

If you tell a potential supporter that you have to raise $250,000 in order to start a new church, you need to be able to justify those expenses with some pretty compelling plans. For example, if you're planning to spend 10% of your first year budget on outreach, it would be wise to justify the necessity of those outreach expenses. Generally, churches will not be excited about buying your new church a state-of-the-art sound system when they are using a sound system that they bought from a garage band at a yard sale. They also will not want to hire you as a full time staff member if they do not know that you will be a good pastor. Those kinds of requests will not compel them to give sacrificially.

## Working Toward Sustainability

A high budget will reduce the chances of financial sustainability. Financially speaking, the goal is to get your new congregation to a point of self-sustainability as soon as possible. Very few supporters sign on to support your work indefinitely. Every expense you add to your initial budget has implications for your future budgets. If you start off with two full-time paid staff members, you are ultimately saying that within a few years, this new congregation will be able to fully support those full time staff members. I am not saying that you should not have big dreams for your new church, but I am saying that every decision you make now has future financial implications. The higher your budget is, the less likely it is that you'll be able to support your future budget with congregational giving.

Asking for an exorbitant amount of money from a potential sponsoring church can come across as arrogant. Anyone can run an organization on a huge budget; no special skill is required for that. But with church planting must come a willingness to make personal sacrifices to obey God's call on your life. A year or two ago, an aspiring church planter made a pitch to me in my tiny office, which I share with a used tire shop. He sat down on my ripped chair, looked over my $89 IKEA* desk, and told me that to start a new church, he had to raise $400,000. As I looked at his budget, I noticed that his total church budget for that year was about $10,000 higher than my church budget. As if that weren't enough, his salary was $30,000 higher than mine! Now, I'm not opposed to someone else making more money than I do, but it was offensive that he would ask me to contribute to his unnecessarily high salary and church budget. Needless to say, I didn't agree to support him.

## Your Personal Budget

Completing an accurate personal budget is a prerequisite for creating an accurate church budget. Your salary is the first and wisest investment your new church will make. Churches need pastors more than meeting locations, equipment, other staff, or computers. For this reason, I recommend starting with your personal budget and determining exactly what amount of money you need to live on for the next few years. Forget what you have made in the past or what you hope to make in the future. This first budget is all about finding your personal budget threshold, the minimum amount necessary to properly care for your family. I have provided a Personal Budget Worksheet in Appendix I to help you determine the amount you need.

> I have completed the Personal Budget Worksheet.

> I have done a cost of living comparison between the
> church plant location and my current location.

## Your Church Plant Budget

Once your personal budget is finished, you can begin determining church budget items. As each item is added, keep in mind that your goal is to reach financial self-sustainability as early as possible. I suggest breaking your church budget into two categories: ongoing monthly expenses and start-up funds. Ongoing monthly expenses are those items that will be a regular part of your church budget into the foreseeable future. Include such items as personnel, facility rent, insurance, missionary support, outreach, and teaching materials in this portion of your budget. Another budget should be created for start-up funds, which are those costs that you will incur at the beginning of your church planting journey but are not likely to burden your monthly church budget. See Appendix J for a Sample Church Plant Budget.

You will find that some financial supporters are willing to support you monthly for a specific amount of time. Other supporters will prefer to give a one-time gift or to take up a special offering for your new church. Make a goal for each category and apply one-time gifts from churches and individuals to your start-up funds and ongoing monthly support to your monthly expenses.

Operating this way will ensure that you don't build your budget with dependency on one-time gifts. After you reach your thresholds in each category, you can move on to the next step. Even when a threshold is reached, you may find that one-time gifts and monthly supporters continue to come through. These gifts will provide you with extra margin for things you would like to do but are not necessary.

> I have completed my church plant budget.

Your church planting prospectus is an important part of the preparation to start a new church and will be your greatest aid as you approach churches and other potential supporters for financial support, prayer support, and additional accountability.

> I have completed my church plant prospectus.

# GATHER

After your plan is complete, it's time to start talking about it with other Christians. Unless you're independently wealthy or have a George Müller-like prayer life, you will need to gather some support. You will want co-laborers to join you in the day-to-day work of ministry, prayerful people to regularly call on God for you, and generous people to contribute financially. Most church planters consider this the most distasteful aspect of planting a new church. Generally speaking, church planters are intimidated by the idea of asking others for money and are afraid that their fundraising attempts will come up short.

In my observation, church plants rarely fail because of money, and this has proven to be true! New churches fail for all sorts of reasons, but money is generally not one of them. There are sufficient funding sources available to assist new church planters until the church is financially self-sustaining, but many church planters don't feel comfortable approaching churches, individuals, and other organizations for assistance. We don't feel comfortable seeking financial support from others because we are simply not accustomed to it. Fundraising feels surprisingly like begging. In our culture, most people who directly ask for money from others are either down-on-their-luck, kids, or politicians. Everyone else earns or borrows the money they need. Asking people for money feels very uncomfortable. Before we discuss the nuts and bolts of talking to others about money, I'll suggest a few mindsets we should adopt to give us a better perspective on fundraising for church planting.

## Healthy Mindsets for Gathering Resources

Financially supporting missionaries and church planters is a centuries-old practice in Jesus' church. Even now, virtually all healthy churches and committed Christians dedicate a portion of their monthly income to the spread of the Gospel. For this reason, you do not have to approach potential sponsor churches with timidity. You are asking them to do something that God has already told them to do. The Apostle Paul expressed his gratitude to the Philippian church for their monetary support: *"I have received full payment and more. I am well supplied having received from Epaphroditus the gifts you sent, a fragrant offering, a sacrifice acceptable and pleasing to God"* (Philippians 4:18). Paul's gratitude to the church at Philippi provides a good model for expressing gratitude to those who support you. Here are a few things to keep in mind as you approach potential financial supporters for help.

**You Are Not Entitled to Anyone's Support.** It is important to remind yourself that no church, organization, or individual owes you support simply because you have decided to plant a church, Guard yourself from the temptation to grow frustrated with churches and individuals who choose not to support you. If a church chooses not to sponsor you, it does not necessarily mean that they are evil, inwardly focused, or ignoring the Great Commission. It could mean that they feel a greater obligation to support another missionary and do not want to divide their efforts. It could even mean that they have not yet been convinced of your mission and church planting endeavor. No matter the reason, churches are entitled to choose whom they will and will not support.

**Church Planting is Free.** At the core, church planting is an absolutely free endeavor. It doesn't cost anything to start a new church. Churches are groups of gathered Christians, and inviting someone to gather is free. There are thousands of buildings in your community available to host your worship service free of charge—they are called homes! If a home is not what you are looking for, then you can probably find a sufficient public place to meet free of charge if you try hard enough. I have helped start new churches in furniture stores, funeral homes, community centers, houses, restaurants, and church buildings—all completely free of charge.

A few years ago I visited Temple Baptist Church in Halfmoon, New York. By New York standards, Temple is a large church with a large facility. While I was there, they told me the church started and met for free in the basement of a local bank until construction was completed on their current facility.

My own church held its first public services under the pavilion in a community park. Although people thought that it was important to start paying for an inside location once winter arrived, until then the pavilion worked just fine. Just because well-known churches are dropping piles of cash to hold their services in trendy warehouse spaces or high-end clubhouses doesn't mean you have to do the same thing. The majority of the world's churches meet in completely free worship spaces.

You are asking for God's money, so you might need to lower your expectations about what is actually necessary to fund the ministry of your church plant for the first few years. This is true for both your salary and the general budget of your new church. Bob Thune, a church planter in Omaha, Nebraska, tells the story of a defunct church planter:

> A few months ago a church planter I know had to close up shop. As I scrolled through his fire-sale ad on Craigslist, I couldn't help but wonder whether he really needed all this stuff. If he had allocated funds differently, could he have stayed in the game a little longer and reached a place of viability? It's not my place to question his decisions; *"before his own master he stands or falls"* (Romans 14:4). But I'm concerned that lots of young, starry-eyed church planters are easy prey for the salesmen of church plant capitalism. You don't have to be. Stand firm, church planter, and don't take the bait. We're four years in, and I just now ordered business cards. Letterhead? Maybe next year.

Business cards and sound systems are not the most important aspects of your new church—ministry is! Be very careful with the money that has been entrusted to you by God and His church. Remember that Scripture teaches that those who are faithful when given a little are considered trustworthy before God (Luke 16:10). Remember that excellence is not about what you have, but about what you do with what you have. Fight the temptation to compare yourself to the fastest growing church in America, or any other church for that matter. Instead, strive to do the very best with what God has given you.

Being a good steward doesn't mean you can't spend money on ministry. It just means you may have to get a bit more creative about accomplishing tasks and projects. If you work at it, you can become proficient at finding creative ways to accomplish ministry projects on small budgets. For example, you may find a few churches that are verbally supportive, but unwilling to give financially. I have found that churches that fall into this category are often willing to directly fund specific projects for new churches even if they will not commit to giving monthly. When I started Pillar Church in 2005, I made a pictorial wish list of the items we wanted for the first year of ministry. The list varied from very inexpensive things, like stamps and nursery toys, to very expensive things, like a 24-foot trailer and a sound system. I was amazed how generous the once resistant churches became when they were asked to give money to a very specific cause rather than a general one. In some cases individuals and churches had connections that made it significantly cheaper to obtain the supplies we needed. In the end, a church or individual provided nearly every item in my catalog, totaling more than $60,000 in equipment and supplies.

> I have made an equipment wish list for potential supporters.

## Financial Accountability

Before you collect your first dollar, it is important that you secure an accountant or another church to help you with financial responsibilities: accepting donated funds on your behalf, producing giving records, generating financial reports, and processing your payroll. You can not simply head over to the local bank, open a church account with your social security number (as if you were starting a small business), and begin accepting donations into that account. If you do this, you may find yourself starting a prison ministry as your next endeavor! The best scenario is for those responsibilities to be handled through your sending church. Having your funds administered by a third party adds a layer of financial accountability and gives your contributors confidence that everything is being handled in an upright manner. If you don't have a church that is willing to take care of this for you, I suggest using a ministry accounting service.

> I have secured accounting services.

## Cleaning Up Personal Debt

I recommend that anyone preparing to fundraise for a church plant has less than $10,000 of personal debt (excluding his home). I realize this may knock many people out, but I think this is an important factor to consider in the planning process. Church planting is not a lucrative occupation, and successful fundraising depends on the generous support of others. Though you may have many reasonable explanations for your personal debt, no church or denomination wants to pay the interest payments on the choices of your past. If you are in this situation, your first priority is to get a good job and get busy paying down your debt. Having a high amount of personal debt doesn't disqualify you from planting, but it should delay you from planting. Once you are in a reasonable financial situation, you can start to raise money for your church planting efforts.

I realize that this type of advice could sound pretty judgmental and legalistic, but this advice was birthed out of my own experiences planting with debt. At the time I began planting Pillar Church of Dumfries, I had more than $40,000 of personal debt from student loans, credit cards, and car loans. We had no savings, no emergency funds, and no contingency plan. To make matters worse, my wife and I had just purchased a new home that was significantly more than we needed or could comfortably afford. These bad decisions combined with the unique stress brought on by church planting led to some terrible experiences that could have been avoided had I not been in that financial position. Eventually, after the pain and stress of spending years financially overwhelmed, we made some drastic decisions and got completely out of debt (excluding our home). My advice to you is simple: work hard to clean up your personal debt before attempting to plant a new church. It may seem like an impossible task at first, but, trust me, it will not get any easier once you start planting. The stresses on your time and budget will be greater as time goes on, and Satan will seek to exploit your financial vulnerability to thwart your church planting work.

> Excluding my home, I have less than $10,000 in personal debt.

## Identifying Funding Sources

A church planter's paycheck may come from a variety of sources. Churches, denominations or networks, core team, individual supporters, and even part time employment all commonly contribute to the income of a church planter. By keeping the funds from these different sources in one account, you can get a realistic picture of your income, which will allow you to make wise financial decisions for the progress of the new church.

## Getting Started

Using your new church's monthly budget threshold as a goal, you can now start working to secure funds for your new church's monthly budget. Since no two church planters have exactly the same situation, it's important to start with the monthly goal and then work backward from that number. For example, if your total annual budget for your new church is $100,000, then you have a monthly budget need of $8,333.33. Your monthly budget may look something like this:

Personnel – $4,500
Meeting Space – $1,300
Insurance – $200
Operating Expenses – $1,100
Missionary Support – $200
Outreach – $1,000
Savings – $533.33

To meet that monthly budget, you will depend on a variety of sources. In order to fund the above budget, your income sources may look something like this:

Sending Church – $1,000

Supporting Churches – $3,000
Denominational Support – $1,500
Networks or Associations – $1,000
Core Group – $1,000
Individual Supporters – $1,500

Your most variable category by far will be your supporting churches category because everyone's circumstance is different. I know one planter who had ten supporting churches, each giving between $100 and $1,500 per month. Another planter received significant funds from the government for his former military service, which lowered the total amount he needed to raise. Yet another guy lived debt free for years in anticipation of planting a new church. He saved so much money that he was able to accept a much lower salary during the formative years of his new church. Each unique situation will require a customized funding approach. In Appendix K you will find a Sample Funding Summary to keep track of your progress.

## Whom to Approach

Your sponsorship search should begin as close to home as possible. Put your greatest effort into securing partnerships within your own church, community, and denomination before venturing outside. These are your most likely sources of funding, and they are the ones that will stand to benefit most by partnering with you.

- **Your Sending Church** – Since church planting is a Great Commission activity, and churches should be about fulfilling the Great Commission, you should work hardest to secure the partnership of the church you currently attend. After you have received their affirmation, be sure to ask the elders what amount they anticipate giving toward your monthly budget.

  My sending church has committed to support me.

- **Your Denomination** – Nearly every denomination has a church planting budget of some kind. Unless you already have a relationship with denominational leaders, take your pastor with you when you approach them. If they have a formal program and application process, follow it quickly and completely to leave a good impression. Denominations and networks that plant large numbers of churches are likely to have a robust application and approval process, so be sure to start the application process several months before you plan to begin.

> My denomination has committed to support me.

- **Other Churches** – Make a list of churches with which you have some connection. Some examples might include churches with an interest in your planting location, your parents' church, or other churches you have attended in the past. You may also have success connecting with churches attended by family members or friends.

> I have made a list of 30 churches that could support me.

- **Friends and Family** – Former associates, friends, and family often want to contribute in some way. Find a way that they can give regularly to your work. Be sure to ask each of them directly instead of sending out a letter or a group email. Emails and letters are easy to ignore, but direct contact requires a response. This may feel uncomfortable, but many things associated with church planting are uncomfortable. You may need to develop some skills and humility in this area. Don't be afraid to reach out to friends and family for help.

> I have made a list of 30 individuals who could support me.

- **Other Possibilities** – Your employer, your seminary, ministerial associations, and mission agencies may also consider supporting your effort. I have included a list of Church Planter Networks in Appendix L.

> I have researched church planting networks and denominational funding sources and have applied to the ones with which I wish to work.

## Making a Donor Database

I started working with new churches in 1996. Since then I have been involved in dozens of church planting projects and have raised hundreds of thousands of dollars for new churches. That would not have been possible if I had a "take the money and run" approach. Instead, I have worked hard to create ongoing relationships with those who support my church planting endeavors. Over the years I have spent a significant amount of time managing a database of supporters. If you and I have ever met, emailed, or talked on the phone, there is a good chance that you are in my database. Some people in the database have never been contacted, while others have been contacted dozens of times. The database only gets used once or twice a year, but every time I use it, the results get better and better. Past supporters have had the positive experience of hearing the results of their investment through ongoing communication. This drastically increases the odds of them giving again in the future.

Church planters often tell me they hate fundraising or they aren't good at it. It's true that asking others for money is uncomfortable, but remember that you are not raising money for yourself. You are raising money for the mission. If you feel timid about asking for support, it is likely that potential supporters will sense your apprehension and will be less likely to believe in your cause. On the other hand, if you speak confidently and persuasively about the need for new churches in the place or people group that you are trying to reach, your enthusiasm will likely be infectious.

After fundraising for more than fifteen years, I am periodically contacted by supporters. Someone will call, "We have $5,000 left over in our missions account this year. Are there any church planting projects you know of that are in need right now?" or "I just bought a new car, and my old one is in good shape. I was thinking about donating it to the church for you to give to a church planter who needs one." Once someone even gave our church a vehicle that we quickly liquidated to assist a church planter in Indonesia. Another friend once got a call from a couple who said, "We've just received an inheritance from a family member, and we want to give

64

you $40,000 because we know we can trust you to use the money to plant new churches."

These kinds of relationships don't happen by accident. They develop when others have confidence that their money is being used wisely for Kingdom purposes. Unless you plan to plant one church and never need the help or support of others again, I encourage you to begin building a supporter database now.

> I have started a donor database.

> I have created a plan to communicate with my supporters regularly.

## Be Content

You can plant a church without raising money, but if you choose to seek support from other people and ministries, be sure to be grateful and gracious to every supporter. Be content with the resources that God brings you, and avoid the temptation to expect the same type of blessings another church planter has received. As soon as the first check is deposited into your church's account, you have a stewardship responsibility before God. God will give you what you need for the day, so trust in Him for provision. Consider church planter Paul's secret for contentment:

> *For I have learned in whatever situation I am in to be content. I know how to be brought low, and I know how to abound. In any and every circumstance, I have learned the secret of facing plenty and hunger, abundance and need. I can do all things through Him who strengthens me* (Philippians 4:11-13).

## A Note to Prospective Sending Churches

While we're thinking about how to gather church planting resources and from whom, I thought this would be a good opportunity to discuss matters from a sending church's perspective.

## The Benefits of Being a Sending Church

Financial support of missionaries and church planters has been a hallmark of Christ's church from the beginning. Virtually all healthy churches and committed Christians dedicate a portion of their income to spreading the Gospel. For the congregation, the benefits of supporting a new church far outweigh the costs. Our church, for example, gives a hearty portion of our income to support church planters. I'll admit at times it's difficult to allocate so much to other churches when we have real "needs" in our own congregation, but we've clearly seen that the more we have prioritized Kingdom growth, the better off we are as a people. We've simply concluded that it's impossible to out-give God. Let me share some very real benefits associated with financially supporting new churches.

- **Gospel Priority** – The struggle to restrict spending on personal preferences in order to allocate generous portions for establishment of other churches is good for a church. It's an act of corporate worship. Just as personal sacrifices for the sake of generosity benefit the individual Christian's soul, corporate sacrifices benefit the soul of a congregation. When a church gives its resources for the spread of the Gospel, it's affirming that the Gospel is more valuable than their personal comfort.

- **Relational Accessibility** – Financially supporting a particular church planting family will personalize the mission. When a church supports entities and organizations (a good thing), it sometimes misses the privilege of personally knowing the individuals it supports.

- **Faith in God's Provision** – "Give, and it will be given to you" (Luke 6:38). This scriptural principle is as applicable to churches as it is to individuals. When a church gives sacrificially to help spread the Gospel, the congregation will experience unexpected blessings, which will build the congregation's faith in God and decrease their dependence on means and methods they can explain and control.

## Advice for Sending Churches

As important as it is to give generously and sacrificially to spread the Gospel, it is equally important to ensure that the money given is being put to good use. Sending churches should put the following safeguards in place.

- **Require Fiscal Transparency.** Before deciding how much to give, a sending church should make sure it has a clear picture of the new church's budget and income and who else is giving to the new church. If a church planter is unwilling to be transparent about his support from other individuals, churches, and entities, a sending church should be wary of supporting him.

- **Manage Expectations.** A sending church should be sure its expectations for communication, accountability, and success metrics are clearly understood before making a commitment to support a new church. Entering a simple written covenant that outlines specific expectations will help avoid miscommunication and frustration.

- **Meet Regularly.** If the church planter is local, a sending church should ask him to give a report at its leader or member meetings. Inviting the planter to preach or simply setting a time to meet for coffee can give the sending church regular opportunities to check in with him. The more a sending church knows about what's going on in the church plant, the better. If a church plant is far away, the sending church should budget some money to bring in the planter at least annually and use technology to have more frequent face time with him.

- **Devise an Exit Strategy.** Almost any project tends to be more expensive, difficult, and laborious than expected. A clear exit strategy will motivate a church plant to achieve fiscal independence within a reasonable time.

In 1910, British author and theologian G. K. Chesterton wrote, "If a thing is worth doing, it is worth doing badly."[13] Today, the quip often includes a qualifier: "If a thing is worth doing, it is worth doing badly—at first." That's good advice for churches getting started in church planting. As with any new skill, proficiency comes with time. A sending church should embrace the process of learning how to plant churches because little it does as a church will have as much lasting significance as church planting.

# ASSEMBLE

Churches most naturally give birth to other churches. Sure, it's possible to get a church started without another church being involved. It's also possible to have a healthy baby without the dad being around. While it may be possible, it isn't best.

Some church planters overreact to the unhealthy patterns they see in existing churches by wrongly concluding that they would be better off planting their own church without any previously churched people. They seek to build a new church on a foundation of newly or not-yet converted people. They often follow the mantra, "Belong, then believe!" While I agree that churches should aggressively pursue those who are far from God, I think there are some unhealthy ideas behind a mindset that forsakes including mature Christians in the church planting process. Let me explain.

- **Christian Hypocrisy** – While at times Christians may have the reputation for being a difficult and quarrelsome bunch, they definitely are not the enemy of the church. The Bible tells us that Christians possess love, joy, peace, patience, kindness, goodness, faithfulness, gentleness, and self-control (Galatians 5:22). Christians with a genuine faith in Christ, living spirit-filled lives, are an absolute pleasure to work alongside. Be careful not to confuse genuine Christians with the posers who make it their mission to oppose the cause of Christ from the comfort of their spot in the pew. Jesus didn't call such people Christians; He called them wolves and tares (Matthew 7:15, Matthew 13:24-30). I don't suggest putting those guys on your missionary team, but I do suggest putting some true Christians on there.

- **Pastoral Snobbery** – Being a church planter means being a pastor to all kinds of people. You may be turned off by some churches' dysfunctionality and some people's hypocrisy, but refusing to pastor them is a form of pastoral snobbery. Good pastors care for the sheep who are entrusted to them by the Chief Shepherd. God may have more in mind for your ministry than simply the conversion of sinners. He may also want to use you to help others grow to maturity in the faith.

- **Rugged Individualism** – Throughout the New Testament we see commands to live out the Christian life with one another, encouraging one another to grow (Hebrews 10:24). How can a church practice the "one anothers" if everyone involved is immature in the faith or unconverted? Can the blind lead the blind? Churches need mature Christians to help disciple less mature Christians and evangelize the lost.

## Establishing a Missionary Team

The process of assembling a missionary team can be one of the most enjoyable aspects of starting a new church. A missionary team is the leadership core of your new church. Though they are not paid staff, they are mature missional Christians who sense a similar call to serving in the establishment of a new church, and they are an essential part of your team. Some will uproot their lives to join the team at great personal sacrifice. They may quit jobs, sell houses, liquidate assets, and seek new employment positions all for the honor of starting a church for Jesus. Each of them will sense a unique call to the work.

Allow me to use a sports analogy to explain what I mean. Let's pretend you were a basketball player. For years you played ball around your hometown. You played on every court, and you know all the ballers in every neighborhood. One day, the coach of the high school team calls you and says, "You know we won the state championship last year, and we're about to start the new season. We need some real competition to see if we're still on our game. Would you be willing to put together a team with the best street players you can find, and we'll see if we can beat you?" I imagine your dream team would include the best point guard, the best long shooter, and the best dunker you know. You would do everything possible to put together a team who would crush the reigning state champs. You might even call some guys from out of town and ask them to drive in for the game.

This is the same approach you should take in assembling your church planting team. It's an all-star team of missional Christians. I have seen many church planters make the critical mistake of begging for team members instead of recruiting them. This would be like putting an ad on Craigslist. You might get a lot of players, but you would probably lose the game. Plus, no decent player wants to be on a mediocre team. After seeing that you have some duds on your team, the great players won't be interested in joining. The same is true in church planting. You should approach the assembly of your missionary team with similar quality standards.

As you start working, other people will grow interested in your work and desire to join it. Be sure to differentiate between those on your missionary team and those who attend your Bible studies, small group meetings, church outreach events, and preview services. One way to do this is to have a "Missionary Team Meeting" once or twice a month specifically for those who are leading different aspects of the ministry.

## Starting Your Search

The first step to assembling a team of missionaries is determining what positions need to be filled. This decision is in part dictated by your personal gifts and passions. For instance, if your strength is in teaching and leadership, consider the position for public teaching filled by you, and then look for others who are strong in evangelism, discipleship, outreach, children's ministry, music, technology, and financial management. Begin by making a job description for each position you wish to be filled by a volunteer. In Appendix M you will find a sample list of ministry job descriptions. Be sure to include your partner and mentor in this process.

It may also be helpful to talk to other church planters about the team members who have played key roles in their church planting efforts.

> I have determined what leadership positions need
> to be filled on my missionary team.

Once your job descriptions are complete, list the Christians you know who have the gifts to adequately fulfill the positions. Be sure not to limit your list only to those you think would consider joining your team or those who already live in your mission field. Rather, list everyone you can think of, regardless of where they live, their current occupation, or whether you think they would consider joining your team. Remember, this is a dream team. You may not be able to think of people to fill all of the positions, but list those you can think of and leave the others blank.

You may want to consider contacting some friends already serving in ministry to ask for recommendations for people to fill specific positions. I remember once calling my childhood pastor and telling him that I was looking for someone to fill a specific position. I described the role and he said, "I've got just the guy for you!" After a just a few phone interviews and the endorsement of a trusted pastor, we invited a young man whom we had never even met face-to-face to join our team, and it worked out great. Once your list of possible teammates is complete, it's time to begin recruiting.

> I have made a list of possible teammates to fill each
> of the positions on the missionary team.

## The Big Ask

Before you begin contacting possible teammates, make sure you have spent adequate time in prayer seeking God's confirmation of your selections. In the process, God may bring others to your mind or even reveal new possible teammates. If you're not sure about someone, wait until you are. It's very easy to put the wrong person in a position, but it is extremely painful to get them out of it. Once you are sure about your selections, set up a meeting. Here is some advice for making "the big ask."

- **Ask boldly and specifically from the start.** As soon as you sit down for a conversation, you can say something like this: "The reason I've asked you to meet with me today is that I'd like you to consider quitting your job and moving with me to (insert city) to plant a new church." Drop "the ask" like a bomb. Don't beat around the bush, don't qualify it, and don't leave them with the responsibility of interpreting your intentions. This kind of directness leaves no room for uncertainty. Potential teammates needs to know that you are absolutely certain that they are right for the job, so your certainty about the matter will help them make a decision. While they are still stunned by your bold ask, list a few specific reasons you believe they are right for the position.

- **Avoid discussing logistics.** One of the biggest mistakes you can make at this point is to discuss logistics. The logistics of a decision like this are often overwhelming. While it is very likely that the potential teammate will have a lot of questions about moving and finding housing or jobs, avoid those questions for now, and ask them to commit to pray with you about whether this is God's will. You can say something like, "I'm not exactly sure how all this will work out right now, but I know if this is God's will, He will provide." Urge your potential teammates to seek direction from the Lord and to be ready and willing to obey the Lord's call.

- **Set a timeline for follow up.** You might ask, "Would you and your wife commit to pray about this for a week? Then if you are sensing God's calling, we can begin discussing the details." Don't leave the invitations hanging indefinitely. Put a deadline on the decision by making a follow up plan.

- **Don't make the decision for them.** If you don't hear back, don't assume that the answer is no. Require an answer and offer reassurance along the way that you believe he or she is the right person for the role.

> I have met personally with those I wish to invite onto my missionary team and have issued a "Big Ask."

## The Walk-Ons

You may not be able to fill your entire team by just asking people you know, so be looking for "walk-ons," those who hear about your church planting work and are drawn to it. Shortly before planting Pillar Church in the suburbs of Washington DC, I was in South Florida attending the wedding of a good friend. During the reception, I saw a girl named Amanda whom I had met once or twice during my college years, but had not seen in a long time. I knew she was an outstanding musician and a passionate Christian, but I didn't know much more than that at the time. We greeted one another and she introduced me to her husband Tim, an impressive young professional with a big smile and a friendly demeanor. A few moments into the conversation she asked me what I was doing these days. I used the opportunity to briefly share my dream of planting a church near a military base and using the natural movements of service members to plant churches around the world. They affirmed my work with nodding heads and nice comments before we parted ways. A month or so later, Tim called to tell me they were looking for jobs in the DC area and were considering moving to help us get the new church started. I was floored! Sure enough, they relocated, bought a house a few miles from our meeting location, and began serving right away. Today, Tim is an elder in our church and Amanda leads us in worship each Sunday.

You never know whom God will call to join you in your work. If God has called you to plant a new church, there's a good chance he is also calling others to the task as well. This new church is much less about you than you might think. God is building a church for Himself, and while you will play an important role in that church, you can't build the church alone. Seek others to join you in the work and always be looking for the unexpected people God will call.

A small group of committed and faithful Christians can accomplish a great deal more than a large group of half-hearted ones. You need not look further than Jesus' disciples to prove this point. When you start gathering teammates, you may be tempted to invite anyone with a pulse, but that will not help you reach your goal of planting a faithful church. Just as the quality of a cake's ingredients affect the taste of the finished cake, the quality of your mission team will affect the outcome of your ministry. Seek quality over quantity when it comes to assembling a missionary team, and you will be thankful you did.

> I have filled all of the positions on my missionary team.

## Term Commitments for Missionary Team Members

It is wise for you to seek term commitments from members of your missionary team. Term commitments allow people to participate even if they are not entirely sure this is a long-term commitment. This is especially important for those who come from other churches. Often, church members want to help with a new church planting effort, but they cannot bear the idea of leaving indefinitely the familiarity of the church they love. Offering commitment terms of six, twelve or eighteen months allows members to serve wholeheartedly in the new church planting team without worrying that they will disappoint someone when they return to their home church.

Term commitments can help the church planter as well. Sometimes people will take on a particular role on your missionary team and, for whatever reason, it ends up not working out. The end of a term is a nice opportunity to place someone else in the position without causing a great deal of conflict. For those who do choose to leave at the end of a term, be sure to celebrate the work they have done and express sincere appreciation for their participation.

## Common Problems on Missionary Teams

Before we move to the next stage of the church planting process, I want to identify some common problems that can develop on missionary teams so that you can watch for them and correct them before they get out of hand. Fortunately, many of the problems that commonly develop on missionary teams are not so much an issue with actual team members as they are issues with the church planter.

- **Expectations** – It's important to communicate your expectations to missionary team members clearly and completely. For example, it's not enough to say, "You're in charge of making the website," unless you truly have no expectations for the form and function of the website. Instead, you have to be clear about what you want the website to do and how you want it to look. Give a color scheme and examples of several websites you like. Give a sitemap, a deadline, and a budget. If you fail to communicate these details, you can expect that what the person produces will probably not meet your expectations. Asking for changes after much time and hard work has been invested can be discouraging and frustrating. Lastly, communicate clearly that the project needs your approval before going live. Your team member may assume that he is now in charge of this process and need not seek any further approval. Make sure that you are clear about the path to completion for the project.

- **Micromanagement** – Once you have communicated clear expectations about the job you want your team member to do, be sure not to micromanage the work. Don't ask to review the work every step of the way, and be careful not to nitpick the details of the project. If you set out an expectation that was not met, be clear about that. For instance, referring to the previous website example, if you didn't give any instructions regarding layout, don't criticize the layout chosen. Remember, your goal is for this teammate to oversee this project in the future so that you do not have to. Communicate your desires for the project, and let your teammate run with it.

- **Inspection** – You may have heard the old adage, "People don't do what you expect; they do what you inspect." I have found this to be true on multiple occasions. It is good to set up checkpoints with volunteers to evaluate progress as they work on projects. This can be done in a group setting where everyone shares progress and weighs in on the evaluation, or it can be done in a one-on one environment. Make sure everyone knows when the inspection point will happen so they can adequately prepare. It's not a good idea to do surprise inspections with volunteers; they usually do not take kindly to it. If you are an approachable leader, you will find that people will voluntarily check with you along the way even when there is no inspection point scheduled. Usually this means that they are excited about progress they have made on the project and want your affirmation. Be careful not to "rain on their parade," but if you see something that needs attention, say you'd like the opportunity to look closer at the project at the next scheduled meeting.

- **Territoriality** – In new church environments developing territorial feelings about an area of service within the church can be a big problem. Let's use music as an example. When the church begins, there are only ten people on the missionary team. None are very good musicians, but one guy can play the guitar, and his wife has a pretty good voice, so they end up leading the music for team meetings and preview services. A few weeks before formal services begin, a professional musician joins your team. He is willing to lead but doesn't want to hurt anyone's feelings by taking over. In a perfect world, the guitar-playing guy and his wife would happily step aside and let the professional musician take the lead, but that is not always what happens. Often missionary team members will feel a sense of unhealthy entitlement about their role, and this can be harmful to the forward progress of the new church. To help prevent this from happening, talk in a group setting about the danger of territoriality and remind the group that everything you are doing is so that people might know Jesus. Encourage them to expect that God will send people with exceptional talents and gifts to be a part of this new church, and ask people to consider how they might respond in that situation.

## Whom to Empower and Whom to Avoid

Placing people in positions is easy; removing them is not. Make sure that you choose your team carefully and wisely. The disunity caused by one disruptive team member can be detrimental to the formation of a new church. Before inviting people into the leadership circle in your new church, spend some time in honest evaluation. Following are a few filters I use to guide my assessments.

- Never move forward if you doubt the ***character*** of the person you are considering.
- If you doubt the ***commitment*** of the person you are considering, probe further to confirm it.
- If the person you are considering merely lacks **experience** or **proficiency**, move forward prayerfully, offering him the training and support he needs.

Empower those who serve willingly without seeking a position or title for the work they do. Those who require you to give them an official position before they are willing to serve will not serve well after they are given a position.

You'll find that some people commit easily and others consider commitments carefully before agreeing. Pay attention to this distinction and be cautious of those who commit too easily. When you're starting a new church, you feel desperate for help and participation, but don't let this desperation cause you to place dysfunctional people in positions of authority. Entitlement is an ugly trait, and it is cancer in a young church.

Speaking of dysfunctional people, church plants are a magnet for them. Those who have been refused positions in other ministries or been avoided or marginalized in other churches often see a new church as a new opportunity to have a "seat at the table." I'm not encouraging you to turn these people away, but I am encouraging you not to put them in charge of anything.

Different Christians respond differently in various environments. Someone who was successful as a small group leader in a large church may not work well with the lack of resources and training at a new church.

Some of the best missionary team members I've ever worked with were those who were sitting on the sidelines in other churches. Perhaps they felt their gifts weren't needed in a church with an abundance of people and resources, but when they came to an environment where nearly every person has a significant job, their commitment level skyrockets. In my observation, usually the truly helpful people are those sitting quietly in the back of the room while others vie for attention and position. So choose your co-missionaries carefully and prayerfully. Communicate expectations to them clearly and check in on their work regularly.

> I have set up a way to regularly check up on the progress of each missionary team member.

# BEFRIEND

## Involving Non-Christians

There's a good chance that as you start working and interacting with folks from the community, you will have the occasion to invite non-Christians into your work. Working shoulder-to-shoulder with non-Christians provides a great opportunity to share the Gospel with them, but let me caution you from officially including them on your missionary team. Including a non-Christian on a missionary team is like a Republican taking a Democrat with him on the campaign trail.

Very soon your missionary team will be populated with members of your small but growing congregation. If there are not distinct lines between Christians and non-Christians in your church, non-Christians may function perfectly well there without ever being confronted with the need to trust in Christ for salvation.

I'm not saying there's no place for non-Christians to encounter genuine Christian community. You should be regularly inviting people into the warmth of authentic Christianity, but be careful not to lead them to believe that their physical presence is what God wants from them. Make clear the distinction between those who follow Jesus and those who do not.

## Living in Your Mission Field

Now that you have raised the money necessary to support your family and have enlisted a team of volunteers, you are ready to begin ministry. While you will still be gathering resources and keeping your supporters informed of the happenings of your ministry, you are now at the place where you can turn your primary attention to your mission field. If you haven't done so already, now is the time to pack up the moving truck and move to your mission field. Many church planters, including myself, have tried to minister in a community where they don't live.

When I planted Pillar Church in the suburbs of Washington DC, we owned a beautiful, new home in a rural setting nearly an hour away from Pillar's meeting location. We had a big lot in a gated community, and my back yard was right at the 9th hole of the Meadows Farms golf course. Our whole family loved our house. When God called us to plant the church, we were in the middle of building that particular home. Since there were no comparably priced homes in the community where we were planting the church, we decided to stay in our new home. Over the next several years, the difficulties of living so far from our church overwhelmed us, and we decided to sell our home. We moved into a much smaller, much older townhome less than a mile from our meeting location. This turned out to be one of the best decisions we made in the early stages of church planting.

It's difficult to express how much living in a community helps you understand it. When we moved to our mission field, we immediately formed dozens of relationships with people living there. We had new bankers, a new grocery store, and new neighbors, and our kids had new playmates. The best part was that every one of the people we met lived close enough to our new church that we could easily invite them to a service or to our home for a meal. None of that was possible when we lived so far away.

If the church is being planted in an expensive or difficult place, you may be tempted to live some distance from your ministry field, but I cannot overstate the importance of living in your mission field. I encourage you to do whatever it takes to make this a reality. Participating in the struggles of living in your mission field will give you innumerable advantages in connecting with the very people you want to reach.

> Both my wife and I have committed to do whatever it takes to live in our mission field.

## Seeing Yourself as a Missionary

Moving forward in your church planting journey, you are a missionary. Soon you will win people to Christ, gather Christians together, and become a pastor to them. But you are now and forevermore a missionary. Church planting is all about reaching the lost with the Gospel of Jesus Christ. Everything you do over the next few years is about making disciples and teaching them to observe all the things Jesus has commanded them to do.

You have moved to this community to be the church, not to put on church. When you first arrive in the mission field, you may be tempted to immediately begin conducting worship services, but it is important to first gather people in small groups and one-on-one settings. You should encourage your team to rub shoulders with as many non-Christians as possible. You and your team should work hard to form relationships with lost people by serving in various volunteer and civic capacities.

## No Welcome Wagon

When you begin working in a community, there is a very good chance that no one will care that you are starting a new church. Some may even express disgust over it. The people of your community may not sense there are any needs that could be met by a church. I tell you this so that you're not disappointed when you arrive and there is no Welcome Wagon. Many church planters act as if the mayor should give them an award for starting a new church in the community, and then they are shocked by the lack of interest others have in their new church.

When I first started church planting, I was most surprised by the response that other evangelical pastors had to my arrival. I remember sitting down with the pastor of a fairly large church in the community. This church was the fastest growing church in our region, where literally hundreds of new families were moving into the community each month. When my partner and I began sharing what we were planning to do, I was shocked when the pastor told us that we were "wasting our time" and that a new church in this community was "completely unnecessary" because the programs in his church were meeting every spiritual need of the community. We left his office feeling like we had just been run over by a truck. Not only did he not welcome us, but he told us to go back home!

Amazingly, we received similar responses from many other pastors in the community. Some were kind (in an apathetic sort of way), but most viewed us as competition and encouraged us not to proceed. We did however meet one pastor who received us warmly. He offered use of his facility and copy machine and welcomed us to share with his congregation about our endeavor. He was a breath of fresh air and a bright spot in an otherwise discouraging process.

Going through the process of meeting the pastors in your ministry field will give you a sense of how many good evangelical churches there are in your area and let you know who your allies are. For that reason alone, I suggest taking the time to contact every evangelical pastor in your new community, and when possible, meet with them face-to-face.

> I have contacted the pastors of other churches in my mission field and told them of my plans to start a new church.

## Person of Peace

If you've done much work in international missions, you've likely heard the phrase, "person of peace." A person of peace is someone with a large network of friends or business contacts in your mission field who shows an interest in helping you. This person may or may not be a Christian, but for whatever reason they are friendly toward you and are willing to give you access to their network of relationships. Jesus instructs us how to relate to a person of peace: *"If a man of peace is there, your peace will rest on him; if not, it will return to you. Stay in that house, eating and drinking whatever they give you"* (Luke 10:5-6).

When we started Pillar Church, Quantico had about 600 residents and was completely surrounded by a military base, which cut them off from the sprawling suburbs of Northern Virginia. In order to even get into the town, you had to enter through the base security checkpoint. When we began working in Quantico, there was no church in the town. In fact, as far as we could tell, there had not been a church in Quantico for decades. There was only one church building in Quantico that had long ago been purchased by the Masons.

One day the church planter and I were walking around the town talking with residents and praying for God to open opportunities for ministry. We stopped in a small coffee shop to take a break. After we finished our coffee, we stopped to pray. When we finished our prayer, there was a friendly, grandmotherly woman standing in front of me. She asked what we were praying for. We told her that we had come to start a new Baptist church in the town, and we were praying for God's help. With a look of shock on her face, she introduced herself as Betty and asked if she could sit down and talk with us. Betty and her friend Jerri took a seat near us and explained that they had been meeting in this coffee shop for many years praying for a new church to begin in the town. As it turned out, Betty was one of Quantico's best-known figures, affectionately called Miss Betty by townspeople. Miss Betty and Jerri joined our effort and within weeks had introduced us to dozens of other townspeople. Betty was a person of peace.

On another occasion, as a social worker was visiting a family in our community, they explained how our church had been proactive with helping them through their troubles. The social worker contacted me to ask if we had any invitations to our church that she could give to people she met who were in need of the same type of care. I took her a stack of invite cards, and in the following months we received regular calls from individuals through her referral. She was a person of peace.

> I have made a list of volunteer opportunities in my community, have chosen one to participate in personally, and have passed the list to each of the missionary team members for consideration.

## Befriending Community and Civic Leaders

Sometimes relationships with community and civic leaders find you; other times you must find them. Work hard to meet the community and civic leaders in your mission field. If your experience is like mine, you'll find more receptiveness from community leaders than you will from other church leaders. When you meet a community leader, be sure to express your desire to start a church that is of benefit to the community, offer to help with community events, and show interest in the civic priorities that align with your church's priorities.

You may find greater success in your community by assisting town leadership with existing community functions than you will by creating alternative ones. In most municipalities there is a staff member assigned to plan and execute community events. Reach out to this person and offer your services. The staff of our church is on a first name basis with our mayor and is in regular communication with our town community events coordinator. Both individuals have a very favorable view of our church and rely on us to provide volunteers for most of the community events that take place throughout the course of the year. They even let us wear t-shirts advertising our church. This year our town recognized us as a Community Service Partner of the Year, complete with a plaque and a picture in the local paper.

This type of partnership can also apply to non-profit organizations in your community. Homeless shelters, crisis pregnancy centers, food banks, and other community service organizations are constantly in need of volunteers. Choose one or two of these organizations, and form a relationship with them.

> I have made contact with political, civic, and non-profit leaders in my community and have expressed my desire to join them in any effort to improve our community.

## Evangelistic Training

To be completely honest, I'm not a big fan of personal evangelism programs. Over the course of my life, I have been through many such programs and have found that a memorized method for personal evangelism sounds too much like a used car salesman for my taste. I don't want to manipulate anyone into a profession of faith in Christ with a savvy presentation, but I do want to see people genuinely converted by the power of the Gospel. On the other hand, I am commanded to *"equip the saints for the work of the ministry"* (Ephesians 4:12), and evangelism is definitely part of the ministry of church planting. Therefore, I must equip those in my church to befriend and evangelize others. Here are a few suggestions for equipping your missionary team members to share the Gospel without giving them a script.

- **Clarify the Gospel.** Perhaps the very best thing you can do to equip your core team for evangelism is to make sure they understand the Gospel clearly enough to repeat it. If the members of your church don't know how to explain the Gospel to others, they will not have the confidence to share it. Help them understand and articulate the Gospel by rehearsing it to them often. In the beginning, this might mean articulating the Gospel every time you get together with your team. It may even mean asking others to explain the Gospel to the group as a way of forcing them to work through articulating it themselves.

- **Lead Your Team to Memorize Scripture.** When I planted Pillar Church, I asked our core team to commit to memorizing passages of Scripture together. Virtually all of the passages memorized related to salvation: *"For our sake, God made Him to be sin who knew no sin, so that in Him we might become the righteousness of God"* (2 Corinthians 5:21).

- **Model Evangelism.** The people you serve alongside will follow your example much more than your teaching. Freely and regularly share the Gospel with others you meet, not in an attempt to appear overly pious, but by allowing it to become part of your regular rhythm of life. You don't want to do this only when people are watching, as Jesus warns us against that kind of thing: *"Beware of practicing your righteousness before other people in order to be seen by them, for then you will have no reward from your Father who is in heaven"* (Matthew 6:1). On the other hand, you don't have to be hesitant to engage in spiritual conversations just because someone is with you and watching.

- **Pray for the Lost.** Make praying for the lost a part of every core team meeting. Pray for them specifically and regularly, and encourage others to pray aloud for those to whom they are attempting to witness. You can tell a lot about someone's desires and passions by listening to their prayers. If you have a desire to see lost men and women come to faith in Christ, be sure to pray for them publicly and regularly, and encourage others to pray for their friends and family members who are not yet followers of Jesus.

> I have chosen some Scripture related to salvation that I will lead my missionary team to memorize.

## Avoiding Gimmicks

A man named Charles Bayly wrote an excellent parable in the 1960s called *The Gospel Blimp*. The story is about a group of Christians with a burden for their neighbors and what they do to bring the Gospel to them. I don't want to give the story away, but trust me when I say it's thought provoking and helpful for those thinking about how to reach out to their communities. The book can be found at several online retailers.

> I have read *The Gospel Blimp* by Charles Bayly.

Leading your church to have passion for the salvation of non-Christians in your community will require constant attention. You will have to work to make community involvement and evangelism a culture within your church. There is a strong pull that will be drawing your church to self-centeredness and apathy toward the plight of those without Christ. As the church planter, it is your job to keep your team focused on making new disciples.

To fight this pull, you will need to set aside a portion of your church's budget and your personal creativity for the planning of outreach efforts in your community. The best outreach ideas are those that put members of your church in direct conversation with members of your community. Throughout my time as a church planter, I have tried dozens of different outreach events and programs. Some of them have been fruitful, but many of them have not. Even still, the constant buzz of outreach activity in our church created a culture of concern for the souls of those who live around us.

I'm a regular listener to the podcast "This American Life." The host of the podcast, Ira Glass, is a staunch atheist (his words, not mine) and an outstanding journalist. The subject of religion doesn't come up often on the podcast, but I do remember one particular segment in an episode titled "Bait and Switch," in which Glass interviewed two evangelical Christians about evangelistic strategies. One of the men, Jim Henderson, told the story of how he always felt uncomfortable with formal evangelism strategies because they seemed to make him view people as projects. This didn't seem right to him, so he changed his approach, and now he simply tries to get Christians to notice people, to listen to them, and to "stop being jerks." The part of the interview that really stuck with me was the host's take on the whole matter. At one point Glass asks, "Is it possible that your tactic just leads to… nothing?" The interview highlighted the confusion that results when well-intentioned churches and ministries rely on marketing gimmicks for growth rather than the beckoning work of the Holy Spirit. Marketing can't make Christians—only Christ can do that.

How does a church or ministry encourage and organize faithful evangelistic efforts and avoid the traps of marketing gimmicks? It's a fine line. It starts with the basic belief that Christians who understand the Gospel and who possess the indwelling power of the Holy Spirit will normally and naturally evangelize when in proximity to lost people. If this is true, church leaders should ensure that all their members understand and can explain the Gospel clearly and encourage them all to be in regular interaction with non-Christians—even if that means organizing occasions for church members to interact with the members of the community.

To give you a sense of what I'm talking about, I've listed below a few of the outreach initiatives that our members have organized over the past few years. Each of these outreach events was an attempt to meet and engage those who are without Christ in our community.

- **One Question** – "One Question" was the title of a sermon series in which we addressed difficult questions with biblical answers. In preparation for the series we placed yellow, hand-written sticky notes on thousands of doors in our community: "If you could ask God one question what would it be?" At the bottom of the sticky note was a web address where they could submit their questions for God. We organized the questions and then answered them scripturally. Because the questions were submitted electronically, we were able to follow up with those who submitted questions on the website and engage them personally about their particular questions. We encouraged our members to ask the people they encountered about their one question.

- **Sports Camp** – We have offered free one-week sports camps at county parks and schools in our community. Using local athletes and volunteers to teach the fundamentals of popular sports, this outreach draws both those who wish to participate as well as adults who wish to volunteer. At the conclusion of the camp, we hold a cookout and kickball game for the entire family.

- **Outdoor Movies** – This is our longest-running outreach event. Each summer for most of our church's existence we have offered a free series of outdoor movies. For years we held the movies on the soccer field next to the school where our church met. Hundreds of people would come with lawn chairs and picnic baskets an hour or so before dark. We encouraged our members to come to the movie early to make friends with someone they did not know.

- **Parents' Night Out** – Our church is near several military bases. We found that military families have trouble finding trustworthy babysitters because very few of them live near long-time friends or family members. In response, we offer a free three-hour children's program on a Friday or Saturday night for 20 military families. The program includes games, music, karate instruction, and some type of craft like pottery or tie-dying t-shirts. Before heading out for a few hours of "alone time," each family would receive a $25 gift card to a local restaurant provided by a member of our church. A few days after the event, someone from our church would show up at the family's home to deliver the craft project and invite them to a worship service.

- **Digits** – Using a local phone book (yes, they still exist), members of our church meet twice a month to call families in our community to ask them if there is any way our church could pray for them. We collect prayer requests and pray for them during our church prayer meeting. A few weeks later we call back to remind them that we're still praying for them and ask if the situation we prayed for has improved at all.

- **Teacher Work Days** – Our church met in a public school for five years. Every few months the school calendar included a teacher work day when teachers were required to come to work but students were off. We provided a Chick-Fil-A lunch and sat down to eat with the teachers.

- **Mall Kiosk** – Our community has a huge shopping mall called Potomac Mills, and the center of the mall is lined with small kiosks where vendors sell electronic cigarettes and remote controlled helicopters. We rented one of these kiosks and adorned it with signs offering free Bibles. Members from our church stood near the kiosk to give a Bible to anyone who wanted one. Over the course of a two-week period, we gave away more than 1,000 Bibles and invitations to church. Many of those encounters resulted in conversions.

- **Oil Changes** – For a time, our church rented a building that had two large garage bays. One Saturday each month, men from our church provided free oil changes for single mothers and wives of deployed service members. We partnered with a local auto parts store that provided discount supplies in exchange for advertisement. While the men were changing oil, women from our church served coffee and donuts to the ladies who were waiting and tried to get to know them a bit.

Events like these are not always successful in terms of seeing people actually become Christians, but they do build your church's reputation in the community and deliver a favorable impression on the minds of those who attend. It's not uncommon for someone to show up at our church and tell us that they came to a movie or other event years ago and lately, as they've been considering spiritual matters, they remembered our church and decided to give it a try.

As you consider how to reach out to the non-Christians in your community, I encourage you to build into your church's calendar and budget a few events like this each year. (Be sure that the monthly budget threshold you created a few chapters back can support this outreach plan.) Do everything you can to allow members to organize and staff the event. This will free your staff and elders to focus on the ministry of the Word and prayer (Acts 6:4).

There are many people in your community with no plans to venture to a church, so the church must venture to them. Lead your church to follow the example of The Son of Man who *"came to seek and save that which was lost"* (Luke 19:10; Matthew 18:11). This endeavor will not always be a walk in the park. At times you will experience discouragement when things don't go as planned, and some projects will flop altogether. Yet somehow, in the midst of all of our fumbling, Jesus will continue to call men and women to Himself.

> I have created a written outreach plan for the
> first year of my church's ministry.

# BEGIN

You are now in the home stretch. You have a paycheck to support your family and a great team to work with, and you've even made some progress befriending your community. Now it's time to start planning your weekly worship services. In most churches the weekly worship services are the heart of the ministry. It's the time every seven days when Christians in a community gather to celebrate Jesus' resurrection from the dead and hear from God's Word about the way they should live.

New Testament worship services exist primarily for the benefit and growth of Christians. Unfortunately this purpose has often been misrepresented in modern churches, as it is a common tendency for churches to focus primarily on using the corporate meeting for evangelizing non-Christians. However, this does not follow the model demonstrated for us in Scripture. Early Christians began gathering for worship on Sunday mornings for the very specific purpose of celebrating Jesus' resurrection. In those earliest gatherings of the Christian church, Scripture records that *"with great power the apostles were giving their testimony to the resurrection of the Lord Jesus, and great grace was upon them all"* (Acts 4:33). Another passage tells us that the people" *devoted themselves to the apostles teaching"* (Acts 2:42). When Paul instructs the Corinthian church about public worship, he tells them everything that takes place in that service should be done in an orderly manner and should be for the purpose of building up the church (1 Corinthians 14:26). The author of Hebrews even commands Christians not to neglect meeting together (Hebrews 10:25).

While it is important to give consideration to the non-Christians who will be attending your weekly gathering, keep in mind that your teaching ministry as a pastor is for the equipping the saints (Ephesians 4:12).

## Knowing When to Start

The decision about when to start public worship services is an important one. There are lots of logistics associated with holding a weekly public worship service, so it is good to wait to begin until you are sure you have the manpower to do it well. There is nothing wrong with meeting for worship as a small group for a period of time before attempting to hold services in a public facility.

I advise you to first determine the specific number of committed families that would be ideal to have before beginning public worship services, and then resolve not to begin services until that number has been reached. Having a sufficient number of workers to handle the logistical aspects of public worship will release you from concern about these items and free you to focus your attention on teaching God's Word. In most cases, I recommend having at least ten committed families before attempting to begin weekly services in a public facility.

Once you begin public services, a certain amount of time in your week will need to be dedicated to the maintenance of the service. Since time is such a valuable commodity for a church planter, wait to begin weekly services until you are certain you can handle or delegate this maintenance without skimping on other important aspects of the church planting ministry, such as evangelism, discipleship, and leading your missionary team.

> I will not begin weekly worship services until
> I have ____ committed families.

## Large Launch vs. Gradual Growth

The beginning of a new church is more like a stairway ascent than a rocket launch. Many new churches that begin with a "launch large" strategy spend months advertising and building up to their first worship service like it's the Super Bowl. I took this approach when I started Pillar Church, but if I could it to do over again, I would do things much differently. I spent about ten months planning for my first public worship service. I brought in a great band, friendly greeters, experienced childcare workers, and even a professional camera crew to help run the service. We sent out expensive mailers and put up signs all around our community announcing the opening of our new church. We launched Pillar church on Easter Sunday and even planned a community Easter egg hunt immediately following the service. The day went off great! We had 120 people attend the worship service and more than 300 at the Easter egg hunt. You might be thinking that sounds like a successful launch for a church plant. So why wouldn't I do that again? Well, because of what happened next.

The next Sunday we had about fifty people in attendance, about thirty of whom were already committed to our work long before the Easter launch. The other twenty were repeat visitors from the previous week, but this week we had no band, no great children's ministry, and no friendly, well-dressed greeters passing out warm donuts. Two weeks after our launch we had about forty people in service, and before too long we were back to the faithful thirty Christians we started with, only now they were all depressed because our rocket had launched and then fallen right back to the landing pad.

After the dust settled, I couldn't help but wonder what might have happened if I had spent the same ten months of energy and money focused on leading our team to make personal connections with people in our community. I think if we had connected first, we would have seen a much better long-term outcome. Thankfully, our church did eventually develop a healthy rhythm of slow and steady growth that still characterizes us today.

## Leadership Capacity

I have learned one important leadership lesson through the church planting process: my church will not outgrow my capacity to lead them. Before planting a church, I assumed I had the capability to lead a large number of people. I was wrong. Instead, my capacity to lead grew at the same pace our church did. I'm convinced, in most instances, our churches stay relatively small because God knows our capacity to lead people is limited. Before He will increase the size of our congregation, He must increase our capacity to care for people. Virtually every pastor I know wishes his congregation were larger. Pastors of churches with 50 wish they had 100. Pastors of churches with 100 wish they had 200, and so on. Yet, in each of our congregations, there are people who are caught in the clutches of sin, in desperate need of discipleship, and just waiting to be equipped for ministry. How must God view our longing for larger flocks when so many people currently under our care are unattended? If you want your church to be larger, take good care of the people you have now. We must first learn to be faithful with little before we can be faithful with much (Luke 16:10; Matthew 25:23).

## Act Your Age

When starting a new church, others will unintentionally pressure you to start every ministry in the book. Some people will ask about your youth ministry or your women's ministry. It might be tempting to give some sort of elaborate answer because you want to impress them and you hope they visit your church. But, it is extremely important when you talk about the church, especially to other churched people, to be brutally honest about your current stage of development. When they ask about your women's ministry, say, "We don't have an organized women's ministry. Our church is very young and still pretty small. We do hope to have a great ministry to women someday, but it will probably be awhile before we do." Your honesty will prevent them from being disappointed with unmet expectations of your church's ministry organizations and will also quickly weed out "consumer Christians."

## Refusing to Settle

As your group of attendees begins to grow, you will probably be tempted to compromise on some important issues in order to have a larger group. After a service, I was talking with a visiting couple who had lived in the area several times before on military assignments. When they moved back and saw that our church was starting in their neighborhood, they felt compelled to get involved. However, they really loved their old church and wanted to stay involved there. Over the next several months, this family would show up every other Sunday like clockwork. They were even giving half of their tithe to each church. One day I called Alex, the husband, to ask if we could meet together. When we met, I told him that I had been thinking about their situation and that I didn't think it was good idea for them to attend both churches. I confessed that while I really hoped they would commit themselves wholeheartedly to our church, if they couldn't, it would be better for their family and for both churches if they committed themselves to their previous church. After some consideration, Alex's family chose to stay at Pillar Church. Since they had the only two teenagers in the church, they worked hard to start a Bible study for teens that eventually developed into our student ministry. Years later, Alex and his family are hardworking and well-loved members of our church and are hosting and leading in many of our ministries.

## Planning Worship Services

In your hurry to begin public worship services, don't neglect your duty to take adequate time to plan for them and consider their content. The patterns and standards you set for your worship services early on are likely to last long into the future. When you begin the worship services, if you are the only preacher, it will be difficult to change that down the road. If you set a pattern of observing the Lord's Supper each week, and later you try to change that, you'll likely run into resistance. This goes for every aspect of your public worship service. Before you begin, take time to consider those elements you want to be a regular part of your weekly worship services and those that you do not. Keep in mind that the Bible has a lot to say about this subject. Take into consideration passages like Acts 2:42-47, 1 Timothy 24:13, and 1 Corinthians 11:2-16, 14:26-40, and 16:1-4, when deciding which elements to include and which ones to leave out. In Appendix N, you will find a worksheet that will help you determine which elements you wish to include regularly in your weekly worship services. Once you've determined which elements you wish to include, begin working on a service order for your first preview service.

> I have chosen the elements I wish to include in each of our weekly worship services.

## Who Will Lead

Next you'll need to consider what types of people God's Word permits to lead in various aspects of public worship. Should only pastors handle leading the worship service, or should your members and elders also be included in the service? Can those who are not members lead in aspects of worship? Does God's Word allow women to lead prayers, read Scripture, share announcements, and lead in musical worship, or are those jobs only to be handled by men? Make these determinations with the help of your partner, your mentor, and the elders of your sending church, so you are prepared to answer those who ask.

> I have studied the Bible's teachings on public worship format and have a clear understanding of which individuals will be permitted to lead various aspects of our public worship services. I am prepared to defend my positions.

## Preaching

Charles Spurgeon repeatedly compared the Gospel to a caged lion, explaining that it "does not need to be defended it just needs to be let out of the cage."[14] As a church planter your ability to accurately and confidently explain the Gospel to others will have a profound effect on the overall well-being of the church you are planting. The Gospel is the agent used by the Holy Spirit to dissolve the corrosion that lines the walls of the human soul, and it's a healing medicine used to coat the soul with the type of faith that pleases God. So the church planter's job in regard to preaching and evangelizing is simply to open the lion's cage, simply to release the Gospel in all of its power and splendor to do the work that God desires it to do. Such confidence in the Gospel should mark the life of a church planting pastor, but sadly it often doesn't. Many modern pulpiteers have abandoned simple and clear gospel proclamation in exchange for other religious messages.

Like hiding a pill inside a marshmallow to trick a child into taking it, these well-meaning orators hide a simple gospel truth in a tasty candy shell. Sin becomes merely a struggle, depravity becomes merely weakness, God becomes merely a wish-granting genie, and the Holy Spirit becomes merely our conscience. This sugarcoated approach comes from a lack confidence in the Gospel's power to rebuke, correct, exhort, and instruct in righteous living. If you find yourself feeling the need to defend or enhance the Gospel with your oratory skills or your ingenuity, the problem is not with the Gospel, instead, it's with your confidence in its power. Your ministry should be marked by an underlying assumption that the Gospel itself is powerful and an unwavering commitment to simply proclaiming it. When a preacher assumes the Gospel is weak, outdated, and only truly effective when properly animated by his oratory skills, he will lead many people astray. The Gospel needs no help. It is *the "power of God for salvation to everyone who believes"* (Romans 1:16)—plain and simple.

Remember, you have been called to preach God's Word, not your word. The better you know the Gospel and the more submissive you are to the Gospel, the more genuine life change you will see in your ministry. If you desire to see lives changed, preach the Gospel. If you desire to see families healed, preach the Gospel. If you desire to see Christians mature, preach the Gospel. As Francis Schaeffer said, "Christianity is not merely religious truth, it is total truth—truth about the whole of reality."[15]

You may be tempted to join the cascade of preachers in our day who forsake the hard work of study and preparation, arguing that it would quench the work the Holy Spirit plans to do through you on Sunday. If so, ask yourself whether it is any more likely that God will speak to you in the pulpit on Sunday than He will in your office on Thursday? Of course not! This approach produces terrible preachers. Their thoughts are disorganized and, more notably, their hearts have not simmered in the truths of the Gospel before standing before God's people. Any carnal man can give good advice, but you are not called to give good advice; you are called to preach. Limited study gives little time for an understanding of the setting, context, and or even the meaning of the words in the text. Scripture proclaims, *"faith comes from hearing, and hearing through the Word of Christ"* (Romans 10:17). Faith does not come by hearing the word of man. For the new preacher, this is especially important. *"Do your best to present yourself to God as one approved, a worker who has no need to be ashamed, rightly handling the word of truth"* (2 Timothy 2:15).

In addition to study and preparation, you must remember your environment and your audience. I have observed preachers who seem completely oblivious to the awkwardness of their presentation. It's not awkward because of what they say, but because of the way they say it and the environment in which they say it. For example, I have attended tiny church plants in large high school auditoriums and movie theaters with zealous young pastors preaching through a sophisticated sound system to just a dozen or so souls. They have the "if you build it they will come" mentality, believing that simply working out the logistics of a church meeting will attract crowds. This approach simply doesn't work and has a terribly disappointing outcome for the optimistic church planter.

In my early years church planting, I spent far too much time putting on church (spending energy on making sure that all of the elements of the meeting were just right), and I spent very little time being the Church (actually loving and serving those who were gathering). If you will place your energy on transferring the Word of God from your heart to the hearts of the people you are leading, you will find that your church will respond to the Word of God. Spend your time studying God's Word so that you know it well, and then freely dispense it to others. Scripture promises and I firmly believe that if you will place your energy on being a well-studied, faithful preacher of God's Word, that Word, when dispensed, will work dramatically in the hearts of those who hear it. Remember that God said, *"So shall my word be that goes out from my mouth; it shall not return to me empty, but it shall accomplish that which I purpose, and shall succeed in the thing for which I sent it"* (Isaiah 55:11).

The bottom line is that many things will contribute to the overall health of the church you begin—small groups, meeting location, and the quality of your leadership to name a few—but nothing will affect the overall health of your congregation nearly as profoundly as time well spent in the pulpit. The hour you spend before the people of God each weekend can have a profound impact on the habits and hearts of those who regularly attend. Preach the Word and your hearers will begin to share your confidence in the power of the Gospel.

## Sermon Preparation

I am fully aware that sermon preparation is an art rather than a science, and great preachers and pastors through history have employed a variety of different study tools and disciplines to become great at what they do. Appendix O contains helpful hints for sermon preparation. There is clearly no "best way" to prepare for preaching that applies to all preachers. I am also aware that I am not the world's greatest preacher and probably not even good enough to be offering this advice, but I at least want you to know some approaches that have proven helpful for me in preaching. I pray they will help you as you prepare to preach God's Word in personal evangelism, formal preaching, and small group teaching.

## Write a Manuscript

The very strongest advice I can give, especially for a new preacher, is to write a manuscript of your sermon. Writing my sermons out word-for-word is the single most helpful habit I have formed as a preacher. There are two primary reasons that the manuscript is helpful for me.

First, writing my thoughts forces me to think through the very best way to communicate them. When I use an outline, I can capture an idea in a bullet point to remind me what I should say, but when it comes time to actually say it, I may or may not be able to articulate my ideas as well as I want. When I write out the idea, however, I am forced to consider the very best way to convey it. Writing sermons in manuscript form is my regular practice, and I find myself now repeating phrases verbatim that were first conceived on paper in preparation for a sermon. These well thought out phrases become part of my daily speech and help me to articulate my thoughts on a particular subject in a logical manner without having to carefully choose my words as I am speaking.

The second reason I write sermons in manuscript is to capture them. Many preachers lose the usefulness of their studying by not capturing it in writing. As a pastor you may spend 8-12 hours or more per week in sermon preparation, jot down your notes in outline form or on a napkin, preach from it on Sunday, and then lose it so it can never be used again. When you write your teaching in a manuscript before presenting it, you have the luxury of sharing it with others as an article, blog post, or an email to a suffering church member. If you capture a series, it can be used in the future as a small group study guide or even a book. Have you ever wondered how well-known pastors have time to produce multiple books each year and still lead vibrant church ministries? It's because they don't waste their study, they capture it. Choose a system that works for you and force yourself to capture your study into a form that can be easily used in the future.

## Aim for Clarity and Simplicity

I began preaching before my 20th birthday. I should not have. I was inexperienced and fully endowed with every negative character trait common to young men. I was preaching to people much older, wiser, and more educated than myself, and I felt the constant strain of inferiority and self-consciousness in my preaching and preparation. I attempted to compensate for my inadequacy by being louder and employing vocabulary that I believed would impress those who were listening to me. In truth, I only confirmed my youthful folly to those who had the misfortune of enduring my early sermons.

As my confidence in the Gospel grew, my self-consciousness diminished. When I stopped trying to impress those I was preaching to and started trying to impress the One I was preaching for, I found myself searching for the simplest and clearest way to convey an idea, not the most elaborate and sophisticated way. What I learned is that preaching isn't about the transfer of information. It's about transformation, and transformation comes from the Word of God. C.S Lewis gives some helpful advice for writing that also applies to preaching.

- Always try to use the language so as to make quite clear what you mean and make sure your sentence couldn't mean anything else.
- Always prefer the clean, direct word to the long, vague one. Don't *implement* promises, but *keep* them.
- Never use abstract nouns when concrete ones will do. If you mean "More people died" don't say "Mortality rose."
- In writing, don't use adjectives that merely tell us how you want us to feel about the things you are describing. I mean, instead of telling us the thing is "terrible," describe it so that we'll be terrified. Don't say it was "delightful"; make us say "delightful" when we've read the description. You see, all those words (horrifying,

wonderful, hideous, exquisite) are only like saying to your readers "Please, will you do my job for me."

- Don't use words too big for the subject. Don't say "infinitely" when you mean "very"; otherwise you'll have no word left when you want to talk about something *really* infinite.[16]

## Get Feedback From Others

Most preachers I know get very little feedback from others about their sermons. If they do, it's in the form of an angry email or a self-appointed theological watchdog. Very rarely do pastors ask other theologically astute individuals or fellow elders to offer feedback. Pastors often critique themselves each week by watching the video or listening to the church's podcast, but I want to warn against this. I think feedback comes better from a faithful brother than from you. Never underestimate your ability to deceive yourself with pleasantries or to berate yourself with unnecessary self-criticism. If you are your own evaluator, you will likely make assessments about yourself that you are not qualified to make. Since pastors also tend to spend time listening to and reading other pastors, you will likely find the comparison game difficult to avoid. British theologian and pastor, John Stott, encourages pastors to avoid listening to and watching themselves:

> If you look at yourself in the mirror, and listen to yourself on tape, or do both simultaneously on videotape, I fear you may find that you continue to look at yourself and listen to yourself when you are in the pulpit. In that case you will condemn yourself to the cramping bondage of preoccupation with yourself just at the time when, in the pulpit, it is essential to cultivate self-forgetfulness through a growing awareness of the God for whom and the people to whom you are speaking. I know actors make use of glass and tape, but preachers are not actors, nor is the pulpit a stage. So beware! It may be more valuable to ask a friend to be candid with you about your voice and mannerisms, especially if they need correction. An Indian proverb says, "He who has a good friend needs no mirror." Then you can be yourself and forget yourself.[17]

## Avoid Excessive Commentary Use

Commentaries are tremendous resources for the pastor and should be used to the extent that they are helpful. But commentaries are a late game activity. Early in your study, your time is best spent in the text itself. Reading and re-reading the text allows you to marinate in it and to consider its implications. Study the words in the text to ensure that you understand their meaning and biblical usage. Search for themes. Remember that you are preaching to see transformation, not merely to convey information. Information alone will not produce the outcome you desire. Give yourself to meditation and reflection. If you do, you will notice that the text will come alive to you throughout the week, and God will teach you lessons concerning the text as you go about your usual business.

I begin reading the passage for Sunday's sermon very early in the week. By Tuesday or Wednesday, I have moved on to studying the words and doing the necessary language work to understand the text. I talk about the passage with other Christians and ask questions of the text. Sometimes I read a book on the theme of the text. By the end of the week, it's time to start writing the manuscript. Only after my manuscript is well underway do I peek into commentaries to see interpretations from theologians I respect. Most of the time, I find that I have come to similar conclusions about the passage. Periodically, I will find something I totally missed and add it to my manuscript. Either way, I have personally experienced the text and can speak about it with firsthand knowledge.

## Personal Study vs. Sermon Preparation

I have often been warned of the danger of mixing my personal study and reflection on God's Word with my preparation for an upcoming engagement, and I want to publicly admit that I have completely rejected that advice. The fact is, when I am preparing to teach, I find I do a much better job when I am personally connected with the text. If, in recent days, God has ministered to me through a text or taught me some glorious truth about His Son, I am noticeably better at preaching it. So when I'm preparing to preach the Sermon on the Mount, that's what you'll find me reflecting on, and it's not a sin no matter what your hermeneutics professor says. The sin would be preaching a text that you have only interacted with on an intellectual level.

As you prepare to dispense God's Word to His people, do so with care. Study to show yourself approved to God. The Gospel is the most concentrated weapon you have for the establishment of a church in any location. Wave it like a banner before the people wherever you have been called to minister. The public preaching of God's Word is the heart of the church's ministry. No other aspect of your church's ministry has the potential to shape the congregation like preaching does. I will not attempt in this material to give an adequate treatment to the subject of preaching, as many other excellent resources already exist. I will, however, encourage you to get into the practice of receiving critical feedback on your preaching every week. I'm not saying you should receive criticism from just anyone, but rather you should be open to criticism from those who are respected for their ministerial effectiveness and wisdom.

## Service Review Team

One of the most practical ways to obtain consistent, constructive feedback is the formation of a service review team. At the start, this team could be your missionary team, but eventually it should include other pastors and elders within your church. Create a simple service review form like the one in Appendix P, and go over it each week following the worship service. Try not to get offended by the criticisms you receive, and work to improve your preaching by working on those critiques that you consider valid.

> I have formed a service review team and will plan to
> have a service review after each worship service.

## Creating a Preaching Calendar

Planning your preaching calendar well in advance will help you become purposeful about the preaching *"the whole counsel of God"* (Acts 20:27). It's far too easy to preach the texts and topics that we enjoy without giving consideration to the duty we have to teach our people to *"observe all things"* that Christ commanded us (Matthew 28:20). Additionally, when starting a new church, there is such a rich reservoir of instruction from God's Word in the New Testament that it would be an oversight not to align our teaching with the church's life stages. What better instruction is there for the missionary team than the book of Acts? What better wisdom is there for establishing biblical polity than that found in 1 Timothy and Titus? Take some time to look over your calendar and anticipate what passages from God's Word will be most useful to your congregation in its formative stages. Don't undertake this task alone. Be sure to include your partner, your mentor, and your sending church's elders in the process of planning your church's preaching calendar.

> I have created a preaching calendar for the first year of our church's weekly worship services.

## Preview Services

One way to test your readiness for weekly worship services is to hold a few public preview services. This is a common practice for new churches. Often team members will encourage you to move to weekly services more quickly than planned. Holding a series of preview services satisfies their appetite for public worship services. Some church planters even choose to hold monthly preview services until they are ready to begin meeting weekly. Preview services accomplish two important purposes.

- **Trouble-shooting** – Leading your missionary team to conduct a preview service is the best way to give them a sense of how much work goes into holding a public worship service. Be sure to have a lengthy service review after each one, inviting a select few who were present at the service. Make a list of all the things that could have gone better in the service and work to correct those problems before the next preview service.

- **Engaging the Community** – As you plan the service, contact the leaders from your sending and supporting churches and ask them to encourage their congregations to attend. You will probably want to hold your service at some time other than Sunday morning to allow for Christians from other churches to participate without skipping their responsibilities at their own church. Utilize free and inexpensive advertising outlets to get the word out about the preview service. If possible, hold the service in the same location you intend to hold your weekly services in the future.

Treat your preview service just like a weekly service. Follow up with visitors, pray for other churches, take up an offering, sing corporately, and preach the Word. You're likely to pick up a few new team members through this process, so be prepared to welcome new attendees to your other weekly activities. It's okay to hold your preview services before reaching your committed families threshold, but I suggest waiting until that goal is within sight before planning the weekly public services.

> I have scheduled one or more preview services.

## Sunday Afternoon or Evening Services

In the event that you are planting a new church near your sending church or another church that is providing a significant number of attendees, you may consider starting weekly services on Sunday evening rather than Sunday morning. If you choose this plan, I recommend doing it only for a short time. Until you move to Sunday mornings, you are not likely to know who's really committed to your new work and who is not. Since your ultimate goal is to meet on Sunday mornings, make that move as soon as possible, but not until you have reached your committed families threshold.

> I have reached my goal of ____ committed families and am ready to begin weekly worship services.

## Advertising Weekly Services

Once you reach your committed families threshold and schedule the date for your first weekly service, do everything you can to let your community know. Take whatever money you have set aside for advertisement in your startup fund and create a plan for informing your community that your church is now holding weekly services. You don't have to go overboard with this, but you want to make sure people know. Create a press release for the local media outlets, and make sure your church website is fully functional.

Nothing is more effective than a personal invitation, so encourage your team to personally invite those they have connected with over the past few months. Lastly, make sure your sending and supporting churches know in advance when and where the service will be held so that they can encourage their members to celebrate this memorable day with you.

> I have communicated with my sending and supporting churches about our plans for weekly worship and invited them to attend.

> I have advertised our church's first worship services and encouraged the missionary team to invite friends and family.

# ORDER

New churches often begin with a great deal of unity. When a group of Christians gets together to start a new church, there's a lot of excitement, and members often exercise exceptional grace toward one another. Team members are overjoyed to work together and are often willing to make great personal sacrifices in order to accomplish the mission. There's lots of prayer, lots of faith, and lots of sacrifice involved. Just as happy newlyweds have difficulty imagining themselves ever being overcome with anger and hatred toward their spouse, church planting team members are often naïve about the inevitable conflict, sin, and disunity that arises within the body. Then the honeymoon ends, and reality dawns.

As you lead this new church, it is imperative that you plan for conflict before it even begins. Being unprepared for conflict and disunity leaves the church vulnerable to Satan's attacks and schemes. The New Testament warns us as pastors to be on the lookout for "wolves." Wolves are men and women who come into your new church posing as allies but who secretly have ulterior motives. They grow to be loved and trusted by you and your team, and then they eat you alive (metaphorically speaking). As a pastor in this new church, it is your job to keep watch over your sheep and to rid the flock of those with malicious or divisive motives. You have been given the honor of serving as a shepherd, and a shepherd's highest responsibility is to protect sheep (Matthew 7:15; Acts 20:28-31). Having a clear, biblical leadership structure will be a crucial benefit to as you navigate the difficult sin issues the church is sure to face. It may even save your church when you face conflict and crisis.

It's helpful to consider Paul's instruction to Titus during the formation of the church in Crete. As Paul's ministry is winding down, he reminds his disciple of the reason he left him in Crete: *"This is why I left you in Crete, so that you might put what remained into order, and appoint elders in every town as I directed you"* (Titus 1:5).

What does Paul mean when he instructs Titus to "put in order what remained"? He offers a clue in the last half of the verse: "appoint elders in every town." It seems that Paul believes that the new Christians resulting from his evangelistic ministry need to be put "in order" and put under spiritual leadership and authority. In other words, a church needs to be formed out of these individual Christians. This verse suggests that, although there are individual Christians in this region, churches are still needed. Obviously, Paul believes that evangelism isn't enough, and those who become Christians need to be organized into local churches with leadership and accountability.

This is exactly what a church planter is to do—win the lost and shepherd the found. Church planters bring order, leadership, and accountability to Christians whom they gather and win, thus creating an environment where many people for many years may become disciples of Jesus Christ.

This will be an uphill battle because much of today's Christian teaching focuses exclusively on a Christian's personal relationship with God and places almost no emphasis on the Christian's relationship to the church. American Christians often feel no particular identification with a local church, nor any sense of duty to the other Christians in their city or in their church. They don't see themselves any more connected to the person sitting next to them in church than they do to the person standing behind them in the grocery store line. However, that mentality is not in sync with Scripture's call and commands for Christians. The New Testament is packed with instructions for Christians:

- Love one another – John 13:34-35
- Build up one another – Romans 14:19
- Be kind to one another – Ephesians 4:32
- Be at peace with one another – Mark 9:50
- Admonish one another – Romans 15:14
- Bear one another's burdens – Galatians 6:2

- Comfort one another – 1 Thessalonians 4:18
- Forgive one another – Ephesians 4:32
- Confess your sins to one another – James 5:16
- Show hospitality to one another – 1 Peter 4:9
- Give preference to one another - Romans 12:10
- Speak to one another in psalms and hymns – Ephesians 5:19
- Encourage one another – 1 Thessalonians 5:11; Hebrews 3:13
- Pray for one another – James 5:16
- Have fellowship with one another – 1 John 1:7
- Spur one another on to love and good deeds – Hebrews 10:24
- Do not slander one another – James 4:11
- Do not grumble against one another – James 5:9
- Live in harmony with one another – 1 Peter 3:8
- Lay down your life for one another – 1 John 3:16-18
- Restore one another - Galatians 6:1-3
- Bear with one another – Colossians 3:12-14
- Do not lie to one another – Colossians 3:9
- Disciple and teach one another – 2 Corinthians 2:2
- Please one another – Romans 15:2
- Accept one another – Romans 15:7
- Suffer with one another – 1 Corinthians 12:26
- Rejoice with one another – Romans 12:15
- Honor one another – Romans 12:10

The "consumer Christian" mentality does not fit with this list at all. In fact, it stands for against God's design for how Christians should interact with one another. The driving consideration for the average American churchgoer is what the church can do for them, expecting that the church should cater to and fulfill their expectations, needs, and wishes. When a church ceases to meet those needs or no longer provides the services they desire, they simply move on to another church or decide to abandon organized religion altogether. I have heard many stories of Christians who have left churches over trivial issues such as style preferences, meeting times, or general discomfort. This lack of allegiance to a church family results from pastoral leaders catering to this consumer Christian mentality by creating worship environments that require virtually no involvement with hurting or sin-captured Christians. Many churches work hard to create environments free from discomfort by removing any requirement to share in the sufferings and difficulties of other Christians.

## The Church is a Family

For the church to be the family of God that Scripture describes, we have to adopt a familial mindset, while growing more patient and loyal to one another. Good parents don't abandon their child on the side of the road simply because they don't like the type of music their child is listening to in the car. Good husbands don't leave their wives merely because they disagree on politics. We suffer through difficulty and discouragement with others because we've made a commitment to one another, and that commitment binds us "for better or for worse, in sickness and in health." A church's ability to bear with and suffer long with one another is much more attractive to outsiders than our ability to offer pleasing and non-threatening worship environments. Jesus never claims that our kindness to outsiders will cause people to know we belong to Him, but He does claim that our love for one another will (John 13:35).

Many people think of the church as a business, a non-profit organization, or a social club, but we know Scripture teaches that the church is like a family (1 Timothy 3:15), a body (1 Corinthians 12), and a bride (Ephesians 5:22-23). If the church is like a family, a Christian without a church is like a spiritual orphan. If the church is like a body, a Christian without a church is like a hand without an arm. If the church is like a bride, then it's essential for the health of our marriage that we stay close to our groom. The modern church, just like the early church, is intended to be an interdependent family of diverse individuals bound together by one great thing that overshadows every possible difference we could notice. That great thing is the Gospel. Jesus doesn't intend for His people to live separately, doing their own thing. He's not in the business of making freelance Christians or spiritual independent contractors. He's building a people for Himself.

We live in a unique period in Christian history when it is acceptable (even preferable) to be a Christian but not be identified with a particular local church. There's an ancient church saying that rightly summarizes the relationship between Christians and churches: "Those for whom God is father the church is mother." I'm not trying to be rigid, but it's important that we teach the flock that both church history and the Bible lead us to understand that Jesus and His church are a package deal. You cannot take one without the other. However, lots of people in our society would argue this point, saying they don't have to go to church to be a Christian. Although in a technical sense this may be true, asking if a Christian is required to go to church is a bit like asking if a husband and wife must live together in order to be married. Obviously they don't have to, but it's difficult to imagine a married couple living separately and having a very good marriage.[18]

Just as it is healthy for married people to live under the same roof, it is healthy for Christians to be part of a church. Just for a moment, imagine asking your spouse how many times you must kiss or say "I love you" in order to remain married. If I asked my wife these questions, she would be disgusted and probably roll her eyes and leave the room. Lovers don't ask questions like this because love focuses not on what it has to do, but what it gets to do. Begrudging love isn't love at all. Christians are people who have been rescued from Hell by the grace of God. We love God because of His great mercy towards us, and we serve Him because we want to.

To be clear, I am not claiming that being part of a church will ensure that you have a vibrant walk with Christ any more than I'm claiming that to be married ensures that you will have a wonderful relationship with your spouse. What I am claiming is that the church is God's gift to the Christian, and all Christians should, out of reverence for Christ and for the good of their own spiritual lives, give themselves in committed service to a local church. If you've been part of a church for any length of time, you have probably noticed that churches have a fair amount of problems. Pastor Kevin DeYoung writes:

> Churches can be boring, hypocritical, hurtful, and inept. The church is full of sinners. Which is kind of the point. Christians are worse than you think. Our Savior is better than you imagine.[19]

Pastors and elders are vital to Christians and to churches because every church is made of recovering reprobates. Godly leaders use God's Word to organize God's people to accomplish God's purposes. Without faithful elders, we should expect ecclesiastical anarchy. Conversely, when church planters *"put in order what remains,"* we impose a system by which sinful saints live in unity, and we set before our churches a mirror to reflect the glory of Christ to the communities we serve.

## Where to Start

Church planters often struggle to decide which piece of church polity to put in place first. I want to spend a bit of time suggesting a course for establishing biblical polity. Note that this plan of action supports a Congregationalist view of church membership and holds to a congregational eldership form of church government. In a nutshell, the Congregationalist view of membership holds that, as born-again, baptized Christians, the members of a church should play a role in affirming the direction of the church. Members are the highest authority in the local church and should not be ruled exclusively by elders, church councils, staff, or individual pastors. The Bible gives clear precedent concerning member authority over important matters such as disputes, doctrine, discipline, and membership. A congregational eldership is the most biblical form of church government and the one modeled most clearly by the church in the New Testament. Appendix Q provides models for church governance.

## Establishing Congregational Eldership in a New Church

If you wish to establish a congregational eldership in the church you're planting, allow me to suggest a five-step path to help you accomplish this goal. You may find that others have reordered these items and been successful, but this is the order that I have found to be most efficient, and I invite you to consider it. The speed of this process will depend on the raw materials you have available. If you are starting a church with a pastoral partner and a team of committed Christians, you'll probably progress fairly quickly through the process. If you're working alone, it may take several years to accomplish all five. The length of time it takes is not nearly as important as the quality of the decisions you make in this stage of your church's life. For me, the process from start to finish took three years. Hasty, shortsighted decisions about church structure will almost certainly need to be corrected in the future when the group is larger and opinions are stronger, so it is important that your leadership structure is biblical, thorough, and affirmed by trusted advisors before implementation. Following is a quick overview of the five-step path:

DOCTRINE ❯ COVERNANT ❯❯ MEMBERSHIP ❯❯❯ ELDERSHIP ❯❯❯❯ DEACONATE ❯❯❯❯❯

1. **Doctrine** – Adopt a statement of faith that clearly and concisely communicates your new church's beliefs.
2. **Covenant** – Write a set of vows members are expected make to one another.
3. **Membership** – Institute a process by which attenders can become members.
4. **Eldership** – Examine and affirm member-nominated elders to join you in shepherding the congregation.
5. **Deaconate** – Select deacons who serve the church by taking care of practical, organizational, and administrative needs.

As I have already stated, unity is extremely important when gathering a church planting team. It is vital that the people who gather and join your team are in agreement with you, both on doctrine and conduct. At this point, I recommend constructing a simple document, sometimes referred to as a "Core Team Covenant," that states clearly and concisely your doctrinal positions and provides general expectations for how you will treat one another. This is not a "Constitution and Bylaws," although this will eventually be a part of those documents. Once the church has elders, those elders will write a constitution and bylaws that will be adopted by the members, but this document will guide you until that work is done.

## 1. Doctrine

Unless you are seasoned theologian with a Th.M. or Ph.D., who's dedicated your life to studying theological nuances, I encourage you not to attempt to write a belief statement. Some of the most brilliant minds in Christian history have worked through decade-long councils to form belief statements. There are dozens of excellent belief statements that churches commonly adopt as their own, that form the bedrock for entire denominations, and that are easily accessible for your review. My church has adopted the belief statement of our denomination. It is clear, understandable, and adequately thorough. See Appendix R for Sample Belief Statements.

> I have adopted a statement of faith with the affirmation of my sending church's leaders.

## 2. Covenant

This is where you get to do some writing. Just like belief statements, there are a lot of church covenants available that you could adopt or edit to fit your congregation. On the other hand, there is no danger in being burned at the stake for writing a church covenant, so you may want to attempt to write your own. Church covenants are very personal vows that express the commitment each member has to other members. In this way, they are a bit like marriage vows and should be viewed as personal commitments by every member. If you need help getting started, you can find a Sample Church Covenant in Appendix S.

> I have written or adopted a church covenant that has been affirmed by my sending church.

## 3. Membership

Keep in mind that second to God, the members are your church's highest authority. Congregational polity acknowledges the priesthood of every believer and assumes that a membership comprised of spirit-filled, obedient Christians will appoint godly leaders and elders and will follow their direction to the extent that it is biblical. Therefore, it is important that you do what you can to ensure that those men and women who become members of your church are, in fact, born-again Christians. You may have had the unfortunate experience of participating in a church where individuals were admitted to church membership or remained as members even when it was clear they were not living obedient Christian lives. Every person admitted into the membership of your church should have a clear and credible profession of faith and a clearly expressed desire to live in obedience to Christ. Therefore, you can expect that there will always be fewer members on your rolls than there will be attenders in your worship service.

To maintain a church membership roster, you should have some mechanism to remove members who live in unrepentant sin, move away, stop attending, or die. Many churches still officially offer membership, but it has grown to mean almost nothing. It is not uncommon for churches to have members who no longer attend or who live contrary to the Gospel. In a healthy church, members actively encourage one another to live godly lives, they eagerly restore when possible members who have gone astray, and they excommunicate members when restoration is not possible. I'm not encouraging you to make the process of becoming a member of your church difficult and time-consuming. I'm simply advising you to do everything in your power to admit into membership born-again Christians with common doctrinal convictions, while refusing membership to those who do not have a credible profession of faith in Christ. Don't make becoming a member of your local church drastically more difficult than becoming a member of Jesus' universal church.

## Minimum Age for Members

I don't advise admitting into membership children living in their parents' home, under their parents' authority. This is not to say that children cannot be born again or that children don't need the accountability and encouragement that formal membership provides to the Christian. It's simply a matter of recognizing that parental authority supersedes church authority. Consider, for example, a 15-year-old girl who professes to be a Christian and becomes pregnant. What if the parents and the church disagree on the best course of action for this situation? Whose biblically prescribed authority trumps whose? God places Christian parents as shepherds over their children, and those parents are responsible before God for their treatment of them. The church's elders can and should shepherd such parents through parental struggles, but they should not intrude into those struggles without invitation.

That raises the question of whether we should baptize children if we will not admit them to membership. This is a difficult issue with strong opinions on every side, but I believe baptizing children is permissible when: (1) the child has a credible profession of faith and has expressed a desire to live in submission to parental authority, (2) the parents are members in good standing of our church, and (3) the parents agree to the child's baptism and are willing to express confidence in their child's profession.

## Constructing a Membership Process

There is no formula for constructing a perfect membership process in a new church, but here are some practices that I recommend as you begin thinking about instituting church membership in your young congregation.

- **Hold a Membership Course.** The course doesn't have to be complicated or long, but it should include a thorough explanation of the belief statement and the church covenant. Don't assume that just because you gave out a document containing those items that everyone actually understands and agrees to them. Take time to explain the points in detail and field questions on points of concern. It may also be helpful to explain any denominational or network affiliations the church has as well as the church's history and vision for the future.

> I have written a membership course and am ready to take my church through it.

- **Interview Each Potential Member.** Because it is so important that you permit only born-again Christians into the membership of your new church, you'll need to make it a priority to interview each member personally. Take time to hear their testimonies, allow them to express any concerns they may have about the church, and reaffirm to them your commitment to their spiritual growth and vitality. In Appendix T you will find advice regarding membership interviews.

> I have prepared a document to guide me through conducting a membership interview.

- **Seek Public Affirmation from Existing Members.** Let your current members know when new people wish to join the membership. Explain that you have heard their testimonies and that you believe their professions of faith to be credible. Remind the congregation about the membership covenant and let them know that each candidate has agreed to it. Finally, seek a public affirmation from existing members.

Once your membership process is in place, it's a good idea to hold your first (pilot) membership course with your core team members. It's an effective way to test the content of the course and to clearly transition core team members into church membership. It's not necessary to require membership interviews for core team members. Be sure to make the course and their subsequent membership a point of celebration. This is a milestone for your new church because this group of people officially becomes its founding members.

## 4. Eldership

Since the office of an elder is a biblical one, certain qualifications of spiritual maturity must be met (1 Timothy 3:1-7; Titus 1:5-9; 1 Peter 5:1-4). The Bible indicates that only men should hold this office. Let me encourage you to set from the beginning a precedent of considering only men for this role. This position is likely to be unpopular, so you will need to arm yourself with a strong biblical defense for it. The elders appointed in your new church will lead the church and be its primary teachers and shepherds. If these men are godly and faithful, the church will flourish; if they are not, the church will suffer.

Since their role is extremely important in the life of the church, your sending church's elders should only grant their appointment after a thorough examination. Elders are essentially co-pastors. They have the same job description as you do—to shepherd the flock by providing oversight. Some churches view elders as a pastoral support team, but, biblically speaking, elders are pastors. With this in mind, a helpful question when considering an elder candidate would be whether the candidate has the character to take your place if you were no longer able to serve as the church planter.

## Elder Nomination

Discovering potential elders in your congregation should be relatively easy. Simply teach the biblical qualifications, and then inform the congregation of the need for additional elders, asking them to prayerfully submit names of men they consider to be qualified for the position.

> I have planned a teaching series on biblical eldership.

> I have collected nominations from our members for elder candidates.

## Elder Examination

If you've done a good job teaching, only a few names will surface. Once prospective elders are identified, invite them for examination by your sending church's elders. If a candidate shows both willingness and fitness for the office, he should be confirmed. Use the questionnaire from Appendix E as a starting place for the examination.

> The elder candidates have completed the questionnaire, and my sending church's elders have joined me in examining them.

## Elder Affirmation

Once elder candidates have been confirmed by the elders of your sending church, introduce them to the congregation with your endorsement. Explain the reasons why the candidate has been chosen and express your confidence in their fitness for the office. Provide an opportunity for members to ask questions of the potential elder both in public and private settings. Once everyone has had a chance to ask questions and receive satisfactory answers, ask members to affirm the decision.

> The members have affirmed the elder selections.

## Elder Responsibilities

According to the New Testament, elders are responsible for the primary leadership and oversight of the church through prayerful discernment and the study of Scripture. In his excellent book, *Elders in Congregational Life* (Kregel Minstry 2005), Phil Newton boils down the elder's responsibility into four nicely alliterated points. Newton says elders are to defend and teach proper doctrine, provide overall direction, administer redemptive discipline, and model lives of distinction before the body. These points are easy to remember and have served me well as I have sought to encourage our elders to fulfill their duties. Here are a few clarifying thoughts on each of the points.

- **Doctrine** – Elders are responsible for ensuring that the teaching of the church is in line with the teaching of the Bible. The elders should promote sound doctrine within the church and defend against unbiblical doctrine. Elders are to be *"able to teach"* (1 Timothy 3:2). Although I don't necessarily believe this means they must be able to stand up and deliver a Sunday sermon, I do think it means that they understand Scripture well enough to explain it clearly to someone who has questions.

- **Direction** – Elders are responsible for the overall direction of the church. They will ultimately choose the endeavors the church undertakes and will assign resources to support those endeavors. They are to set the direction of the church, keeping in mind both the spiritual health of the members and the command every church has to make disciples of all nations.

- **Discipline** – Elders are responsible for applying restorative discipline to members who are trapped in sin by ensuring that Jesus' plan for restoration is enacted whenever a member strays from Christ. This does not mean that elders are the "sin police" who need to become personally involved every time a member sins, but it does mean that they encourage members to handle sensitive and sinful situations in a biblical manner. It also means that if a member's sin needs to become a public matter, they would lead the congregation through the process of restoration or excommunication.

- **Distinction** – Elders are responsible for modeling proper Christian living before the body. Obviously they don't need to be perfect Christians, but they do need to be good examples of Christian living both publicly and privately. Members should be able to see that an elder presents a good example of a life that honors God.

## Paul's Advice to Elders in a New Church

> *"Pay careful attention to yourselves and to all the flock, in which the Holy Spirit has made you overseers, to care for the church of God, which he obtained with his own blood. I know that after my departure fierce wolves will come in among you, not sparing the flock; and from among your own selves will arise men speaking twisted things, to draw away the disciples after them. Therefore be alert, remembering that for three years I did not cease night or day to admonish every one with tears." Acts 20:28-31*

- **Be Attentive to Yourself.** Your church needs elders who are wholly devoted to God. Your congregation will be watching to see the Gospel clearly applied in the elders' lives: the way they love, the way they lead, and the way they rebuke and admonish one another. It's no mistake that Paul first advises elders to *"pay careful attention"* to themselves. That may seem counterintuitive because you'd think Paul would put others first, but Paul knew that before an elder can care for the flock, he must attend to his own life.

- **Be Attentive to the Flock.** A good shepherd must be watchful and responsive to the needs of his flock. Likewise, an elder must pray for the members of his church and ask God to show him how their individual and corporate needs can best be met. Such needs may include physical assistance as well as spiritual guidance and instruction. An elder must be present and approachable.

- **Be Alert for Predators.** A security guard who sees a shadow or hears a noise and fails to investigate is worthless. Scripture warns that there will be predators prowling and lying in wait to distract and destroy Christians. Elders have been assigned to guard their particular flock. They must take initiative in both the growth and protection of those God has entrusted to them. Such protection includes managing external threats as well as internal ones: *"from among your own selves will arise men speaking twisted things, to draw away the disciples after them."* Elders are to serve as the congregation's line of defense against harmful people and ideas.

- **Be Willing to Admonish.** Our culture tells us not to judge others and that religion is a private matter. While our walk with Jesus is personal, it is not private. Jesus has put us in community with other believers so that we can grow. Often, we are unable to see our sins and shortcomings without a rebuke lovingly and humbly offered by a godly and trusted friend. Such admonishment is one of the reasons that elders have been given to the church—but that doesn't make it easy. The work of rebuking Christians was difficult even for Paul, who did so *"with tears."* Although he didn't enjoy admonishing others, Paul feared what might happen to them if he refused, and he loved them enough to *"speak the truth in love"* (Ephesians 4:15).

## A Final Note on Elders

It's always easier to put someone on a stage than to remove him. When you have only a few people around, it's easy to fall into the pattern of just selecting the best option at your disposal rather than searching for the ideal candidate for the position. Instead, be patient and prayerful until God provides the right person for this or any role in the church. I have never regretted filling a position with a person who lacked competency but had good character, but I have experienced pain resulting from putting someone in a position primarily because of his competency while ignoring obvious character flaws. If you put a leader with weak character in place because he's the best option, you can expect two things: your faithful, competent leaders will be reluctant to follow him, and you will eventually have to go through the painful process of removing him from the position. Choose character over competency every time.

## 5. Deaconate

As modern people, serving and being served by others is deeply embedded in our way of life. Who doesn't like to go to a posh hotel and have someone in a nicely pressed uniform fluff the pillow and then leave a mint on it? Who doesn't like to go to a nice restaurant and enjoy a good meal prepared by someone else, or to be driven around by a chauffeur, or to have someone else clean the toilets or wash the dog? We love being served so much that we are happy to pay for good service.

On the other hand, most of us also spend a lot of time serving. We know that to maintain the lifestyles we desire, we must spend massive amounts of our time in service to others just so we can have enough money to pay others to serve us. It's called having a job. Some serve in the military so that the rest of us don't have to defend ourselves against terrorists. Some serve in the school system so that the rest of us don't have to educate our own children. Have you ever considered how different your standard of living would be if you were forced to live in a house that you built or drive a car that you put together or wear clothes that you knit? Most of us would be homeless, stranded, and naked!

Our society teaches that our importance is measured by the ratio between our serving and being served. Those who are important in this world are waited on hand and foot by those who are not important. This, however, is not true in the Kingdom of our God. With Jesus' measuring rod, servanthood is ranked far above masterhood. Kingdom mindsets about servanthood are absolutely counterintuitive. Consider some of these ideas from the New Testament:

- The way up is down.
- The way to be first is to be last.

- The way of success is service.
- The way of attainment is relinquishment.
- The way of strength is weakness.
- The way of security is vulnerability.
- The way of protection is forgiveness (even 70 x 7).
- The way to life is death—death to self, society, and family.
- The way God's power is made perfect is in our weakness.
- The way to freedom is surrender to God.
- The way to be great is to be least.
- The way to discover yourself is to forget yourself.
- The way of honor is humility.
- The way to deal with enemies is to bless them, love them, and pray for them.

Service is so glorified in God's Kingdom that the hero of our faith, Jesus, even describes Himself as a servant (Matthew 20:28; Mark 10:45; Luke 12:37, 22:26-27; John 13; Romans 15:8) and tells His followers, *"The greatest among you shall be your servant"* (Matthew 23:11).

## Servanthood in the Church

In Jesus' church, it should come as no surprise that servanthood is exalted. The job of service in the church is so important that the person fulfilling the role is expected to meet some pretty strenuous qualifications in order to have the privilege of being a deacon in God's church. As a church planter, you'll have to invite people into the privilege of servanthood. The default setting for most people who get involved in your ministry will be to simply observe until they are invited to serve.

When Pillar Church began, I was 24 years old. I was a sub-par preacher and a sloppy, partially trained theologian. I tried to compensate for my obvious inferiority by working hard. I assumed that to gain the respect of those around me, I would need to work hard for it. As a result, I did everything myself. Some of the early members jokingly refer to our Sunday morning worship services during our first year as "The Clint Show" because I did nearly everything myself. I towed the trailer full of worship equipment to the school where we met, set up the equipment, printed the bulletins, designed the graphics, played the guitar, preached the sermon, passed out the offering baskets, led communion, said the prayers, uploaded the sermons to the website—you get the point. By the time the worship service started on Sunday morning, I had already been up for six or seven hours. I'd be drenched with sweat and looking completely ragged. When people asked how they could help, I'd tell them to just enjoy themselves because everything was under control.

The problem with this approach was that the most important things about the church's ministry—evangelism, preaching, counseling, and prayer—were receiving only a tiny fraction of my time. Not to mention that I was burning out fast. As a result, our worship services in the early stages of our church amused people more than it ministered to them. Fortunately, some older, wiser people in our church patiently helped me delegate responsibilities to others and encouraged me to focus my attention on the things that were most important. Over time, I began noticing that my focus was producing good results in the lives of those I was serving, and I began to really see the value in dedicating myself to a few things and doing them well.

Before long, servant-hearted people oversaw the practical aspects of operating the church. When I stopped doing all the work, God started working in the hearts of men and women who took on various aspects of the ministry. To my surprise, they did a much better job accomplishing these duties than I did. This was the beginning of our deacon ministry. Today, faithful volunteers serve joyfully in the ministry by taking care of virtually every aspect of the ministry throughout the week and on Sunday mornings.

## Not Everyone Who Serves Is a Deacon

We look again to Scripture for the qualifications of those who get the privilege of serving Jesus' church. One thing is clear when you study the qualifications for deacons in 1st Timothy: the servant's character is of utmost importance to God. The qualities mentioned in this list are character qualities, not competencies. God thinks so highly of service in the church that He reserves the most menial tasks for those with the best character. When people are dedicated to serving the body, they are imitating Christ when He willingly took on the form of a servant (Philippians 2:1-11).

It's important to note that not everyone who plays a service role in the church should be formally recognized as a deacon. There is a distinction in Scripture between the office of deacon and simple servanthood. This distinction can be clearly seen in the appointment of deacons by the apostles in Acts 6. The apostles ask the congregation of disciples to select from among themselves *"seven men of good repute, full of the Spirit and of wisdom"* (Acts 6:3). The role of these seven men was not only to wait tables, but also to take responsibility for the task in order to free up the apostles to dedicate themselves to the ministry of the Word and prayer (Acts 6:4). Therefore, we should view deacons in the church as "lead servants," entrusting them with the responsibility of guiding the accomplishment of administrative, practical, and physical needs within the body.

## Where to Start Your Search for Deacons

In my upbringing, deacons had the unfortunate reputation of being the grumpy, power-hungry old men who ran the church. It seemed they were always at odds with the pastor. Ironically, this is exactly opposite of what the deacons were appointed to accomplish in Acts 6—not simply the serving of tables, but the calming of a disruption. Pastor and author Mark Dever explains:

> If you look at this passage (Acts 6) in a more abstract way, you could ask, "In caring for these widows, what were they really doing?" They were working to make the food distribution among the widows more equitable. That's true, but why was that important? Because this physical neglect was causing a spiritual disunity in the body. That's how the passage begins in 6:1, *"In those days, when the number of disciples was increasing, the Grecian Jews among them complained against those of the Aramaic-speaking community because their widows were being overlooked in the daily distribution of food."* One group of Christians was beginning to complain against another group. This seems to be what arrested the attention of the Apostles.

They were not merely trying to rectify a problem in the benevolence ministry of the church. They were trying to stop the church's unity from fracturing and being broken up, and that in a particularly dangerous way: along traditional cultural lines of division. The deacons were appointed to head off disunity in the church.[20]

With this in mind, I encourage you to search for deacons who have the following three characteristics to be lead servants in the church you are planting.

- **Look for peacemakers.** We're looking for bases, not acids. We don't want to fill the deaconate with volatile, explosive types but with reasonable, level-headed types who are problem solvers, not problem makers. We want the guys who will defuse the ticking relational bombs, not the ones who will detonate them.

- **Look for a healthy home life.** Six of the twelve scriptural qualifications for deacons have to do with the deacon's wife and family. Four of the twelve qualifications are specifically dedicated to the wife's character. For this reason alone, we should pay special attention to the family of a deacon.

- **Look for comfort behind the scenes.** Some in your church will assume that the deaconate is like junior varsity, that they couldn't cut it as elders or are waiting to be called up to fill a vacancy in the eldership. Be careful not to foster this idea. The roles of both deacons and elders are interdependent and equally important, so look for individuals who are happy to serve behind the scenes, with or without recognition.

> Our elders have selected and affirmed deacons as lead servants in the ministry of our local church. Simple job descriptions have been created for them, and they are aware of expectations.

## Deacons' Meetings

Traditionally, most evangelical churches have regular deacons' meetings. In my experience, meetings are unnecessary and potentially problematic. Deacons manage a particular aspect of service in the church. For example, our church has a deacon responsible for overseeing the care of our rental facility. He spends most of his time coordinating cleaning crews, scheduling work to be done, and ordering supplies. This alone takes a great deal of time. His role interfaces with the role of several other ministries, and systems have been created to make those logistics run smoothly between those ministries. He needs to meet with individuals who volunteer to help clean the facility and to make sure they know what to do and where to get the necessary supplies, but he doesn't generally need to meet with the deacon who oversees the website and technical ministry. When we first appointed deacons, we had regularly scheduled meetings for them. With that came the necessity for a chairman and a number of other logistical issues such as childcare, food, and authority within the group. Eventually, the deacons' meetings stopped, but the deacons' service continued. Periodically, our elders do meet with our deacons to work through particular problems, but regularly scheduled meetings seem to be unnecessary.

## Helping Deacons Succeed

As you appoint deacons into service roles in the church, encourage delegation and look for ways to make their jobs as easy as possible. In their job description, clarify your expectation that they help make sure the work gets done, not that they do all of the work themselves. When you see a particular ministry is shorthanded, use your influence to encourage others to join the team. When you see that a simple piece of software or hardware could make their job easier, work to get it for them. Most of all, communicate to them regularly your appreciation, and affirm the importance of their work before the congregation.

## Set Structure Early

Polity is infrastructure. Just as a city needs roads, parks, electrical grids, and sidewalks to ensure its residents can travel, communicate, and work easily, a new church needs infrastructure to ensure its members can live together in peace and unity. If you don't create the infrastructure in a new church, someone else will create it for you. People don't stop walking just because there are no sidewalks; they create their own paths. In the same way, if you don't lead the church to make decisions and handle problems in a biblical manner, you should expect that someone else will make those decisions. You may not feel the need for such formality when the church is small and unified. You may even be tempted to function as the sole decision maker until you feel the need for additional help. That would be a mistake for at least two reasons.

First, you're probably not as good a leader as you think you are. Most young leaders overestimate their ability to lead people well. This was certainly true of me. When I began church planting, my youthful confidence convinced me that I could handle most any situation. I knew my commitment to the success of the church was higher than anyone else's, so I assumed that meant I was the best person to make decisions for the church. In hindsight, I regret many of the decisions I made in the first several years of the church's life. They were shortsighted and hadn't stood the test of scrutiny by other godly men. On the other hand, once our church elected elders, the quality of our decisions noticeably improved. Before working with other elders, all of the decisions were mine alone, which I liked. If the decision I made worked out well, I owned it and felt a sense of pride for my success. If the decision turned out to be a bad one, I felt the full weight of the destruction that decision caused.

I have also learned that successful leaders in business, education, or in the military are not necessarily successful leaders in the church. If you're a more experienced leader going into church planting, you should be cautious about the transition. Leading volunteers in a church environment is much different from leading employees, students, or cadets. Church members generally don't respond well when you bark orders at them. They also don't feel particularly motivated to fulfill your wishes until they respect you, and they won't respect you until you earn their respect.

Leaders in a church environment will be required to bank some "influence equity" with team members before leveraging that influence to get things accomplished. Be careful not to overestimate how much of it you have, and use it sparingly. I've heard Mark Dever say, "Influence is like a bar of soap; the more you use, the less you have." Keep in mind that the people who are serving in this new church also have work and family pressures. This may be your occupation, but it's probably not theirs. Treat them graciously and express lots of appreciation.

Second, when real trouble comes, the weight of decision-making is heavy. Satan is waiting to pounce on you with discouragement and doubt. Sharing the leadership load with others not only divides the weight, but it also multiplies the joy of pastoral leadership. Scripture teaches that there is wisdom in a multitude of opinions (Proverbs 14:11, 15:22); so don't try to lead alone. When you are alone, you are most vulnerable, but partners in gospel work will help provide a measure of protection and spiritual accountability that will be good for the stability of your new church.

While the church is small and unified, institute biblical church governance. As the size of the congregation grows, so does the potential for contention. Setting up a biblical system for making decisions, solving problems, and moving forward in the church will decrease the odds of terminal conflict and disunity in the body and will distribute leadership and work among the saints. Install simple, clear pathways for progress and problem solving. The New Testament provides a rich source of instruction as you write documents and install leaders in the body of Christ.

# REPEAT

Just as with a woman trying to become pregnant, the window of fertility for a local church to reproduce is relatively narrow. The older a church gets, the less likely it is to ever intentionally reproduce, so it's important to begin attempting to plant early. The more a church emphasizes numerical growth, the more difficult it will be to lead that church to reproduce.

Earlier, I mentioned Naethan, my pastoral partner. Naethan served with me as I worked to plant Pillar Church, and he became our first church planter just one year after Pillar began. Our church was very small and, by most accounts, not ready to start another new church. We didn't have a lot of money, we didn't have our church polity in place, and we didn't have a facility, but we did have a qualified and competent leader. Naethan was well-loved by our tiny congregation. He was an excellent Bible teacher with a strong pastoral gifting.

Sending him out to plant seemed counterintuitive. Everything in my experience was telling me to continue to focus my attention on building our congregation rather than worrying myself with the need for other congregations in our region. On the other hand, I believed the Great Commission to be a call to start new churches, and I knew that the numerical growth of Pillar Church was infinitely less important than the growth of Jesus' Kingdom.

By the end of our first year of ministry, Naethan was living in a small apartment in Quantico and leading a Bible study there with townspeople and Marines from the neighboring military base. Though the town was less than five miles from Pillar Church's meeting location, it became clear to us that the group in Quantico had the potential to develop into a separate congregation. We secured permission from the town council to begin renting a community center for services and decided to begin with Sunday evening services. Naethan and I didn't part ways when the new church began; we worked together to develop both congregations simultaneously. On Sunday mornings we met in a public school under the name Pillar Church, and on Sunday evenings we met in the community center as The Church at Quantico. The sermons and music were often the same, but the two congregations were developing independently. Ten years later, the two churches minister to two dramatically different groups of people.

Charles Spurgeon challenged his congregation this way: "We encourage our members to leave us to found other churches; nay, we seek to persuade them to do it. We ask them to scatter throughout the land to become the goodly seed, which God shall bless. I believe that so long as we do this we shall prosper."[21]

## Biblical Rationale for Church Planting

I think the majority of Christians like the idea of church planting conceptually. In fact, I don't recall ever meeting a Christian who was directly opposed to the idea. Even so, the vast majority of Christians and churches will never start a new church or even give serious consideration to doing so. I think one primary reason is that many Christians are unable to pinpoint any biblical foundation for church planting. Just because the average Christian doesn't know where to find scriptural support for church planting, doesn't mean that there is none. So I want to first look at one very well-known passage of Scripture that explicitly commands disciples of Jesus to start new churches.

If you've been a Christian for a while, you've probably read the Great Commission (Matthew 28:18-20) hundreds of times, but you may not have recognized it as the Bible's most explicit command to plant new churches:

> *And Jesus came and said to them, "All authority in heaven and on earth has been given to me. Go therefore and make disciples of all nations, baptizing them in the name of the Father and of the Son and of the Holy Spirit, teaching them*

*to observe all that I have commanded you. And behold, I am with you always, to the end of the age."*

Jesus commands His followers to make disciples, baptize, and teach. Since disciple-making, baptizing, and teaching are activities of the local church, it is reasonable to conclude that, when Jesus spoke the Great Commission, He intended His followers to plant churches.

There was a time when the Great Commission really meant something great. It meant that Jesus' disciples were to travel to other communities to take part in the ongoing process of making followers of Jesus in that community, then, through baptism, to usher those new followers into a life of accountability, service, and commitment with other Christians. In short, there was a time when the Great Commission was about the church, not the individual Christian.

Jesus couldn't possibly be talking about something other than the local church, could He? Are there any other organizations on planet Earth that are responsible for making disciples of Jesus, baptizing people into Jesus' family, or teaching people to observe all the commands of Jesus? Not that I am aware of. Jesus' church is the only organization that He could have been talking about here. So why didn't Jesus just say, "Go therefore into all nations and start new churches, and I'll be with you always, even until the end of the age"? The simple answer is that when Jesus spoke the Great Commission, churches had not yet started.

Here's an analogy. Pretend I recruit you to do a job for me. I say, "Go into the garage and pull the string on the top of the red machine until the engine starts. When it starts, walk around the yard, pushing the machine in front of you. Be careful to push it over every bit of grass in the yard. When you are finished, turn the machine off and put it back into the garage." Wouldn't that essentially be the same as recruiting you to mow the grass? In the same way, the Great Commission is a call to establish local churches. Consider each of the commands individually.

- **Make Disciples.** The word disciple means "learner."[22] Believers are to be busy making learners out of those who place their faith in Christ for salvation. The early church understood discipleship as part of its responsibility. Acts 14:21 says, *"When they had preached* *the gospel to that city, and had taught many, they returned."* Jesus' followers went into various cities and made disciples. Those who followed Jesus in the early days of the Church recognized no distinction between establishing churches and making disciples because making disciples was (and is) a necessary part of establishing churches. After the Great Commission, the specific command to make disciples is not repeated. Perhaps making disciples is so innate to the nature of redeemed life that it need not be repeated.

- **Baptize.** Throughout the New Testament, it is clear that baptism means incorporation into a worshipping community with accountability and boundaries. Paul tells the churches at Rome and Colossae that they were buried with Christ through baptism (Romans 6:4; Colossians 2:12), a practice that we see happening throughout the days of the early church. In Acts we see that all those who accepted Christ's message were baptized (Acts 2:41). It would be a mistake for us to think of baptism as somehow disconnected from the local church.

- **Teach.** The teaching ministry of the local church is its most prominent feature. The leaders of a church must be able to teach, and Paul instructs young pastor Timothy to devote himself to the *"public reading of Scripture, to exhortation, to teaching"* (1 Timothy 4:13). Even the very earliest fellowship of believers devoted themselves to the apostles' teaching (Acts 2:42). [23]

Just in case you're not yet completely convinced that the Great Commission is a call to start new churches, notice that in response to hearing Jesus say, "Go, make disciples, baptize, and teach," the disciples spend the rest of their lives establishing churches. Why would they do this if they didn't think the Great Commission was about new churches? These men were not confused about the nature of Jesus' command. They could have gone on a two-week mission trip, painted a synagogue, tucked tracks into every doorway, and called it a day. But they didn't. They took the Great Commission as a command to start new churches and then gave the rest of their lives to the establishment of churches. For some reason, many modern churches have re-interpreted the Great Commission in a way that is not so great.

If Jesus commands his followers to go, make disciples, baptize, and teach, essentially Jesus is commanding his followers to establish new churches! Jesus' final command to His disciples before His ascension into heaven was to go start new churches—and they did. If this is true, and if the Great Commission is a command from Jesus to start new churches, the implications for modern Christians are clear. Every Christian and every church should endeavor to start new churches.

Notice, I didn't say that every Christian should be a church planter. God does not call every Christian to pastoral leadership, but He does call every Christian and every church to obey the Great Commission, and as we have already established, that means planting new churches. Church planting is the Great Commission, and the Great Commission is church planting. If you are a pastor, this means you should encourage church planting as regularly as you encourage the Great Commission. It means that if your church is involved in Great Commission work that doesn't involve church planting, you're not really involved in Great Commission work. It means that you should lead the people of your church to view an increasing number of gospel churches in your city as an aid to your church rather than competition. It means you should pray for new churches to be established. Educate your congregation on the need for new churches and remind the members of your church that God often calls ordinary people to establish new churches. If you regularly teach the people of your church that "planting new churches is the most effective evangelistic methodology known under heaven,"[24] you will find them eager to support the establishment of other local churches.

If you pay attention as you read, you will see church planting all over the New Testament.

- **Jesus was a church planter.** Jesus, the hero of the Bible, established the universal Church and claimed that the gates of hell would not prevail against it (Matthew 16:18). He also led a small congregation of disciples. He taught them the Word of God,

He shared communion with them, and He commissioned them to plant more churches.

- **Paul was a church planter.** Paul's commissioning by the church at Antioch in Acts 13 marks the beginning of an incredible church planting streak. Over the course of thirteen years, Paul embarked on three missionary journeys in which he traveled more than 7,000 miles and planted at least fourteen new churches.

- **The apostles were church planters.** The book of Acts recounts the apostles' church planting ministry. They planted churches with little support from other churches and against great political and religious opposition. Ultimately, their commitment to obey the Great Commission by planting churches cost them their lives.

## How Churches Began in the New Testament

Today, churches are started all sorts of different ways. Sometimes, Christians in a church disagree and divide over the conflict, other times churches willingly send members to plant a new church in an area of need. Sometimes, groups of people are forced to relocate due to occupation. In his book, Finding Organic Church, Frank Viola points to four ways we see churches begin in the New Testament.

- **Jerusalem Model** – many disciples in a particular location plant one church.
- **Antioch Model** – an apostle enters a town, preaches the gospel, and plants a church from the converts.
- **Ephesian Model** – an apostle disciples and trains men to plant churches and then sends them out.
- **The Roman Model** – Christians from various places relocate in order to plant a new church.

## A Comprehensive Case

Like many doctrines in the Bible, the most compelling case for church planting is not found in any one passage of Scripture but rather in a synthesis of a number of applicable passages. We have many doctrines that fall into this category. Perhaps the most well-known perhaps is the doctrine of the Trinity. Though the Trinity is not mentioned or named in any specific passage of Scripture, it is a commonly held (and very important) doctrine in the church. Why is this? Because of the synthesis of many texts that lead us to a clear understanding of what theologians have for centuries called the Trinity.

Similarly, you will not find the term "church planting" in the Bible, but that doesn't mean that church planting is not a biblical idea. In truth, every Christian and every church is commanded to participate in church planting. There are explicit commands such as Matthew 28:18-20, as well as many places where church planting is implied or assumed. In the book of Acts alone we have dozens of references to church planting.

- Jesus authorizes his apostles to plant the first church in Jerusalem as a base for spreading the Gospel around the world (Acts 1:8, 2:1-47).
- In Acts 8, Philip preaches the Gospel effectively during the persecution and scattering of the Jerusalem church in Samaria. Philip had been previously affirmed both by the church as a whole and its senior leaders (Acts 6:1-7).
- In Acts 9, Saul (Paul), the greatest missionary the world has ever known, converts from a persecutor of the church to a planter of churches. The leaders of the Jerusalem church confirm Saul's calling (Acts 9:26-31).
- In Acts 11, the church at Antioch was born of Christians scattered by the Jerusalem persecution. Barnabas was sent by the Jerusalem church to authenticate and lead this new church (Acts 11:19-26).
- In Acts 13:1-4, Paul and Barnabas were called directly by the Holy Spirit for a mission to launch new churches. The church prayed, fasted, and affirmed their calling through the laying on of hands by other leaders at Antioch.
- Paul's missionary ministry of planting churches forms the rest of the story of Acts. He preaches the Gospel in every city, plants new faith communities called churches, and remains until approved

elders are in place to shepherd the new work going forward (Acts 14:23; Titus 1:5).

- Paul also remained under the authority of the church in Jerusalem which had first sent him out (Acts 15:6-35).

In addition to the book of Acts, many of the New Testament letters were written to encourage, rebuke, or instruct church planters and their congregations. Even the New Testament word for church, *ekklesia*, indicates a called-out assembly or congregation.[25] God's people are called out of society at large to live together as the people of God in local assemblies. Those local assemblies worship Christ, uphold one another, and evangelize the lost. In modern society, the people of God are mobile, and wherever there are new groups of people, churches are needed.

## The Mystery of Church Growth

There's a lot of talk in ministry circles about church growth, but I think there is sufficient reason to doubt the rationale behind much of what we hear and read on the subject. Modern ministerial philosophies teach that we can achieve significant numerical growth in our churches by implementing ideologies and strategies that have proven effective in other places. We're taught that if we implement those strategies in our setting, we will achieve similar results. In fact, there is an entire section of most Christian bookstore dedicated to "church growth."

Don't get me wrong, church growth is important. God cares about the hell-bound masses in our communities, and we should be faithful to do everything in our power to bring the Gospel to them. It's a mistake to assume that this will be achieved chiefly through your own local church. It is a scheme of the devil to convince pastors that their churches are the answer to the problem of lostness in their community. Friend, your church is not the answer. The Gospel your church preaches is the answer. Every church should endeavor to grow not only numerically, but also in establishing other gospel-preaching churches in their own communities and regions and around the world.

Church growth is a mystery. No formula or ideology will enable your church to reach your city for Christ. Regardless of how popular this idea becomes in American Christianity, we have no reason, historically or theologically, to believe that our churches will reach our entire communities for Christ or that people will flourish in our congregations better than they will in other congregations. The Bible clarifies for us that the growth of a church and the growth of the Kingdom have very little to do with us.

Jesus describes it this way: *"The kingdom of God is as if a man should scatter seed on the ground. He sleeps and rises night and day, and the seed sprouts and grows; he knows not how"* (Mark 4:26-27). Notice that He makes a point of mentioning that the man doesn't know how it happened. Later in the New Testament, Paul describes his labor by saying, *"I planted, Apollos watered, but God gave the growth"* (1 Corinthians 3:6). And later, *"Neither he who plants nor he who waters is anything, but only God who gives the growth. He who plants and he who waters are one, and each will receive his wages according to his labor. For we are God's fellow workers"* (1 Corinthians 3:7-9).

Charles Spurgeon understood this mystery and regularly encouraged the people of his church, the Metropolitan Tabernacle, to leave in order to form other churches. Here are a few examples of how he encouraged multiplication in his church:

> My brethren, if you can do more good elsewhere than you can do here, for God's sake, go, and happy shalt I be that you have gone. If you can serve my Master in the little rooms in the neighborhood, if by forming yourselves into smaller churches you can increase the honor of my Master's name, I shall love you none the less for going, but I shall delight to think that you have Christ's spirit in you, and can do and dare for his name's sake. At the present moment we rejoice to know that many a Sunday School in this neighborhood is indebted to the members of this Church for teachers. It is right. We do not want you at home, and are therefore glad to see you at work elsewhere. No matter, so long as Christ is preached, whether you throw your strength into that Church or into this Church. Here, as being members with us, we have the first claim upon you; but when we do not need you by reason of our

abundance of men, go and give your strength to any other part of Christ's Church that may desire you.

This Church will begin to go rotten at the core the moment we are not working for God with might and main. Sometimes I get a pull at my coat-tail by very kind, judicious friends, who think I shall ask you to do too much. My brethren are welcome to pull my coat-tail, but it will come off before I shall stand back for a moment. As long as I live I must serve my Master with my whole soul, and when you think I go too fast, you can stand back if you dare, for mark, you will be responsible to God if you do; you may start back if you will and if you dare, but I must go on, must go, MUST go on, or else you and I that are worthy of the day in which you live will follow me, step by step, in any good project, and though I should seem too rash, you will redeem me from the charge of rashness by the enthusiasm and the earnestness with which you carry out my plans. Here is this great city! Was there ever such spiritual destitution? A million of people who could not go to a place of worship, if they had the heart to go there!

We have undertaken many enterprises for Christ; we hope to undertake a great many more. We have never husbanded our strength; we have undertaken enterprises that were enough to exhaust us, to which we became accustomed in due season, and then we have gone on to something more. We have never sought to hinder the uprising of other Churches from our midst or in our neighborhood. It is with cheerfulness that we dismiss our twelves, our twenties, our fifties, to form other Churches. We encourage our members to leave us to found other Churches; nay, we seek to persuade them to do it. We ask them to scatter throughout the land to become the Godly seed which God shall bless. I believe that so long as we do this we shall prosper. I have marked other Churches that have adopted the other way, and they have not succeeded.

I have seen that the effect of trying to keep all the blood in the heart is to bring on congestion, and very soon the whole body has been out of health.[26]

    Spurgeon actually credits the success of the church to the fact that they have liberally and joyfully given their members away to form other churches! It makes me wonder how different the spiritual landscape of our country would be if pastors and churches were as dedicated to Kingdom growth as they are to the growth of their own congregations.

Think of a drain in a bathtub. Water comes out of the faucet and goes directly down the drain as long as nothing is blocking it. As items get in the way of the drain, the flow of water slows, and more and more water gathers in the tub. As debris is moved from the drain, water begins to flow again. Churches often think that the goal is filling up the tub, so they work to establish leaders and ministries to keep folks attending their churches. Imagine if we stopped trying to gather folks to block the drain but intentionally removed the drain guard to give them freedom and encouragement to go and serve God wherever the drain takes them. Granted, it is entirely possible that you will have less water in the tub. But it's also quite likely that the water passing through will be much fresher. The same can be said of our churches. We have built our entire church system around gathering people, but the heart of Jesus' teaching is scattering people. If you live in a transient area, be grateful for the natural traffic God is bringing through. If you don't, you should work to compel people to carry the Gospel away to places that need it.

## Common Objections to Church Planting

I find sport in asking pastors if they have ever led their church to plant another new church. Although most have not, they have a positive position on church planting. They commonly express to me their desire to lead their congregation to plant new churches. When I ask why they haven't, I generally get responses like these:

- **"We just don't have the people to send."** Usually what they really mean is, "We have a bunch of ministries now that are understaffed. We will have to wait until all the ministries are staffed. When that impossible task is accomplished, we will consider starting a new church." This is teaching people that fulfilling Jesus' mission is equal to staffing the ministries of our church.

- **"We don't have the money."** Church planting is only expensive because we think that, in order to have a legitimate church, it has to be complete with a five piece worship band, a modern facility, a sophisticated sound system, and theater lighting to set the mood. But how much does it cost to share the Gospel with your neighbor? How much does it cost to meet in your living room? Church planting is about making, baptizing, and teaching disciples—all of which are free!

- **"Our people aren't ready for that yet."** This one may be legitimate for a time. Some congregations are genuinely not ready, but priority number one is to get them ready. Mission is at the center of God's design for the church. If you have been the pastor of a congregation for very long and you are still making this excuse, I have to ask what you are teaching your people. As the pastor, you can be leading your congregation to readiness and away from selfishness.

- **"I don't feel God leading us in that direction."** You would find more biblical support for having a concubine than for saying God is not leading you to plant churches. If you don't feel God leading you to obey the Great Commission, what do you feel him leading you to do? A capital building campaign? A clothes closet? Our feelings should never trump our mandate.

Planting early won't be easy, but it won't be any easier down the road either. I wish I had a dollar for every time a pastor told me that they're going to wait until they reach 300 or 500 or 1,000 attendees before they start a new church, believing it will be easier then. But think about it this way.

At that point, your budget is maxed out, your people are accustomed to only thinking about themselves, and you've operated for years doing only what advances your own congregation. Once a church begins thinking primarily about itself—its growth, its comfort, and its facilities—turning its attention back to reproduction is nearly impossible. There is no better way to keep your congregation focused on the mission of spreading the Gospel than to lead them to plant other churches early and often.

## Leader Readiness

If a church doesn't need money, a large congregation, expertise, or a special call from God to start a new church, what does it need? The answer is surprisingly simple. You need a church planter. The most important factor in a church's ability to plant a new church is leader readiness. You can plant a church without money, a big team, and a nice sound system, but you can't plant a new church without a church planter. All that's really necessary for you to lead your new church to plant another church is a competent and qualified church planter.

When I was in college, I went to dinner with a pastor named Cliff. During the meal, our waitress came to the table, and Cliff asked whether the restaurant was open on Sunday. When she replied that it was not, he made some complimentary remarks about the size of the dining room and told her that it would make a perfect location for a church to gather. Then Cliff asked the owner whether he would allow a church to meet there on Sunday mornings. The two men talked logistics for a few minutes before Cliff took his audacity to a new level by asking if the owner would you mind if he stopped by sometime to invite the staff to attend. With one simple conversation, Cliff initiated a new church. When he went to meet the staff from the restaurant, he took a leader from his church and introduced him as the leader of the new congregation. On Sunday, he challenged the members of his church to gather at the restaurant to support their brother in his new ministry.

We have made church planting so difficult and expensive that only professionals can do it. This was never God's intention. Church planting is for the average Joe. That's why Jesus picked up his recruits from the beach instead of the synagogue. The professionalization of ministry has drastically slowed the establishment of new churches. As pastors, we are to press our people to carry the Gospel far and wide and to allow our churches to be known for scattering rather than gathering.

To create a culture of scattering, place an early emphasis on leadership development. There are two helpful acronyms that I have borrowed from the world of international missions that have served me well as I have sought to discover and develop leaders for church planting. Before our church had any training material or a church planting residency program, these two acronyms were the entirety of our recruitment and training methodology for church planting.

## FAT People

The first acronym has to do with choosing whom we should spend our time developing. When we started church planting, the most accessible people in our congregation were the young men who attended our church. These men were growing rapidly in their faith and were eager to do something great for Jesus. Naethan and I started making ourselves available to meet them for discipleship, and soon we found that some of them took our investment very seriously and worked hard to arrange their schedules to spend time with us. Others stood us up or would coast into meetings having done nothing we asked them to do the week before. Out of those experiences, we started to notice faithfulness, availability, and teachability as essential qualities for those we were developing for church leadership. Allow me to make a few observations about these qualities.

- **Faithful** – We noticed that those who were quick to obey Jesus when they knew what He wanted them to do were worth our investment. Some guys struggle with the same sins over and over again and seem unwilling to take the drastic, eye-plucking, hand-chopping (Matthew 5:29-30) measures that are required to really mortify the flesh. Those who were willing to take these measures inevitably grew faster and gained victory over areas of sin in their lives more quickly. I remember sitting with a young man who was confessing that he was addicted to pornography. He said he would do anything to escape from its clutches. I asked him if he was serious, and he claimed he was. I told him I wanted him to

144

promise me that the next time he went to a pornographic website, he would let me toss his laptop into Quantico Creek. He stared at me for a few seconds in deep contemplation then promised me he would. Months later he told me that simple promise helped him gain victory over his pornography addiction. We're not looking for perfect guys. We're looking for guys who are serious about obeying Jesus, even if it's costly. Be on the lookout for faithfulness in your search for leaders to develop.

- **Available** – I live in Northern Virginia where everyone is always busy. Careers are demanding and traffic is atrocious. As a result, there are a plethora of excuses for not being able to meet for personal spiritual growth. When I invite someone to meet with me for discipleship, and they actually do it, I know that their spiritual development is a priority to them. Invest your time in those who stretch to make themselves available to you.

- **Teachable** – This is perhaps the most important piece and also the most difficult to discern at first. A person's teachability has to do with their willingness to implement your instruction, even if they are not convinced it is credible. *The Karate Kid* offers us with a helpful picture. Remember when Mr. Miyagi told Daniel to paint the fence and wax the car when all Daniel wanted to do was learn Karate? Miyagi recognized some areas of Daniel's life that needed development, even though Daniel didn't. The same will be true for those you disciple. Invest your time in those who heed your advice and instruction even when it doesn't make complete sense to them.

> I have identified one or two guys in my ministry that I consider faithful, available, and teachable.

## MAWL People

The second acronym we have used when providing on-the-job training for those with ministerial aspirations is MAWL (Model, Assist, Watch, Leave). This is something you can begin doing right away with FAT people in your ministry who are eager to gain ministerial experience. The process begins with simply allowing those you're training to go with you as you accomplish the work of the ministry.

- **Model** – If you are going to visit someone who is in the hospital, bring a FAT guy with you. If you are going to study for your sermon, invite a FAT guy to study with you. Be sure to explain everything you do, and don't hold back anything you've learned along the way. Say something like, "I try never to leave the hospital without praying for the person who is sick," or "I find that I study best in the mornings so I set aside two mornings a week for sermon preparation." Invite a FAT guy and his family to join you and your family for devotions or dinner or some other opportunity that allows them see how you interact with your family. It's not rocket science. Simply invite FAT guys to see the behind-the-scenes footage of your life.

- **Assist** – Once you have modeled a particular area of ministry, it's important to let your trainee assist you. Maybe have him do some research for your sermon on Sunday. Allow him to join you in teaching a section of the new members course or to help you fill up the baptistery. When it seems like he has a handle on what he's doing, start assisting him. Allow him to take the lead on the visitor follow up, then debrief with him after it's over.

- **Watch** – Once it's clear that he knows what he's doing, just sit back and watch. This might mean allowing a FAT guy to preach a sermon or lead a small group while you sit in the crowd. It might mean allowing him to put an outreach event together from start to finish. Expect that he'll do it a bit differently than you (probably not quite as well), but leaving him alone to make his own mistakes is part of the process of training. Be sure to tell him afterwards what he did well and what areas you think he could improve.

- **Leave** – This part is critical and probably the most difficult because it requires you to get out of the way. It's a much different experience to lead something on your own without the watchful eye of a mentor in the crowd. Your presence could actually prevent those you're training from feeling fully empowered to lead. Eventually, when you feel they have a good grasp on what they are doing, leave and allow them to accomplish the task without you. As always, be sure to talk with your trainees afterward to see how things went. Give them room to grow, make mistakes, and experience firsthand some of the joys and difficulties of pastoral ministry.

In order to prepare your congregation for someone to take on new leadership roles, it is helpful to be transparent about your desire to develop new leaders for church planting. When putting potential leaders in new roles within the church, it's common for me to say something like, "You know Josh, right? Would you mind if he sits in on this meeting? He's preparing for ministry, and this experience might be a big help to him." You'll find that over time this type of training will become part of the culture of the church. The members will expect you to always have someone with you and will feel proud that they play a role in the development of other leaders.

> I have identified at least five pastoral activities
> that I can easily teach to others.

## Choose a Planter

The possibility of failure can cause great hesitation and fear when choosing a potential leader, but at some point you just need to choose someone. The best scenario is that you choose someone from your congregation to be your first church planter, perhaps your pastoral partner, another team member, or one of the guys you've been working to develop. Presumably, choosing someone from within will make it easier to get support from the members and attenders of your church, but if no one is ready internally, don't hesitate to find another planter to support. There is more to be lost by doing nothing than by attempting to do something.

> I have identified someone as our first church planter and
> have a plan to prepare him for church planting.

## Preparing Your Congregation

Since developing this mentality of church planting does not come naturally or easily for a congregation, the pastoral leadership must foster it. Christians joining your team from other churches may already have a good perspective on church planting when they arrive, but those who join you from the community and those you win to Christ will need you to teach them about the priority of church planting. Allow me to share some things that have helped to develop a culture of church planting at Pillar Church.

- **Talk about church planting regularly.** Talking about church planting regularly normalizes it for the people in your congregation. At Pillar Church we feature a church planter every week and spend time in prayer for them publicly. The majority of those church planters were once members of our congregation. This prayer time is a weekly reminder that God calls regular people to plant ordinary churches that do extraordinary things for God.

> I have chosen one or more church planters whom I
> can lead my congregation to pray for regularly.

- **Keep things simple.** Do your job in such a way that those participating in your ministry can imagine themselves ministering in a similar way. If you present yourself in a highly professional manner and create the impression that your skills are specialized, people will have a difficult time imagining themselves serving in a position like yours. Instead, invite people to join you in your work so that they see how rewarding it can be. Consider letting someone else preach, baptize, lead communion, pray, and evangelize. Celebrate when a lay person does something that is normally the job of a pastor.

- **Be Generous.** It is impossible to out-give God. Don't be afraid to encourage members to start new ministries or help struggling ministries. It will be tempting to keep all the resources you gather close to home, but this kind of leadership will never produce Kingdom- heartedness in your people. Many churches are in the habit of saving their best resources for themselves and distributing very little to help prosper or build other local ministries. Commit from the very beginning to hold your resources loosely, and you will find that the more you give away, the more God will entrust to you. One very practical way to do this is to dedicate regular budget money to church planting from the very beginning of your new church. Even if it's a small amount to start with, it's better to start with something. You can start this practice even if you don't have a particular church planter in mind. Set aside money so that when God leads you to support a church planter, you have the funds available to do so.

> Our new church has decided to dedicate $_____
> every month to a church planting fund.

- **Believe for Others.** People will have a difficult time seeing themselves as ministry leaders. Frequently encouraging ordinary people to do extraordinary things for God helps instill a sense of confidence and interest in serving as a ministry leader. Before I entered ministry, faithful men and women of God gave me courage by predicting how God would use me in the future. Their words gave me courage to tread ground that I never would have without their encouragement. Your optimism about their future effectiveness says more about your confidence in God than it does about your confidence in them; so don't hesitate to encourage them.

- **Teach about Church Planting.** As you teach through the Scriptures, you'll find plenty of opportunities to teach about church planting. The New Testament is full of great stories about men and women with missionary zeal carrying the Gospel to other places both far and near. Don't hesitate to say something like, "You know, there are a lot of Spanish-speaking people in our community, and I don't know of any healthy Hispanic churches here. I pray that one day God will allow us to be a part of starting one."

- **Pray for Other Churches.** It's not uncommon for the people in your congregation to assume that other churches are your competitors. You can dismantle this type of view simply by praying for the success of other ministries. Make sure the people of your congregation understand that you want every other faithful church in your community to prosper because you are more concerned about the success of the Gospel than the success of your church. There is nothing wrong with praying for the pastors of those churches by name and encouraging your members to do what they can to bless them.

These are just a few ways that you can work to develop Kingdom-heartedness in your congregation. Your eagerness to see Jesus made known in your community will teach them that the Gospel, not your church, is the real treasure of the Kingdom. If your experience is like mine, you will find that this type of leadership trickles down to every aspect of your ministry and creates a culture of spiritual sensitivity for those living and working around you.

## Dying Churches and Church Mergers

In virtually every community in North America, there are dying, dysfunctional, or terminally ill churches. Often these churches have facilities and a handful of people left in the congregation. You may find that you have the opportunity to be a blessing to a church in this situation by helping them through the difficulty. A few years ago we heard about a church in the neighboring town that had fallen on hard times financially. This congregation had no pastor and was left with only a few people and virtually no money. Since we had an abundance of young preachers, we offered to send some of those men to preach until the church figured out what to do. The experience gave some of our younger men preaching experience and temporarily solved a problem for the struggling congregation. Another time our church conducted an outreach event for churches in our community that didn't have the manpower and resources to pull off the event themselves.

Take time to reach out to the leaders of churches in this situation and attempt to understand what has caused the churches' decline. You may find that a simple friendship between the churches can be mutually beneficial. Occasionally churches in this situation are willing to consider church mergers. Some have found success in combining congregations in order to multiply disciples, but generally speaking these situations are fraught with difficulty. If you choose to pursue a merger, proceed with caution.

> I know of at least one church in my community that is in need of assistance. I have attempted to make contact with the church leadership to offer my assistance.

## Closing Arguments

Like a lawyer's closing arguments just before the jury heads out to deliberate, I present to you four closing arguments for leading your church to plant. I hope you will give some serious thought and attention to them.

## Your Church Is Going to Die

It is my observation that people rarely consider how churches begin and almost never consider how they end. Churches, just like people, have lifecycles. They are born and they die. They close their doors, they sell their buildings, they liquidate their assets, and they stop gathering. If you don't believe me, get on a plane to Jerusalem and look for the church first pastored by James. Then skip over to Turkey and see if you can find the church at Antioch still meeting. Those churches are closed, disbanded, and scattered. American churches are closing too, and not just one or two at a time—they are closing by the thousands. This Sunday morning when you go to church, about 135 fewer American churches will be gathering than gathered the same time last week. That's 600 churches disbanding every month and 7,000 churches vanishing every year.[27] It's a good thing that the human race is not in this same predicament.

Imagine the President of the United States appearing on your television screen one day with an important announcement for the nation: "Ladies and gentlemen, we have a crisis on our hands. The human race is dying out. If current trends continue, the human race will be extinct in less than 200 years." It would be disturbing and unsettling, and my guess is that people would get pretty aggressive about repopulating the world. The church in America is in this exact predicament. We are an endangered species, and if current trends continue, the America of the future will look very similar to the Europe of today.

Western Europe experienced drastic changes over the course of the 20th century. In particular during the 1960s, it experienced terminal decline of virtually all of its large, organized churches and the pervasive Christian culture, which influenced Western Europe for centuries, virtually disappeared. Today the streets of major cities throughout Western Europe are peppered with church buildings that lasted longer than the congregations that erected them. Hundreds of church buildings are now being used as restaurants, nightclubs, concert venues, cafés, modern condominiums, museums, and mosques. They stand as stark proof that western culture is spitting Christianity out of its mouth.

The change is not really that shocking if you think about it. Churches are made up of sinners, and sin kills everything it touches. As long as sinners are going to church, churches will be dying. As long as churches are dying, new churches are necessary. Every year in America about 4,000 evangelical churches begin.[28] Of those started, 35% close before their 5th anniversary,[29] leaving about 2,600 new churches planted annually. While churches are dying at a significantly higher rate, each year in the U.S. approximately 7,000 churches close their doors forever. All things considered, the number of churches in the U.S. is decreasing by about 4,400 churches per year,[30] while our population is growing by about three million people per year.[31]

How is the American church responding to the crisis? We are spending countless millions of dollars erecting buildings and maintaining fruitless ministries. We are building the nightclubs and mosques of tomorrow while tossing pennies to the establishment of new churches. As you get busy with your work, you will be tempted to find the measure of your success based on the number of people you successfully gather for worship. Please keep in mind the mission of the church was to scatter, not to gather. Instead of measuring the success of your church by the harvest you gather, concentrate your energy and measure your success based on the seed that you scatter. Remember that churches have a life cycle and eventually die, and one day yours will too. My prayer is that you would plant a church that is committed to vigorously planting other new churches. I pray that you will stretch the faith of your people, not so that they can have a larger building to worship in, but so that Christ may have a larger Kingdom of worshipers.

## The Shortsighted Apple Farmer

Pretend with me for a moment that we're talking about planting apple trees instead of churches. Let's suppose one morning you stare out at your field with an apple seed in your hand and determine that you'd like to see that field full of apple trees. What would you do? First, you would plant your seed and nurture your little apple tree until it produced fruit. Then you'd take the seeds from your harvest and plant more trees in hopes of eventually having more apple trees.

On the other hand, you could decide that you don't really need a whole orchard because the tree you have now produces enough apples for a season's worth of pies, apple butter, and applesauce. There's not really a need for more trees. Planting is hard work, and you currently have all that you need. But, eventually, there will be an apple shortage. If every orchard develops this mentality, then you can soon say goodbye to those fresh apple treats.

You can use apples for all sorts of other good things, but if you stop using apples to plant apple trees, eventually your tree is going to die, and no one will get any pie. The point remains that apples are for planting apple trees more than they are for making apple pies. Don't allow yourself to fall into the trap of the shortsighted apple farmer who buries his apple in the oven rather than the soil. Dig a hole, plant your seeds and pray for rain.

## New Churches Reach More People

Research confirms over and over again that young congregations reach more young people, marginalized groups, and unchurched people than older churches. New churches naturally focus more of their energies and resources on non-members and reach more unchurched people than more established congregations.

> Dozens of studies confirm that the average new church gains most of its new members (60-80%) from the ranks of people who are not attending any worshiping body, while churches over 10 to 15 years of age gain 80-90% of new members by transfer from other congregations. This means that the average new congregation will bring six to eight times more new people into the life of the body of Christ than an older congregation of the same size.[32]

Since the goal in missions is for people to know Jesus, and more people come to know Jesus (per capita) in newer churches, we should focus our attention not only on the growth of churches but also on the establishment of new ones. Over the past quarter century, we have seen the explosion of the megachurch movement. Thousands of evangelical churches now have a weekend attendance of 2000 or greater, with some churches reaching into the tens of thousands. This phenomenon gives the false impression that Christianity is thriving in the United States, when in actuality every year the percentage of the population that attends church regularly is dwindling. We cannot assume that because some churches are growing larger that more people are becoming followers of Christ. Based on the facts, there is only one clear and logical response: we must plant new churches. Pastor and author Tim Keller argues, "A vigorous and continuous approach to church planting is the only way to guarantee an increase in the number of believers, and is one of the best ways to renew the whole Body of Christ."[33]

## The Math Works Better

If I were to offer you a penny a day doubled for a month or a million dollars all at once, which would you choose? Probably the million dollars, right? But wait… the math is pretty amazing:

- Day 7 – $0.64
- Day 14 – $81.92
- Day 21 – $10,485.76
- Day 30 – $5,368,709.12

The math has clear implications for church planting. Multiplication is more powerful than addition!

As we plant churches that plant churches, we multiply the Gospel in incredible ways. Every Sunday morning that Pillar Church gathers, we have a few hundred people. Not a wildly impressive crowd for a ten-year-old church. However, in those ten years, we've planted twelve Churches, three of which have planted again, and two have merged or closed. In total, thirteen churches gather on Sunday mornings as a result of our church planting initiatives. Combined attendance in all of those churches is somewhere around 1,000 people each weekend. These churches meet in three countries, and about a dozen pastors serve them each week. Harkening back to the penny analogy and imagining every day to be a year, we feel like we're on day ten and just starting to see the power of multiplication. I can't wait to see what years twenty and thirty hold in store!

## Conclusion

If you're not already, very soon you will be the pastor of a small church. You will face all kinds of pressures and difficulties in your role. Don't let those difficulties distract you from the reason you set out to plant a church in the first place. Everyone will have an opinion about what you are doing; members, attenders, supporters, friends, and family will offer advice about how best to lead your new church. Remember, you're not planting a church for them. You're planting a church for Jesus. You are building a people for Jesus, and He's the one you will give account to for your labor. Jesus isn't

155

wringing his hands in heaven wondering if your church is going to make it, and He doesn't want you to do that either. What He wants is clear: baptize, teach, and make disciples, equip the saints, and build a church for the Kingdom of God.

*Jesus, I pray that you would use this material in the lives of those who read it to motivate them to plant faithful churches that will plant other faithful churches for the praise of Your glory. Endow them with sufficient resources for the advance of Your Kingdom and give them faith to trust You as they redistribute those resources to make You treasured around the globe. Protect them from any temptation to make a name for themselves and help them to find joy in making Your Name great. Amen.*

# THRESHOLDS CHECKLIST

STAGE ONE: CONFIRM

- [ ] I have completed the Abandonment Worksheet.
- [ ] I have completed the Scriptural Adequacy Worksheet.
- [ ] I, as well as others who know me well, believe that I have the evangelistic fervor, initiative, tenacity, and vision to plant a church.
- [ ] I have reviewed the Sample Church Planter Commitments and have agreed on something similar with my sending church's elders.
- [ ] I have completed the Prospective Church Planter Questionnaire and given it to the leaders of my sending church.
- [ ] My wife has affirmed my desire to plant a new church and is prepared to join me in the work of church planting.
- [ ] My church has formally and publicly committed to send me to plant a new church.

STAGE TWO: PREPARE

- [ ] I have placed important family events on my calendar before creating a ministry calendar.
- [ ] My weekly schedule includes an appropriate amount of family time.
- [ ] I have completed the Expectations Worksheet and have shared the outcome with the leaders of my sending church.
- [ ] I have chosen a day of the week for rest.

## STAGE THREE: RECRUIT

☐ I have enlisted a pastoral partner.

☐ I have enlisted a church planting mentor.

## STAGE FOUR: PLAN

☐ I have chosen a location for this new church.

☐ I have chosen a name for this new church.

☐ I have researched the demographics of my ministry field and have an accurate picture of the types of people who live there.

☐ I have completed the Personal Budget Worksheet.

☐ I have done a cost of living comparison between the church plant location and my current location.

☐ I have completed my church plant budget.

☐ I have completed my church plant prospectus.

## STAGE FIVE: GATHER

☐ I have made an equipment wish list for potential supporters.

☐ I have secured accounting services.

☐ Excluding my home, I have less than $10,000 in personal debt.

☐ My sending church has committed to support me.

☐ My denomination has committed to support me.

☐ I have made a list of 30 churches that could support me.

☐ I have made a list of 30 individuals who could support me.

☐ I have researched church planting networks and denominational funding sources and have applied to the ones with which I wish to work.

☐ I have started a donor database.

☐ I have created a plan to communicate with my supporters regularly.

## STAGE SIX: ASSEMBLE

☐ I have determined what leadership positions need to be filled on my missionary team.

☐ I have made a list of possible teammates to fill each of the positions on the missionary team.

☐ I have met personally with those I wish to invite onto my missionary team and have issued a "Big Ask."

- [ ] I have filled all of the positions on my missionary team.
- [ ] I have set up a way to regularly check up on the progress of each missionary team member.

## STAGE SEVEN: BEFRIEND

- [ ] Both my wife and I have committed to do whatever it takes to live in our mission field.
- [ ] I have contacted the pastors of other churches in my mission field and told them of my plans to start a new church.
- [ ] I have made a list of volunteer opportunities in my community, have chosen one to participate in personally, and have passed the list to each of the missionary team members for consideration.
- [ ] I have made contact with political, civic, and non-profit leaders in my community and have expressed my desire to join them in any effort to improve our community.
- [ ] I have chosen some Scripture related to salvation that I will lead my missionary team to memorize.
- [ ] I have read *The Gospel Blimp* by Charles Bayly.
- [ ] I have created a written outreach plan for the first year of my church's ministry.

## STAGE EIGHT: BEGIN

- [ ] I will not begin weekly worship services until I have ____ committed families.
- [ ] I have chosen the elements I wish to include in each of our weekly worship services.
- [ ] I have studied the Bible's teachings on public worship format and have a clear understanding of which individuals will be permitted to lead various aspects of our public worship services. I am prepared to defend my positions.
- [ ] I have formed a service review team and will plan to have a service review after each worship service.
- [ ] I have created a preaching calendar for the first year of our church's weekly worship services.
- [ ] I have scheduled one or more preview services.

☐ I have reached my goal of ____ committed families and am ready to begin weekly worship services.

☐ I have communicated with my sending and supporting churches about our plans for weekly worship and invited them to attend.

☐ I have advertised our church's first worship services and encouraged the missionary team to invite friends and family.

## STAGE NINE: ORDER

☐ I have adopted a statement of faith with the affirmation of my sending church's leaders.

☐ I have written or adopted a church covenant that has been affirmed by my sending church.

☐ I have written a membership course and am ready to take my church through it.

☐ I have prepared a document to guide me through conducting a membership interview.

☐ I have planned a teaching series on biblical eldership.

☐ I have collected nominations from our members for elder candidates.

☐ The elder candidates have completed the questionnaire, and my sending church's elders have joined me in examining them.

☐ The members have affirmed the elder selections.

☐ Our elders have selected and affirmed deacons as lead servants in the ministry of our local church. Simple job descriptions have been created for them, and they are aware of expectations.

## STAGE TEN: REPEAT

☐ I have identified one or two guys in my ministry that I consider faithful, available, and teachable.

☐ I have identified at least five pastoral activities that I can easily teach to others.

☐ I have identified someone as our first church planter and have a plan to prepare him for church planting.

☐ I have chosen one or more church planters whom I can lead my congregation to pray for regularly.

☐ Our new church has decided to dedicate $_____ every month to a church planting fund.

☐ I know of at least one church in my community that is in need of assistance. I have attempted to make contact with the church leadership to offer my assistance.

# ABANDONMENT WORKSHEET

In my opinion, the single greatest factor in the success of a new church is the endurance of its church planter. It is not uncommon to hear of a new church closing within the first year or two of public services. A church planter's unmet expectations can cause discouragement and fatigue. Sometimes a major setback, like a rift in the missionary team or the loss of a meeting space, can terminally upset the fragile ecosystem of a new church. These problems, and others, can lead church planter to throw in the church-planting towel too quickly.

This exercise is designed to help you identify what your pain threshold is for church planting. What are you willing to endure in order to start a new church? What is your spouse willing to endure? Church planters, using the left column, mark the box next to any of the statements that would cause you to quit church planting. If you are married, ask your wife to answer using the right column.

I would quit church planting...

PLANTER        SPOUSE

☐    ☐    When I no longer enjoy the work.
☐    ☐    When I suspect my wife would be happy if I quit.
☐    ☐    When my wife actually asks me to quit.
☐    ☐    When I no longer have vision for the church.
☐    ☐    When I am convinced that I am not good at it.

- [ ] [ ] When others tell me I'm not good at it.
- [ ] [ ] When the elders of my sending church ask me to.
- [ ] [ ] If after the first year we have less than 10 people.
- [ ] [ ] When I can no longer afford to support my family financially.
- [ ] [ ] If after three years we have fewer than 30 people.
- [ ] [ ] When someone I respect within the new church tells me I should quit.
- [ ] [ ] When someone whom I perceive will do a better job is available.
- [ ] [ ] When I feel like a failure.
- [ ] [ ] When I act out in violence or rage toward someone else.
- [ ] [ ] When I become addicted to pornography.
- [ ] [ ] When I have an extramarital affair.
- [ ] [ ] When I steal money from the church.
- [ ] [ ] When I get offered a position at a larger church.
- [ ] [ ] When my kids are unruly/rebellious
- [ ] [ ] When my wife is uninvolved in the churches ministry.
- [ ] [ ] When my kids tell me they want me to quit.
- [ ] [ ] If after one year no one has been baptized.
- [ ] [ ] If after three years no one has been baptized.
- [ ] [ ] If after three years no one I've baptized is still walking in the faith.
- [ ] [ ] When my financial supporters back out.
- [ ] [ ] When the people in my church are constantly bickering and fighting.
- [ ] [ ] When I no longer meet the Bible's qualifications for pastors.
- [ ] [ ] When need to move to meet the needs of my extended family.
- [ ] [ ] When I doubt my faith in Christ.
- [ ] [ ] When I begin to mistrust the teaching of the Bible.
- [ ] [ ] When my family is being neglected.

# SCRIPTURAL ADEQUACY WORKSHEET

*Shepherd the flock of God that is among you, exercising oversight, not under compulsion, but willingly, as God would have you; not for shameful gain, but eagerly; not domineering over those in your charge, but being examples to the flock.* 1 Peter 5:2-3

The Bible provides clear standards for those who serve in the office of church elder. If you wish to become a church planter, carefully evaluate your adequacy for the job by considering these qualifications. Before you begin this worksheet, make two additional copies, one for your spouse and one for a trusted pastor. Ask them to honestly evaluate your life against these qualifications. Collect their responses and compare them to your self-evaluation.

**Instructions:** In the box beside each scriptural qualification, rate yourself /the planter with one of four marks.
- **Q** = I'm confident I/he meet(s) this qualification.
- **U** = I'm unsure if I/he meet(s) this qualification.
- **S** = I/he struggle(s) to meet this qualification
- **N** = I do not believe I/he meet(s) this qualification.

Biblical qualifications from 1Timothy 3:2-7, Titus 1:6-8, and 1 Peter 5:2-3:

☐ Above reproach
☐ Husband of one wife
☐ Believing children
☐ Sober-minded
☐ Not arrogant
☐ Not quick-tempered
☐ Self-controlled
☐ Respectable

- ☐ Hospitable
- ☐ Lover of good
- ☐ Upright
- ☐ Holy
- ☐ Disciplined
- ☐ Holding firm to the Word
- ☐ Able to give sound instruction
- ☐ Able to refute bad instruction
- ☐ Able to teach
- ☐ Not a drunkard
- ☐ Not violent, but gentle
- ☐ Not quarrelsome
- ☐ Not a lover of money
- ☐ Not greedy
- ☐ Good manager of household
- ☐ Keeping children submissive
- ☐ Not a new convert
- ☐ Well thought of by outsiders

**Brief Explanations of Each Qualification:**

**Above reproach** means that no one could bring a credible claim against the elder and that he is not given to ungodly attitudes and actions that could discredit his Christian testimony.

**The husband of one wife** qualification has sparked a great deal of debate in the church, primarily because the meaning of the phrase is unclear. The phrase could be a reference to polygamy (not married to more than one woman at a time), fidelity (faithful to the woman he's married to currently) or exclusivity (only one marriage to one woman). Most churches today interpret this qualification as fidelity in current marriage. A pastor must love his wife exclusively with his thoughts, attitudes, and actions.

**Believing children** is commonly interpreted in one of two ways: (1) an elder is disqualified from formal pastoral church ministry if his son or daughter turns away from Christ or (2) an elder is not qualified for formal pastoral church ministry if his children are lawless and unruly. A pastor's first flock and proving ground is his family.

**Sober-minded** means an elder possesses wisdom and keeps his mind from extreme judgments or thoughts. It is self-awareness and self-control in his thought life.

**Not arrogant** means an elder has a proper view of himself, awareness of his own weaknesses and shortcomings, and a willingness to communicate about them humbly. A pastor must be willing to admit his mistakes and repent of sinful attitudes and actions.

**Not quick-tempered** means an elder has the ability to control his emotions and to remain calm in stressful or volatile situations. Those who are easily angered are not good candidates for pastoral ministry since they must serve as godly examples to the flock.

**Self-controlled** means that an elder manages his words and actions well. The man of God controls his physical desires and brings them under discipline.

**Respectable** means that an elder's attitudes and actions are worthy of admiration.

**Hospitable** means that an elder cares about others and invites them into his home and his life in such as way that people enjoy being with him and are at ease in his company.

**Lover of good** means that an elder desires and pursues the things that God calls good. He gives his thoughts to things that are true, noble, right, pure, admirable, and praiseworthy (Philippians 4:8).

**Upright** means that an elder must have impeccable character so that he sets a good example to the flock. He can be trusted to make God-honoring choices even when no one is paying attention.

**Holy** means set apart. An elder must live a life of distinction and godliness in the midst of a crooked and perverse generation.

**Disciplined** means an elder has command over his body, mind, and speech. By the power of the Holy Spirit, he has tamed his tongue and suppressed his evil and glutinous desires in order to live a life pleasing to God.

**Holding firm to the Word** means that an elder must trust and proclaim the Word of God against immense pressure to equivocate, concede, and exchange the clear teaching of Scripture in order to placate worldly men.

**Able to give sound instruction** means that an elder is endowed by God with the ability to understand God's Word and the wisdom to discern and explain its meaning to others.

**Able to refute bad instruction** means that an elder should possess the ability to detect false teaching and the courage to challenge it with clarity and patience.

**Able to teach** means that an elder should possess the capacity to teach the God's Word in a winsome, accurate, and persuasive manner which draws believers to obedience and faith. Note that this is the only ability-based requirement in the list of elder qualifications; all others relate to an elder's character.

**Not a drunkard** means that an elder must not drink alcohol in excess and should avoid becoming intoxicated.

**Not violent, but gentle** means that an elder is to be kind, calm, and peaceable. Those who are given to violence, cruelty, or brutishness are not fit for service in God's church. Violent men are not eligible for pastoral ministry.

**Not quarrelsome** means that an elder seeks peace rather than controversy. Pastoral ministry often requires patience and grace. Involvement in petty skirmishes is not becoming of a man of God.

**Not a lover of money** means that an elder cannot love money more than God. Those who lead God's church must pursue God above wealth and fortune.

**Not greedy** means that an elder must be generous. A miserly man doesn't understand the gift of grace Christ has given.

**Good manager of household** means than an elder's home generally runs smoothly and that his wife and children are well taken care of. The man who is unable to manage his household affairs is unfit for the pastoral ministry.

**Keeping children submissive** means that an elder's children must follow his leadership as he submits to the leadership of Christ. An elder's children need not be perfect, but they should be respectful and submissive to authority. Children who are unwilling to submit to their fathers are poor models of the gospel life. In such a case, the elder should focus his ministry on his home and willingly step away from pastoral ministry for a season.

**Not a new convert** means an elder should not be a new Christian. Many fall away from the faith, and there are many false converts. The one who seeks the office of elder should have a proven record of faithfulness.

**Well thought of by outsiders** means that an elder is to be respectable both inside and outside the church. His business dealings, hobbies, and friendships should lead non-Christians to a favorable view of his character. That is not to say he must please everyone or make everyone happy, but it is imperative that he works hard to maintain his witness to those outside the faith.

# CHURCH PLANTER COMMITMENTS

1. Until the church I am planting has a second local elder and a ratified constitution, I will cheerfully submit to and cooperate with the [SENDING CHURCH'S] elders concerning all major personal and church decisions.

2. I will consult the elders (via email or in person) on any unbudgeted purchase of more than $250.

3. I will consult the elders of my sending church on matters related to public teaching in the new church. These include, but are not limited to, a preaching calendar, the invitation of guest preachers, and the frequency with which I preach.

4. I will lead my new church to support other new church plants and planters financially from our very earliest stages, giving priority to those church planters within our church planting network.

5. I agree to participate regularly in the recruiting, training, and mentoring of other church planters, and will use the resources of my church and my own expertise to benefit other church planters within the [CHURCH PLANT'S] network.

6. In the event that I no longer agree with the doctrines or practices of [CHURCH PLANT], or am dissatisfied with the current direction of my sending church's ministry, I will make it known to the elders and will work diligently to a reach a mutually agreed upon resolution. In the event that an agreement cannot be reached, I will resign my position as planter, and the elders will appoint a replacement.

7. I commit to be present in person or by video or phone conference once a month with the [CHURCH PLANT'S] elders. This meeting is currently scheduled for _____. In preparation for that meeting, I will accurately and honestly answer the questions below:

- Do you have any important updates since our last meeting?
- What step are you on in the planting process? When do you expect to accomplish the next step?
- What was the church's total income for the last calendar month?
- What were the church's total expenses for the last calendar month?
- Has the church met all of its financial obligations over the past month?
- Have you had any conflict in the church or on the core team?
- Who are your committed core team families at the present time?
- Have you participated in any activities in the following month that, if they became public knowledge, would bring shame to our church and our Lord?
- (If paid) Did you receive the full agreed upon amount for your pay in the last calendar month?
- Are you personally abiding in Christ? Are you spending time regularly in Scripture reading and prayer? How are things going in your spiritual life?
- Are your wife and children receiving an appropriate amount of your attention?
- Are there any areas where you are failing to pastor your family?
- Are your wife and children experiencing any obvious negative effects as a result of your service as a church planter?
- Are you financially or otherwise supporting any other church planting efforts?

- Do you feel that we are doing an adequate job supporting you and your family as you plant this new church?
- Is there anything we could do to better help you?

8. If the elders of my sending church deem me unfit for the work or otherwise disqualified from pastoral ministry and ask me to resign or take a leave of absence, I will honor their request.

# PROSPECTIVE CHURCH PLANTER QUESTIONNAIRE

You are being considered for a leadership position at [SENDING CHURCH]. Since God's Word teaches that there are standards of character for those who serve in church leadership, we want to do the best we can to understand your theological convictions, personal practices, family life, and your walk with God. Please help us start this conversation by answering the questions below, using a separate sheet as necessary.

## Personal Information:

**Name:**
**Phone Number:**
**Email:**
**Age:**

## Relationship With God:

1. Briefly describe when you became a follower of Christ?

2. Do you actively participate in spiritual disciplines such as prayer, Bible reading, fasting, tithing, corporate worship, and evangelism?

3. Do you consider yourself to be scripturally qualified for pastoral ministry according to 1 Timothy 3 and Titus 1? ☐ Yes ☐ No

4.  Please describe the greatest struggles that you face in the Christian life?

5.  What spiritual gifts do you believe you possess?

6.  Have you been baptized by immersion since becoming a Christian?
    ☐ Yes ☐ No

7.  Since becoming a Christian, has there ever been a time when you significantly rebelled against the Lord, or has there been a time when you abandoned your faith all together? ☐ Yes ☐ No – If so, explain.

8.  In what ways is it obvious that you have a love for Jesus Christ and His Gospel?

9.  Have you ever personally discipled another Christian and seen them experience significant spiritual growth?

10. What do you think a pastor's responsibility is before the Lord?

## Your Theological Positions:

11. Can you wholeheartedly affirm [YOUR DENOMINATION OR NETWORK DOCTRINAL STATEMENT]? ☐ Yes ☐ No (If no, please comment on the areas if disagreement.)

12. Please explain the Gospel of Jesus Christ to me as if I had never heard it?

13. Do you have any formal (seminary) or church-based theological education? ☐ Yes ☐ No – If so where and when?

14. With what denominations or networks have you been affiliated in past churches?

15. What do you consider the role of church membership in a healthy local church?

## Your Family Relationships:

16. If you are married, would your spouse support your endeavor to become a church planter? ☐ Yes   ☐ No   ☐ Not Married

17. If married, please describe one or two ways your spouse has supported you in previous church roles.

18. Have you ever been divorced or had a marriage annulled? ☐ Yes ☐ No

19. Have you ever had an extramarital affair? ☐ Yes   ☐ No

20. Do you feel that you are a good manager of your home?

21. Are you now, or have you ever been, in the regular practice of viewing pornography?

22. Have you ever been in a homosexual relationship or taken part in homosexual sex? ☐ Yes ☐ No (If yes, please explain.) Has your spouse? ☐ Yes ☐ No (If yes, please explain.)

23. Have you or your spouse ever been sexually molested by a friend, family member, or stranger? ☐ Yes ☐ No (If yes, please explain.)

24. Have you ever been through a bankruptcy or foreclosure? ☐ Yes ☐ No (If yes, please explain.)

25. Other than your home, what is the total amount of your personal consumer debt, including credit cards, car loans, student loans, etc.?

## Personal Practices:

26. Are there any areas of your life that, if exposed, would bring shame to our Lord and our church? (For example: Do you make a habit of

becoming intoxicated? Do you commonly view pornography? Do you operate ethically at your work place? Do you commonly steal or lie? Have you ever been convicted of a felony or imprisoned?) ☐ Yes ☐ No (If yes, please explain.)

## [SENDING CHURCH] Particulars:

27. Please explain the reason you are considering participating in church leadership at [SENDING CHURCH]?

28. Can you wholeheartedly support the vision, structure, and government style of [SENDING CHURCH], as you currently understand it? ☐ Yes ☐ No (If no, please explain.)

29. Are you currently a member in good standing of [SENDING CHURCH]? ☐ Yes ☐ No (If no, please explain why not.)

30. [SENDING CHURCH] is committed to participating in church planting locally and globally. If you successfully plant a new church, will you endeavor to lead that new church to plant other churches? ☐ Yes ☐ No (If no, please explain.)

31. Our church has chosen to cooperate in missions with the [CHURCH PLANTING NETWORK OR DENOMINATION]. Can you support our partnership with this organization? ☐ Yes ☐ No (If no, please explain.)

# ORDINATION PROCESS

Congratulations on your call to gospel ministry. Your ordination is an important milestone in your preparation. Our church elders will arrange a date to hold an ordination council, when we will invite pastors and elders from our church and other likeminded churches to examine your fitness for gospel ministry. During this council, you will be expected to explain your doctrinal positions and be prepared to give a defense for them.

[YOUR CHURCH NAME] practices ordination because we believe it is important to do the best job we can to ensure that the men we set aside for the gospel ministry are spirit-filled, well- studied, and faithful shepherds. During your ordination council, a group of experienced pastors and elders will:

- Examine your fitness to the office by examining your doctrinal positions, your philosophy of ministry, and your positions concerning marriage and family.
- Question you on general areas of concern.
- Warn you against potential pitfalls and blind spots that could render your ministry less effective.
- Recommend to our church whether they believe we should proceed with the planned ordination.
- Commend resources and practices to you that they believe will help strengthen areas of weakness.
- Pray for you as you begin a life of vocational service to Christ.

# Preparing for Your Ordination

## I. Prepare an Opening Statement

You need to be prepared to give a 5-minute explanation of your call to gospel ministry. This explanation should also be submitted in written form. Please include your future plans and aspirations as well. This is also a good time your opportunity to point out why you feel compelled to dedicate yourself to gospel work. The council should know the answer to the following questions after this speech:

- Why you want to go into ministry?
- What (if any) Scripture did the Holy Spirit use to convince you of your calling?
- What evidence is there that you have dedicated yourself to this task?
- Why are you so confident that God has called you into ministry?
- What have you already done to prepare yourself for a lifetime of ministry?

Be prepared to defend what you say in your opening statement.

## II. Prepare a Theological Position Paper

Your theological position paper will be the heart of your ordination. Give great time and attention to preparing it. You will provide a written theological statement about each of the following areas of theology: God, Man, Salvation, Scripture, Missions, the Church, and end times. Your statement should be as concise as possible, while still being thoughtful and thorough. You are not expected to write or speak like a seasoned theologian, but you are expected to have a clear understanding of each of these major areas of theology and be able to provide a sensible and biblically sound defense of your positions. Two or more paragraphs are expected for each area, but no one doctrine should be more than one page in length. At the beginning of each section, you will read your positions (in the order listed above), and then there will be an opportunity for questions and comments from the council after each section. Each statement should be written in your own words and not "copied and pasted" from any other source. You will be asked to defend your statements against those with opposing viewpoints, and the council members will be testing you to ensure that you have a clear understanding of the theological matter at hand. This discussion will continue for each of the six areas. Make sure you have 20 copies of this position paper ready for distribution on the day of your council.

**Tip:** You are strongly encouraged to submit your paper to trusted theological advisors beforehand in order to receive feedback and correction. The council will be looking for your ability to articulate and defend important doctrinal positions. Areas where you seem uncertain or unclear will be explored in greater detail.


## III. Prepare a Philosophy of Ministry

You will write a statement expressing your ministry philosophy. Be as brief as possible while still covering all areas you consider important. You may put this section in bullet points, outlining the general principles you will follow as a minister of the Gospel. Here is an example.

I am to equip the saints for the work of the ministry (Ephesians 4:11-12)
- This means I am to focus on ministering to those who minister.
- This means that teaching is my primary responsibility.

I am to shepherd the flock of God (1 Peter 5:2)
- This means I am to spiritually protect those under my care.
- This means I am to lead them and know them.
- This means that my primary ministry is to those within the Kingdom of God.

## The council should know the answer to the following questions after this speech:

- What principals/beliefs will drive you as a minister of the Gospel?

- What will stop you from being "driven about by every wind of doctrine?" (Ephesians 4:14)
- What will your focus be as a minster of the Gospel?

Again, the council will interact with you about your philosophy of ministry. They will affirm statements you make that they have seen as true in your life, and they will challenge areas where they question your philosophy. Be prepared to defend what you say about your philosophy of ministry.

## IV. Prepare a Statement on Marriage and family

Briefly write your views about the role of a husband and father who is serving in full time ministry. Again, be prepared to defend your statements. Include some commentary about how you expect your family to participate in the ministry that you will lead and ways that you will shepherd them along with the church.

## Dismissal:

When you have finished all your statements, you will be asked to leave the room while the council deliberates about what they have heard. The moderator will call for a recommendation from the council concerning weather to proceed with ordination plans. When a decision is reached, you will be invited back into the room, and the moderator will summarize the council's recommendation.

## Open Floor for Council:

After the recommendation is read, the counsel will give you some closing comments, advice, instructions, or warnings about what they have heard. Each council member will have an opportunity to speak. When all are finished, the men will gather around you for prayer.

# EXPECTATIONS WORKSHEET

Every new church planter has expectations about how things will turn out in the early stages of church planting, but not all expectations will become reality. How well a church planter manages his expectations will contribute a great deal to his sense of personal effectiveness in ministry. Two new church planters were asked the same question: How would you feel if, one year from now, your church has an average weekly attendance of 75? The first church planter responded positively by saying, "I'd be amazed that 75 people would come to hear me preach." The other one honestly confessed, "I'd quit." Their expectations make the difference. If they both had the exact same experience, one would finish the year ready to give up, and the other would be encouraged.

Spend some time exploring your expectations for your first year of ministry. Below is a list of questions that will help reveal your expectations. After you understand your expectations, you can begin to consider how you will respond if and when your expectations are exceeded or unrealized.

The wise church planter remembers Scripture concerning the accomplishment of our plans and will evaluate his success not on his own accomplishments but on the promised guidance provided by our Savior.

- "Many are the plans in a person's heart, but it is the Lord's purpose that prevails."[1]

[1] Proverbs 19:21

- "The heart of man plans his way, but the Lord establishes his steps."[2]
- "I am with you always, even until the end of the age"[3]

Review the following list of expectations, marking the ones you expect will be true by the end of your first year of public worship services.

EXPECTATION   REALITY

☐  ☐  My family will settle into a "normal" rhythm for our life and ministry.

☐  ☐  I will enjoy the work.

☐  ☐  My family will be settled into stable housing and school situations.

☐  ☐  The church will have a strong, committed base of at least 10 families.

☐  ☐  I will be as excited about the ministry as I am now.

☐  ☐  We will have other significant ministry partners serving with us.

☐  ☐  The church will have held its first baptism service.

☐  ☐  The church will have a stable meeting location.

☐  ☐  The church will average more than 100 people in weekly worship services.

☐  ☐  The church will have a quality worship leader.

☐  ☐  The church will have affirmed at least one other elder.

☐  ☐  Our church constitution will be written and agreed upon.

☐  ☐  The church will have deacons.

☐  ☐  The church will have members.

☐  ☐  The church will have a membership course.

☐  ☐  The church will have given monetary support to another planting or revitalization project.

☐  ☐  The church will have identified and helped to prepare another church planter.

---

[2] Proverbs 16:9
[3] Matthew 28:20

- [ ] [ ] The church will have organized and participated in a foreign mission trip.
- [ ] [ ] Our worship services could be described as joyful and spiritually meaningful.
- [ ] [ ] The leaders of each ministry are spirit-filled, obedient Christians.
- [ ] [ ] The men and women who serve closest to me in the work respect my leadership.
- [ ] [ ] The men and women who serve closest to me in the work respect my walk with God.
- [ ] [ ] The men and women who serve closest to me in the work are my closest friends.
- [ ] [ ] People who attend our church will invite others to attend regularly.
- [ ] [ ] I will be able to see the result of my preaching in the lives of those who attend regularly.
- [ ] [ ] I will have had a major conflict with a key member of the core team or staff.
- [ ] [ ] I will have angered someone so much they left our church.
- [ ] [ ] I will have a good relationship with the other church planters in my network.
- [ ] [ ] I regularly help other church planters with advice or encouragement.
- [ ] [ ] I will have at least one major regret concerning the way I have led so far.
- [ ] [ ] I read and study regularly.
- [ ] [ ] My prayer life is meaningful and consistent.
- [ ] [ ] I am pastoral in my home with my wife and family.

# RESOURCES FOR RESEARCH

## Association for Religious Data Archives

The Association of Religion Data Archives (ARDA) strives to democratize access to the best data on religion.
- Website: www.thearda.com
- Provides religious data for North America

## Christianity Today

*Christianity Today* equips Christians to renew their minds, serve the church, and create culture to the glory of God.
- Website: www.christianitytoday.com
- Provides social commentary, religious trends, statistics, religious resources

## City-Data

By collecting and analyzing data from numerous sources, City-Data creates detailed, informative profiles of all cities in the United States.
- Website: www.city-data.com
- Provides crime statistics, local weather patterns, school reviews, property tax assessments, sex offender registry, restaurant guides, statistics, housing data, demographics

## Expatistan

Expatistan is a cost-of-living calculator that allows you to compare cities around the world. The comparisons give a better understanding of the costs of living in any city before you move there.
- Website: www.expatistan.com
- Provides cost of living calculator, salary conversion tool

## Federal Bureau of Investigation

The FBI is an intelligence-driven national security and law enforcement agency, providing leadership and making a difference for more than a century.
- Website: www.fbi.gov
- Provides crime statistics, background checks, sex offender registry

## Gallup, Inc.

Gallup delivers analytics and advice to help leaders and organizations solve their most pressing problems. With more than 80 years of global experience, Gallup knows more about the attitudes and behaviors of employees, customers, students, and citizens than any other organization in the world.
- Website: www.gallup.com
- Provides research and statistical data

## GreatSchools

GreatSchools is a non-profit organization with profiles of more than 200,000 preK-12 schools – public, public charter, and private – and over one million reviews from parents, teachers, and students about the schools they know best.
- Website: www.greatschools.org
- Provides educational resources, school reviews

## Joshua Project

Joshua Project is a research initiative highlighting the ethnic people groups of the world with the fewest followers of Christ. Accurate, updated ethnic people group information is critical for understanding and completing the Great Commission.

- Website: www.joshuaproject.net
- Provides research on the people groups of the world

## Noodle

Noodle is an education website helping parents and students make better decisions about learning. Using interactive search tools, users can find the right preschool, college, tutor, or any other learning resource. In addition, users can read expert-authored articles, ask questions, and get answers from some of the leading minds in education. They can also connect with others in their communities.

- Website: www.noodle.com
- Provides local educational resources, school reviews, training

## North American Mission Board, SBC

The North American Mission Board works with churches, associations, and state conventions in mobilizing Southern Baptists as a missional force to impact North America with the Gospel of Jesus Christ through evangelism and church planting. Send North America is their national strategy for mobilizing churches to plant churches and mobilizing church planters and other missionaries to assist with those efforts.

- Website: www.namb.net
- Provides demographic research, statistics, training and funding

## Numbeo

Numbeo is the world's largest database of user contributed data about cities and countries worldwide.

- Website: www.numbeo.com

- Provides cost of living calculator, housing indicators, local health care information, traffic conditions, crime statistics, pollution levels

## PEOPLEGROUPS.info

Peoplegroups.info is a joint initiative of the North American and International Mission Boards of the Southern Baptist Convention. This site casts a vision for engaging unreached people groups and equips individuals and churches to fulfill the Great Commission where they live.
- Website: www.peoplegroups.info
- Provide research on the people groups of the world

## Pew Research Center

Pew Research Center is a nonpartisan fact tank that informs the public about the issues, attitudes, and trends shaping America and the world. We conduct public opinion polling, demographic research, content analysis, and other data-driven social science research.
- Website: www.pewforum.org
- Provides demographic research, religious trends, social commentary, statistics

## United States Census Bureau

The Census Bureau provides data about the nation's people and economy.
- Website: www.census.gov
- Provides statistics, demographics, interactive maps

## Zillow

Zillow is the leading real estate and rental marketplace dedicated to empowering consumers with data, inspiration, and knowledge about the place they call home and connecting them with the best local professionals who can help.
- Website: www.zillow.com
- Provides real estate help, housing trends

# PERSONAL BUDGET WORKSHEET

F ill in the information below about your personal and household expenses. In the left column enter the amount needed to live comfortably in that category. In the right column enter the lowest amount on which you could survive.

| CATEGORY | IDEAL | THRESHOLD |
|---|---|---|

**Home:**
- Rent/Mortgage
- Utilities
- Phone
- Insurance
- Cable/Media
- Internet
- HOA/Condo Dues

**Auto:**
- Fuel
- Repairs
- Insurance

**Personal Care:**
- Hair Cut
- Clothes

- Education     _____     _____
- Personal Items     _____     _____
- Doctor Visits     _____     _____
- Dentist Visits     _____     _____

**Food:**
- Groceries     _____     _____
- Restaurants     _____     _____

**Fun:**
- Vacation     _____     _____
- Family Fun     _____     _____
- "Mad" money     _____     _____
- Christmas     _____     _____
- Birthdays     _____     _____

**Debt Payments:**
- Car Payment     _____     _____
- Credit Cards     _____     _____
- Student Loans     _____     _____
- Other Loans     _____     _____
- Birthdays     _____     _____

**Wisdom**
- Tithe/Giving     _____     _____
- Savings     _____     _____
- Investments     _____     _____
- Charity     _____     _____

**Miscellaneous**
- Other     _____     _____
- Other     _____     _____
- Other     _____     _____

Total Monthly     _____     _____

# SAMPLE CHURCH PLANTING BUDGET

To help project your new church's budget, fill in both the "Ideal" amount needed to operate comfortably and the "Threshold" amount needed to cover only the necessities.

| CATEGORY | SAMPLE | IDEAL | THRESHOLD |
|---|---|---|---|
| **Personnel** | | | |
| • Planter Salary | 40,000 | | |
| • Planter Housing | 15,000 | | |
| • Assistant | 25,000 | | |
| • Education/ Training | 6,000 | | |
| • Auto Reimbursement | 2,400 | | |
| **Facility** | | | |
| • Rent | 30,000 | | |
| • Insurance | 3,250 | | |
| • Utilities | 4,800 | | |
| • Maintenance | 2,400 | | |
| **Trailer & Equipment** | | | |
| • Trailer Maintenance | 600 | | |

- Equip. Maintenance 1200 _____ _____
- Equip. Purchase 5000 _____ _____

## Ministry
- Curriculum 1200 _____ _____
- Supplies 1000 _____ _____
- Outreach 14,000 _____ _____
- Evangelism 2,000 _____ _____
- Small Groups 1,200 _____ _____
- Hospitality 600 _____ _____
- Events 18,000 _____ _____

## Missions
- Missionary Support 2,400 _____ _____
- Trip Scholarship 4,000 _____ _____
- Planter Support 6,000 _____ _____
- Planter Support 6,000 _____ _____
- Denominational Giving 3,600 _____ _____

## Communications
- Website 1000 _____ _____
- Email 600 _____ _____
- Mailing 3000 _____ _____
- Signage 4300 _____ _____

## Miscellaneous
- Other _____ _____
- Other _____ _____
- Other _____ _____
- Other _____ _____

Total Monthly Expenses: $_____ $_____

Ideal Amount      Threshold Amount

# SAMPLE FUNDING SUMMARY

This worksheet is intended to help you keep track of your fundraising efforts. Record totals here and be sure to update all your partners whenever there is a change in your partnerships.

Planter: _____ Planter's Spouse: _____

Church Plant Name: _____ Year Started: _____

| SUPPORTER | YR1 | YR2 | YR3 | YR4 |
|-----------|-----|-----|-----|-----|
| Denominational Support | | | | |
| Church Plant Income | | | | |
| Sending Church | | | | |
| Supporting Church #1 | | | | |
| Supporting Church #2 | | | | |
| Supporting Church #3 | | | | |
| Supporting Church #4 | | | | |

Supporting Church #5

_____    _____    _____    _____    _____

Supporting Church #6

_____    _____    _____    _____    _____

Individual Supporters Total

_____    _____    _____    _____    _____

Other Support
Total Support         _____    _____    _____    _____

# PLANTER NETWORKS

- 21st Century Strategies – www.effectivechurch.com

- Acts 29 – www.acts29network.org

- Aletheia Network – www.aletheianetwork.com

- Association of Related Churches – www.arcchurches.com

- Calvary Nexus – www.calvarynexus.org

- CityReach Network – cityreachnetwork.org

- Church Multiplication Associates – www.cmaresources.org

- Church Multiplication Network – churchmultiplication.net

- Church Multiplication Training Center – www.cmtcmultiply.org

- Church Planting By Nexus – www.nexus.us

- CoachNet – www.coachnet.org

- Converge – www.convergeworldwide.org

- Dynamic Church Planting International – www.dcpi.org

- Evangelical Free Church of America – www.efca.org

- Exponential Network/Passion for Planting – www.church-planting.net

- Fellowship Associates – www.fellowshipassociates.org

- Global Church Advancement – www.gca.cc

- Glocalnet – www.glocal.net

- Harvest Bible Fellowship – www.harvestbiblefellowship.org

- Kairos Church Planting – kairoschurchplanting.org

- Liberate – www.liberate.org

- Liberty Church Planting Network – www.libertycpn.com

- Multiply Group – multiplygroup.org

- New Breed Church Planting - newbreedcp.org

- North American Mission Board – www.namb.net

- North American Church Planting Foundation – http://northamericanchurchplantingfoundation.org

- Northwest Church Planting – www.nwchurchplanting.org

- Pillar Network – northamericanchurchplantingfoundation.org

- Pillar Planting – www.pillarchurchsbc.com

- PLNTD Network – www.plntd.com

- Praetorian Project – www.praetorianproject.org

- Redeemer City to City – www.redeemer.com

- SBC State Conventions List – http://www.sbc.net/stateconvassoc.asp

- Sent Network – www.sentnetwork.org

- Sojourn Network – www.sojournnetwork.com

- Soma Family of Churches – www.wearesoma.com

- Sovereign Grace Ministries – www.sovereigngraceministries.org

- Stadia – www.stadia.cc

- The Association of Related Churches – www.weplantlife.com

- The Summit Network – www.thesummitnetwork.com

- Treasuring Christ Together Network – www.tctnetwork.org

- V3 – www.thev3movement.org

- Verge Network – www.vergenetwork.org

- Vineyard Church Planting – www.vineyardusa.org

- Vision360 – www.vision360.org

- Waterhouse Church Planting Network – www.waterhouse.org

# MISSIONARY TEAM JOB DESCRIPTIONS

**P**rayer Advocate – The Prayer Advocate is responsible for promoting personal and corporate prayer in the life of our new church. This person should (1) maintain a healthy and growing spiritual life and lead others to do the same; (2) establish a monthly church-wide prayer meeting for members and attenders; (3) create of an efficient means of communicating time sensitive prayer concerns to the congregation; (4) create of an efficient means of communicating church prayer needs to our supporters and partners; and (5) work with other ministry leaders to ensure that prayer plays a key role in their ministries.

**Worship Leader** – The Worship Leader is responsible for magnifying the greatness of God and Jesus Christ through the planning, conducting, and promotion of the music and worship programs of our church. This person should (1) maintain a healthy and growing spiritual life and lead others to do the same; (2) participate regularly in leading worship music at our gatherings on Sundays and at other events from time to time; (3) recruit, develop, and lead a worship team; (4) work with our pastor to select worship song sets that are Gospel centered and Christ exalting; (5) establish and lead rehearsals; and (6) help in the oversight and coordination of other areas related to worship—sound, lights, video, etc.

**Discipleship Director** – The Discipleship Director is responsible for promoting discipleship in our church to help people grow in both knowledge of and obedience to the Word of God. This person should (1) maintain a healthy and growing spiritual life and lead others to do the same; (2) equip mature Christians with the tools and resources necessary to disciple others; (3) identify less mature Christians in need of discipleship; and (4) establish and facilitate disciple-making relationships throughout the congregation.

**Outreach Coordinator** – The Outreach Coordinator is responsible for the overall planning, development, and deployment of the outreach ministries of our new church, including the local, national, and international mission fields. This person should (1) maintain a healthy and growing spiritual life and lead others to do the same; (2) develop and maintain local and international mission programs; (3) recruit, train, and support a network of volunteers to lead various outreach opportunities; (4) plan and lead mission trips, both locally and abroad; (5) work with our church leadership to establish a presence for our church at community events; and (6) network with various small groups and individuals to accomplish the outreach goals of the congregation.

**Children's Ministry Coordinator** – The Children's Ministry Coordinator is responsible for the planning, conducting, promoting, and evaluating a comprehensive and balanced ministry to our children and their families. This person should (1) maintain a healthy and growing spiritual life and lead others to do the same; (2) plan programs and activities for the spiritual, emotional, and intellectual development of our children and their parents or guardians; (3) enlist and equip ministry leadership and volunteers; (4) evaluate and secure literature, resources, and teaching material; (5) develop and implement policies for the safety and security of our children: and (6) coordinate and staff the care of young children during worship services and special church-wide events.

**Communications Coordinator** - The Communications Coordinator is responsible for ensuring that the media and message of our church is consistent, biblical, and clear. This person should (1) (1) maintain a healthy and growing spiritual life and lead others to do the same; (2) manage content and aesthetics for all forms of church communication including web, social media, and print; (3) act as the funnel through which all communications pass before being released; (4) work with various ministry heads to produce a consistent, articulate message to our community and to our congregation; (5) manage the church membership database, keeping track of visitors and those who attend outreach events hosted by our church; (6) regularly inspect our website for outdated information and broken links; (7) provide content for any of our church's social media posts or campaigns; and (8) ensure that we are utilizing the best communication methods available to reach the largest number of members and attenders.

**Technical Director** – The Technical Director is responsible for leading a team of volunteers to provide high quality support for audio, video, and lighting used during worship gatherings and other events as needed. This person should (1) maintain a healthy and growing spiritual life and lead others to do the same; (2) recruit volunteers; (3) provide training opportunities for volunteers to gain the necessary skill set for success in their area; (4) initiate and plan ongoing training on a regular basis; (5) schedule the needed volunteers for each service or event and communicate their responsibilities in advance; (6) initiate repairs and replacements for critical equipment; and (7) establish a plan to prepare and execute quality video, display, and lighting elements for each service or event.

**Service Coordinator** – The Service Coordinator is responsible for planning, implementing, and evaluating the church worship services including service formats, order, themes, and special programs. This person should (1) maintain a healthy and growing spiritual life and lead others to do the same; (2) manage the logistics of all worship services; (3) work alongside the preaching pastor and the service leaders to create a cohesive presentation of service elements; (4) act as the point of contact for all elements of the worship service; and (5) develop a team and a system that will keep everyone involved informed.

**Student Ministry Director** – The Student Ministry Director is responsible for planning, conducting, promoting, and evaluating a comprehensive and balanced ministry to our youth and their families. This person should (1) maintain a healthy and growing spiritual life and lead others to do the same; (2) plan programs and activities for the spiritual, emotional, and intellectual development of our youth and their parents or guardians; (3) enlist and equip ministry leadership and volunteers; (4) evaluate and secure literature, resources, and teaching material; (4) develop and implement policies for the safety and security of our youth; (5) plan and conduct special projects, such as camps and retreats; and (6) coordinate youth outreach and mission trips.

**Treasurer** – The Treasurer is responsible for properly receiving, dispersing, accounting, and safeguarding church funds within policies established by the church. This person should (1) maintain a healthy and growing spiritual life and lead others to do the same; (2) develop and implement policies and procedures related to receiving, accounting, and dispersing church funds; (3) maintain records of funds received and dispersed; (4) enlist volunteers to receive, count, and deposit money; (5) maintain records of contributions and prepare and distribute contribution statements; (6) reconcile monthly bank statements and correct ledgers as needed; and (7) make regular reports to the church or leadership as directed by church policies.

**Small Group Coordinator** – The Small Group Coordinator is responsible for organizing our small group ministry for the development and care of disciples, the encouragement of biblical community, and the ministry to the lost. This person should (1) maintain a healthy and growing spiritual life and lead others to do the same; 2) collaborate with church leadership to build and implement a system of small groups; (3) develop and implement procedures that promote attendance and participation in small groups; (4) be familiar with curriculum resources and make recommendations for classes and groups; (5) recruit and develop leadership for future groups; (6) provide accountability and further training for current small group leaders.

# WORSHIP ELEMENTS WORKSHEET

Below is a list of potential worship elements you might consider including in your worship services. Keeping in mind the length and context of your service, weigh the pros and cons of each element to determine which ones will work for your services. This is not a complete list, and you might not be able to include every element from this list in your service.

## General Views On Worship

As you decide which elements you will use during your worship services, wrestle through which principle of worship best represents your understanding of Scripture. Below, I have included a brief introduction of each principle; however, I also recommend doing additional personal research on these principles. As you decide to include or exclude certain elements in your worship services, having a sound understanding of these principles will help you make wise choices and articulate your reasoning to inquisitive members and leaders.

- **Regulative Principle of Worship** – In brief, the Regulative Principle of Worship is the understanding that, through the Bible, God has specifically prescribed how He is to be worshiped corporately by man, and that any attempt to corporately worship Him that is not specifically stipulated or exemplified in Scripture is unacceptable. This approach to worship is an attempt to honor Scripture and avoid antinomianism.

- **Normative Principle of Worship** – In contrast, the Normative Principle of Worship is the understanding that God has not limited how He is to be worshiped corporately, and that only those actions or forms of worship specifically prohibited by the Bible are unacceptable. This approach to worship emphasizes our freedom in Christ and is based on passages including 1 Corinthians 10:31 and Colossians 3:17.

## Worship Elements

**Music** – Music is the primary method by which most congregations throughout history have engaged in corporate worship. Much of Psalms and several passages in the New Testament provide both the precedent and prescription to worship the Lord through singing and music. As a church planter, you will need to decide when you will begin including a musical worship element into your services and determine which style of music best fits your context and your understanding of Scripture.

**Preaching** – For many churches, preaching constitutes the primary teaching and discipleship ministries of the church. In some cases, pastors will also use the sermon as a key evangelistic tool as well. There are two primary methods of preaching, topical and expository. Topical sermons typically explore a single idea across a variety of scriptural texts. The goal of the topical sermon is to understand what Bible says about the topic. In contrast, expository sermons typically focus on a single text and may include a variety of ideas. The goal of expository sermons is to understand what the Bible text says. As a church planter, you will need to wrestle with which approach to preaching best fits your context and your understanding of Scripture.

**Prayer** – Prayer is an important part of the individual Christian's life as well as the life of the congregation as a whole. Including prayer as an element in your worship service will provide an opportunity to elevate the importance of prayer in the life of the church. Prayer also empowers the ministry of the church. As a church planter, you should consider giving prayer a prominent place in your worship service. Additionally, you will need to determine when and how often you would like to pray during the service and who will lead those prayers. Finally, you should consider how you would like the congregation to pray. Some churches provide opportunities to pray at the altar, kneel at their seats, or pray in small groups.

**Baptism** – Baptism is one of the two ordinances of the church. Baptism should be one of the first steps of obedience for a new believer. It is the new believer's opportunity to identify publicly with the body of Christ. According to your understanding of Scripture and your context, you will need to determine your method of baptism and how prominently you want to feature baptisms. You will also need to communicate to the congregation any expectations you have for how they should encourage the newly baptized believer.

**Communion** – Communion is one of the two ordinances of the church. Christ modeled communion in the Gospels, and regular participation in communion is both scripturally mandated and historically practiced. As a church planter, you will need to wrestle through a few questions related to communion. First, while wine has been historically used in communion, many modern congregations opt to use grape juice instead to be sensitive to those struggling with alcoholism. You will need to decide which drink best fits your context and your understanding of Scripture. Additionally, you will need to decide how often you would like to offer communion. Most congregations partake in communion weekly, quarterly, or annually. Finally, as a planter, you should decide how you would like to conduct communion. Churches and denominations participate in communion in a variety of ways. Research or visit several churches from different backgrounds to develop a communion method that best fits your context and your understanding of Scripture.

**Scripture Reading** – Many churches read passages of Scripture during their services. Reading Scripture during worship has rich historical precedence and serves to highlight the Word of God in the life of the believer. Churches approach Scripture reading in a variety of ways, sometimes including music, videos, or congregant participation. As there are a variety of ways to present Scripture, you should consider which methods best highlight the passage being read and best fit your context.

**Missions Focus** – Many churches opt to highlight missions during their services. One of the most common ways churches do this is by praying for a specific missionary or church planter or by praying for a country or people group. Some churches show a missions related video or invite a missionary or church planter to speak for a short time. Providing a missions element to the worship service can help develop a congregational passion for missions.

**Offering/Tithe** – Giving a portion of one's resources back to God has been an integral element of worship for both Christians and Jews. Giving provides congregants an opportunity to worship God through trusting Him with their resources, and giving funds the ministry work of the church. Both the Old and New Testaments provide ample instruction to give. Some churches focus on offerings of general gifts of any amount, while other churches actively encourage a tithe, the Old Testament expectation that each person should give 10% of their income. Churches collect offerings and tithes in a variety of ways, including passing collection plates/buckets, providing convenient drop boxes, online giving, etc. As a church planter, you will need to decide which method of collecting gifts best fits your context and your understanding of Scripture. You must also wrestle with whether the Old Testament command to tithe is expected in New Testament churches.

**Baby Dedication** – Baby dedications provide opportunities for congregations and parents to stand together in accountability for raising and discipling the children of believers. Across denominations, there are a variety of opinions on baby dedications and similar functions, including paedobaptism. As a church planter, you will need determine your stance on this element, and give careful thought to the structure and timing of this ceremony.

**Children's Participation** – Some churches engage children in the service by bringing them to the front for a short lesson from a pastor or children's director. These lessons usually include visual elements and are easy for children to understand and apply. As a church planter, you will need to consider whether such an activity is an appropriate element for you context.

**Theatrical Element** – Theatrical Elements include dramas and interpretive dances often accompanied by music. When performed well, theatrical elements can provide a unique and creative opportunity for worship and reflection. As a church planter, you will need to assess whether your team can effectively carry such a production and whether the result will be worth the effort.

**Testimony** – Some churches include testimonies as part of their services. These testimonies may be in person or on video, and may include the person's salvation story or a testimony of God's provision during a trial. Testimonies can be an encouragement to the congregation, and those giving their testimonies should be thoroughly prepared to share.

**Video** – Some churches, especially larger churches, regularly use videos during their worship services. The topics and functions of these videos vary. They may be used to introduce the sermon topic or to provide teaching, useful information, or a good laugh. As a church planter, if you decide to use videos in your service, you will need to carefully select videos that enhance the worship experience.

**Announcements** – Part of being a good leader is communicating well to those you are leading. To accomplish this during worship services, many churches communicate announcements at various times and in various ways, including announcement slides, church bulletins, videos, and speech. As a church planter, you will need to decide how and when you will communicate announcements.

**Altar Call** – Born out of the Great Awakening, altar calls have become a staple in Evangelicalism. Altar calls are listeners' opportunities to respond to the preacher's message. Some preachers offer anonymity by asking the congregation to close their eyes, while others express the need to respond publicly before the congregation. As a church planter, you will need to assess whether there is scriptural support for altar calls and decide which method best fits your context and understanding of Scripture.

# PREPARING TO PREACH

By Jonathan Ransom – Pillar Church of Okinawa, Japan

## PRAY

You need the Holy Spirit to speak to you through God's Word. Ask God to show you what the text means. Ask Him how it applies for your audience today. Ask Him to help you faithfully communicate the text and to protect you from saying anything silly or confusing. Ask Him to keep you humble and listening. Ask Him to reveal any changes you need to make in your own thoughts/life/beliefs before you go preaching to others. Repent quickly and completely of anything the Holy Spirit reveals to you. Embrace the text. Live in it. Learn it. Think about it. Pray it. Ask God to keep His glory central. Ask Him to help you focus on Christ and His Gospel and to keep the cross central in all your preaching. We preach to point people to the cross, the Gospel of Jesus Christ, and the grace we so desperately need. We do not preach to make good people better. We preach to point rebels to their redeemer. Pray! Ok, now begin.

## READ

Read the passage multiple times. If possible, read the entire book at least once. The more the better! If you do not have time to read the entire book, make sure to at least read the passages surrounding the verses you intend to preach. CONTEXT IS KEY. If you don't have a handle on context, you may end up preaching something other than what the author intended. Needless to say, that's not good. Seeing the whole picture protects a preacher from distorting the parts that make up the whole. Basically, if you can't summarize what the book or letter is about (who wrote it, to whom it was written, and the author's intention in writing), you probably don't yet have a handle on its context. Ideally, you want to be able to explain the argument, overall point, or general message of the particular book or letter. If you can do that, you are well on your way to understanding context.

If you do not have the time to study the context of a book, or if you just feel like you've been unsuccessful in this endeavor (which happens, so don't beat yourself up), read what other trusted scholars have written about the text from which you will be preaching. **But— and this is important— please do not to read expositional commentaries about the verses yet**. You have some work of your own to do before you read what others have preached about the text. If you have a study Bible, that's a great place to start reading about the context of a passage. If you don't own a study Bible and you don't have access to commentaries, the Internet is a great place to go for this information. The following link provides an introduction to every book of the Bible: <u>blueletterbible.org/study/intros/esv_intros.cfm</u>

## PRAY AGAIN

## OBSERVE

As you prepare, here are some great questions to ask yourself about your text:

- Who wrote it?
- Who received it?
- What is the book about?
- When was it written?
- Where was it written?
- Why was it written?
- Is there a key word, idea, doctrine, theme, etc.?
- Who are the main characters in the book?

# PRAY AGAIN

## Journey from Text to Sermon

After reading and making some basic observation about your passage, you are ready to take the next steps, which will lead you from raw text to ready sermon.

1. Read your passage in the translation you plan to use while preaching. (Pray)
2. Jot down initial observations and/or questions you may have about the text. (Pray)
3. Read the passage in other translations; sometimes this will help clarify something in the text. (Pray)
4. Determine the meaning of the verses leading up to and immediately following your text. You're not trying to write sermons about these additional verses, you're just making sure you generally understand them and could explain them to someone. I know this sounds tedious, and maybe you feel like you already did this in the steps above, but remember, context is key! (Pray)
5. Diagram your text, separating the sentences within the verses you will study and preach. (Pray)
   a. Identify the subject and verb of each sentence. Since the verbs are used to advance the argument or story, you must find those verbs.
   b. If you see the word "therefore," ask yourself, what's it there for?
   c. Conjunctions (but, and, or, for, nor, yet, so) are very important since they point your attention to the flow of a conversation or argument.
   d. Other clues in the text include so that, for this reason, and then.
6. Outline your passage, allowing it to flow from the text. Simply write the main clauses (subject and verb) on one line, and then write below them, in indented lines, the dependent clauses (which modify and/or explain the main clauses). This format will help you see the main points and how the author employs everything else

in the passage to explain or describe the main points. Make sure your main points flow from main points in the text. You don't want to make up something or preach something that simply is not there. (Pray)

7. Word study time! Now that you have identified the main verbs and other key words, it's time to make sure you understand what they mean. Make yourself a list of words, and then do a little research on each one. Again, if you don't have access to any Bible study tools of your own, visit blueletterbible.org/index.cfm or olivetree.com/pc/. (Pray)

8. Biblical theology time! What are the key theological themes in your text? Mercy, grace, sin, sanctification, etc.? Make sure you can find them and explain them. No need to write papers about these themes, just make sure you can explain them in a sentence or two.
   a. See what else the author of your passage has to say about those same words elsewhere in this same book or letter.
   b. If your author has written other books/letters, search those for any theological ideas that show up in your passage.
   c. Next, conduct a full Bible search for those themes. Again, the Blue Letter Bible site is a great tool.

9. Write a rough draft using your outline. Concentrate on the following guiding questions as you develop your outline further.
   a. What does the text say?
   b. What does the text mean?
   c. What do I need to know, believe, do, or stop doing in response to this text?

10. After doing all of this work, read some respected commentaries. This is important because you want to make sure your message contains no inaccuracies. If any of your interpretations differ from even a few of the commentaries you read, you are probably the one who is wrong.

# SERVICE REVIEW FORM

- Report for the week of:

- Did the service start on time: ____ Yes ____ No (What Time: _____)

- Did we end on time? ____ Yes ____ No (What time: _____)

- Were there any technical problems? ____ Yes ____ No

- What were the technical problems?

- Who is assigned to correct this problem?

- Who preached the sermon?

- What was the text?

- Was the point of the text the point of the sermon?

- Was the Gospel proclaimed at any point in the sermon?

- Were there particularly strong points to the sermon?

- Is there any constructive criticism for the preacher?

- How long was the sermon?

- Was the Lord's Supper conducted in a way depicted the Gospel?

- Is there anything we can do to improve our presentation of the Lord's Supper?

- Were clear instructions given concerning who may take the Lord's Supper?

- Was the offering pictured as an act of worship?

- Were the songs scripturally sound?

- Was there anything distracting about the service that turned attention from God to man?

- Who is present at review?

- How many adults were in worship?

- How many children were in worship?

- What was the total attendance for the week?

- What was the total weekly offering amount?

# THREE CHURCH GOVERNMENT MODELS

By Clint Clifton

C hrist is the head of the Church (Colossians 1:18). He is the source of all that the Church is and does. His Word, the Bible, is the church's guide for every decision. The worldwide church exists for the pleasure and purpose of Jesus alone. All Christians are ministers and priests of God (1 Peter 2:5-10). They have received spiritual gifts from God (Romans 12:3-6) and a special place of service in the church body of Christ (1 Corinthians 12).

Some of God's plans for local church leadership are depicted in the pages of the New Testament. Local churches should closely follow the examples modeled by the early Christian church. Where Scripture is silent, churches should use the wisdom of faithful leaders and the application of biblical principals to effectively mold the structure for God's work.

Two offices existed in the early Christian church: elder and deacon. The term elder is used synonymously with the terms bishop, overseer, and pastor in the New Testament. For the purpose of this document, the term elder will represent all four terms. Elders have the responsibility to lead, teach, and oversee the church, and deacons serve the body of Christ.

## Three Historical Models

Throughout church history, churches have governed themselves in three basic ways. Although there are many nuances and variations of each of these church governance systems, episcopal, congregational, and Presbyterian are the prevalent ecclesiastical models.

## Episcopal

By the 2nd century, the eldership church governance model found in the New Testament churches was replaced by an episcopal model, in which one man, a bishop, is appointed to govern multiple congregations. Dr. Erwin Lutzer explains:

> The church has frequently mimicked the political constructs of the presiding culture, with its strengths and flaws. Evidenced by the numerous writings of the church fathers, solitary church leadership (also known as episcopal church government) strongly correlated with the Roman Empire's leadership. As the emperor was supreme over the physical, the bishop/elder/pastor was supreme concerning the spiritual, presiding over all others (deacons and members).*

Catholic, Anglican, Eastern Orthodox, and Lutheran churches all presently govern themselves through episcopal polity. Although it has obvious advantages, such as efficiency and uniformity, the model itself seems to create an environment where corruption can easily take root.

## Congregational

By far the protestant church's most popular form of government, the congregation model emphasizes the priesthood of every believer, a core conviction of Baptist churches worldwide. Collective congregational wisdom becomes the deciding factor in virtually all major decisions and directional objectives for the local church. The hiring and firing of pastors, the acquisition of property, the annual budget, and all other major decisions are submitted to the congregation for consideration, discussion, and approval. This level of influence by every member has both positive and negative effects on a congregation. Positively, the congregation is protected by the additional layers of accountability provided by the dissemination of authority. On the other hand, with more opinions comes the increased opportunity for petty infighting and disunity in the body.

## Presbyterian

The Presbyterian form of governance combines the episcopal and congregational forms. The foundation of Presbyterian polity is the "presbytery" or the "elder board," a group of biblically qualified and congregationally appointed leaders charged with providing direction, oversight, and accountability to one congregation. In most instances, the church body has some influence over major decisions, but biblically qualified elders carry the lion's share of the leadership responsibility. This model is consistent with the New Testament churches and seems to maintain a good balance of efficiency and accountability.

## Conclusion

Churches are vulnerable to all sorts of difficulties and challenges. Church polity is the mechanism designed to carry a local congregation through the turbulent waters that often accompany ministry, change, and growth. Episcopal, congregational and Presbyterian forms of church government have stood the test of time as functional forms of church polity. A church planter must determine which form of church government seems most biblical.

*Lutzer, Erwin. "Different Forms of Church Government." Church Leadership and Government. Accessed January 8, 2016. http://www. moodymedia.org/articles/different-forms-church-government/.

# SAMPLE BELIEF STATEMENTS

## Pillar Church of Dumfries Statement of Beliefs, Adapted from the Baptist Faith and Message 2000

### God

God is the creator and ruler of the universe. He has eternally existed in three persons: the Father, the Son, and the Holy Spirit. These three are co-equals and one God.

The Father: God the Father reigns with providential care over His universe. He is all-powerful, all knowing, all loving, and all wise.

The Son: Jesus Christ is the only Son of God. He is fully God and fully man. He was born of a virgin, lived a sinless human life, and offered himself as the perfect sacrifice for the sins of all by dying on a cross. He arose from the dead after three days to demonstrate His power over sin and death, and ascended into heaven where he sits at the right hand of God.

The Holy Spirit: The Holy Spirit is present in the world to make people aware of their need for Jesus Christ. He lives in all Christians from the moment of salvation, providing them with power for living and guidance in doing what is right.

*John 16:7-13; Galatians 5:22-25; John 4:24; 1 Corinthians 15: 3-4; Philippians 2:5-11; Genesis 1:1; Deuteronomy 6:4.*

## Scripture

The Bible is God's Word to us. Human authors wrote the Bible under the supernatural guidance of the Holy Spirit. Because of its divine inspiration, the Bible is the supreme source of truth for all people. We believe that every word of the Bible is inspired and that, in its original form, the Bible has no error. We also believe that the Bible plays an indispensable role for the follower of Christ. It builds up, transforms, encourages, corrects, and protects the Christian as he or she studies and applies it.

*Psalms 119:11; Acts 20:32; Ephesians 5:26; 6:17; Exodus 24:4; Psalms 40:8; 2 Timothy 3:15-17; Hebrews 4:12; Psalm 119:105; 1 Corinthians 2:7-15; John 16:12-15*


## Man

Man is the special creation of God, made in His own image. In the beginning man was innocent of sin and was endowed by his Creator with freedom of choice. By his choice man sinned against God and brought sin into the human race. Man's decision to sin caused a division between Creator and creation leaving man in need of a Savior.

*Genesis 1:26-30; 2:5,7,18-22; 3; 9:6; Psalms 1; 8:3-6; 32:1-5; 51:5; Isaiah 6:5; Jeremiah 17:5; Matthew 16:26; Acts 17:26-31; Romans 1:19-32; 3:10-18,23; 5:6,12,19; 6:6; 7:14-25; 8:14-18,29; 1 Corinthians 1:21-31; 15:19,21-22; Ephesians 2:1-22; Colossians 1:21-22; 3:9-11.*


## Salvation

Salvation involves the redemption of the whole man, and is offered freely to all who accept Jesus Christ as Lord and Savior, who by His own blood obtained eternal redemption for the believer. In its broadest sense salvation includes regeneration, justification, sanctification, and glorification. There is no salvation apart from personal faith in Jesus Christ as Lord.

1. Regeneration, or the new birth, is a work of God's grace whereby believers become new creatures in Christ Jesus. It is a change of heart wrought by the Holy Spirit through conviction of sin, to which the sinner responds in repentance toward God and faith in the Lord Jesus Christ. Repentance and faith are inseparable experiences of grace. Repentance is a genuine turning from sin toward God. Faith is the acceptance of Jesus Christ and commitment of the entire personality to Him as Lord and Savior.

2. Justification is God's gracious and full acquittal, upon principles of His righteousness, of all sinners who repent and believe in Christ. Justification brings the believer into a relationship of peace and favor with God.

3. Sanctification is the experience, beginning in regeneration, by which the believer is set apart to God's purposes, and is enabled to progress toward moral and spiritual maturity through the presence and power of the Holy Spirit dwelling in him. Growth in grace should continue throughout the regenerate person's life.

4. Glorification is the culmination of salvation and is the final blessed and abiding state of the redeemed.

*Genesis 3:15; Exodus 3:14-17; 6:2-8; Matthew 1:21; 4:17; 16:21-26; 27:22-28:6; Luke 1:68-69; 2:28-32; John 1:11-14,29; 3:3-21,36; 5:24; 10:9,28-29; 15:1-16; 17:17; Acts 2:21; 4:12; 15:11; 16:30-31; 17:30-31; 20:32; Romans 1:16-18; 2:4; 3:23-25; 4:3; 5:8-10; 6:1-23; 8:1-18,29-39; 10:9-10,13; 13:11-14; 1 Corinthians 1:18,30; 6:19-20; 15:10; 2 Corinthians 5:17-20; Galatians 2:20; 3:13; 5:22-25; 6:15; Ephesians 1:7; 2:8-22; 4:11-16; Philippians 2:12-13; Colossians 1:9-22; 3:1ff.; 1 Thessalonians 5:23-24; 2 Timothy 1:12; Titus 2:11-14; Hebrews 2:1-3; 5:8-9; 9:24-28; 11:1-12:8,14; James 2:14-26; 1 Peter 1:2-23; 1 John 1:6-2:11; Revelation 3:20; 21:1-22:5.*

## Evangelism and Church Planting

It is the duty and privilege of every follower of Christ, and of every church of the Lord Jesus Christ, to endeavor to make disciples of all nations. We believe that disciples are most effectively made in the context of the local church. Therefore, church planting and missions are of utmost importance. The Lord Jesus Christ has commanded the preaching of the Gospel to all nations. It is the duty of every Christian to seek constantly to win the lost to Christ.

*Genesis 12:1-3; Exodus 19:5-6; Isaiah 6:1-8; Matthew 9:37-38; 10:5-15; 13:18-30, 37-43; 16:19; 22:9-10; 24:14; 28:18-20; Luke 10:1-18; 24:46-53; John 14:11-12; 15:7-8,16; 17:15; 20:21; Acts 1:8; 2; 8:26-40; 10:42-48; 13:2-3; Romans 10:13-15; Ephesians 3:1-11; 1 Thessalonians 1:8; 2 Timothy 4:5; Hebrews 2:1-3; 11:39-12:2; 1 Peter 2:4-10; Revelation 22:17.*

## Ordinances

There are two ordinances for the New Testament church. The first, baptism, is the immersion of a believer in water. It is an act of obedience symbolizing the believer's faith in a crucified, buried, and risen Savior, the believer's death to sin, the burial of the life, and the resurrection to walk in newness of life in Christ Jesus. Second, the Lord's Supper is a symbolic act of obedience whereby followers memorialize the death of the Redeemer and anticipate His second coming.

*Matthew 3:13-17; 26:26-30; 28:19-20; Mark 1:9-11; 14:22-26; Luke 3:21-22; 22:19-20; John 3:23; Acts 2:41-42; 8:35-39; 16:30-33; 20:7; Romans 6:3-5; 1 Corinthians 10:16,21; 11:23-29; Colossians 2:12.*

# SAMPLE CHURCH COVENANT

## New Covenant Bible Church -- St Charles, IL
## Church Covenant

Having been brought by God's grace to repent and believe in the Lord Jesus Christ, we now, depending upon the Holy Spirit, establish this covenant with one another.

In all we do, we will aim to glorify and enjoy the God of our salvation, from whom and through whom and to whom are all things: to Him be all glory forever! (*1 Cor. 10:31; Rom. 11:36*)

We will eagerly maintain the unity of the Spirit in the bond of peace by walking together in love and in the Spirit and by putting away all bitterness, anger, and injurious speech. (*Eph. 4:3; Gal. 5:16, 25; Eph. 4:29, 31*)

With humility and gentleness, patience and love, we will be kind to one another, tenderhearted, forgiving each other, even as God, for Christ's sake, has forgiven us. (*Eph. 4:1-2; Luke 17:3; Col. 3:13; 1 Thess. 5:11; 1 Pet. 1:22*)

We will carry each other's burdens, rejoicing with those who rejoice and weeping with those who weep. (*Gal. 6:2; Rom. 12:15*)

We will train our children in the instruction of the Lord, seeking to walk in a way that adorns the Gospel of Christ before our family, friends, and neighbors (*Prov. 22:6; Eph. 6:4; 1 Pet. 3:1*).

We will strive to live self-controlled, upright, and godly lives in this present age, as we wait for the blessed hope, the appearing of the glory of our great God and Savior Jesus Christ. (*Gal. 5:22-24; Titus 2:12; 1 Pet. 1:14*)

We will not neglect to gather together, but will support and treasure the biblical preaching of the whole counsel of God, the faithful observance of baptism and the Lord's Supper, and the loving exercise of church discipline. (*Heb. 10:25; 2 Tim. 4:2; Acts 2:38; 1 Cor. 11:26; Matt 18:17; 1 Cor.5:13*)

We will contribute cheerfully and generously to the expenses of the church, the relief of the poor, and the advancement of the gospel both to our neighbors and the nations. (*Matt. 28:19; Luke 12:33; 2 Cor. 9:7*)

We will, when we move from this place, unite as soon as possible with some other church where we can carry out the spirit of this covenant and the principles of God's Word.

In all these things, we rely on our God who has made a new and everlasting covenant with us, saying:

> "They shall be my people, and I will be their God. I will give them one heart and one way, that they may fear me forever, for their own good and the good of their children after them. . . . I will not turn away from doing good to them. And I will put the fear of me in their hearts, that they may not turn from me. I will rejoice in doing them good . . . with all my heart and all my soul." (*Jer. 32:38-41*)

In and because of Jesus we pray, Amen.

# MEMBERSHIP INTERVIEWS

*How to Conduct an Effective Membership Interview*
*By Mike McKinley*

At the outset, it may be helpful to acknowledge that there are no specific verses in Scripture that require a church to conduct an interview before recognizing someone as a member of its congregation. In the days of the New Testament, the process for becoming a member of the church seems to have been fairly brief and organic. A new member professed faith in Christ, was baptized, and was added to the church (cf. Acts 2:41).

But for good reason many churches have found it helpful to set aside a time to talk with a membership candidate before he or she joins the church. In my experience, these interview sessions represent an extremely valuable pastoral opportunity. It's a chance to ask questions, provide pastoral care, and shape the candidates' understanding of their role in the church.

The purpose of this article is to provide some practical guidance on how to make the most of these interviews for the benefit of the member and the health of the church. And while there's no one set way to conduct a membership interview, I've found it helpful to try to achieve three things in the course of a one-hour meeting:

1. Get to know the candidate for membership.
2. Help the candidate understand the church.

3. Begin pastoral care for the candidate.

## Get to Know Them

After opening in prayer, I usually begin asking questions that will help me get to know the individual better. Sometimes I interview persons I know quite well, like former members who have moved back to the area. Other I'm interviewing those who are, for all intents and purposes, complete strangers. So while I might tailor my approach to those specific situations, here are four things I normally ask of every membership candidate (with some brief comments):

### 1. What makes you want to join the church?

This question is a good ice-breaker. It helps get at people's motivations and can occasionally raise some red flags (such as the person who once answered, "Because I'm sick of looking for a good church").

### 2. Where are you from?

People don't arrive in your office *ex nihilo*. They're formed for good and ill by their backgrounds, their experiences, and their families. As a pastor, this information will help you care for the new member, as she becomes part of your flock. Someone from a legalistic Christian background will probably have different needs, reactions, and temptations than someone raised by atheist parents.

### 3. How did you become a Christian?

This is the most important piece of information to get in a membership interview. A church must be confident its members are genuinely converted, and a person's understanding of their conversion will often reveal quite a bit about their spiritual maturity. More than once this question has been used by God to reveal that the potential member may very well not be converted at all.

### 4. Can you briefly explain the gospel to me?

You may be surprised how many Christians cannot clearly articulate the good news about Jesus. They may believe the gospel but not understand it well enough to communicate it. Or, more commonly, they might leave out an important part of the gospel, such as the need for sinners to respond in repentance and faith. This question allows you to gently inform or correct their understanding of the good news.

## Help Them to Know the Church

After taking time to get to know the potential member (and believe him to be converted), I move the conversation toward helping him to understand the church he's come to join. While we have a membership class that covers many of these subjects, it's helpful to walk through them one-on-one.

### 1. Answer any questions the candidate might have.

People often have questions about the church that range from the small ("Why is the church logo green?") to the weighty ("What does the church teach about divorce?"). This is a good opportunity to let folks explore whatever questions might be nagging them.

### 2. Review the statement of faith and church covenant.

This subject is normally covered pretty thoroughly in our membership classes, but the interview occasionally generates good opportunities to explain some point of doctrine or correct a misunderstanding.

### 3. Review expectations of church members.

The membership interview is a great time to clearly set expectations. We tell our new members the congregation expects six things from all its members:

- *Attend* - For our church, this means Sunday morning and (if at all possible) Sunday evening. You can't be part of something if you're not present.

- *Pray* - We ask and expect our members to pray for each other.
- *Give* - Giving is an act of worship and obedience.
- *Serve* - Use your Spirit-given gifts to edify the body.
- *Live holy* - Your actions, in private and in public, affect the health of the body. Fight sin by God's grace and be quick to confess and ask for help when you need it.
- *Evangelize* - You're a missionary sent by our church into your neighborhood, home, and workplace.
- *Reinforce any distinctives important to your church culture.*

The membership interview is a prime time to ensure new members really "get" the church culture. I usually review our approach to Christian liberty, the priority we give in our budget to church planting, and our emphasis on every-member ministry rather than programs. It's helpful for everyone in the church to be on the same page with these kinds of issues.

## 5. Review the membership process going forward.

This part is simple; walk them through the next steps in your church's membership process. It may be helpful to address questions they have about timing as well as any public statement they may be asked to give.

## Begin Pastoral Care

At this point in the conversation, I should have a pretty good idea about what a candidate might need as he enters into the life of the congregation. At the end of the meeting, it's good to set up a plan for ways the candidate can integrate into the church. In our congregation, this can mean arranging to set him up with a small group and a one-to-one Bible-reading partner. In some special cases, it becomes clear the person would benefit from some special follow up (like counseling, a program of Bible study, or even an evangelistic course). In those cases, I prefer to start the ball rolling on that process before the candidate leaves my office. At the conclusion of the meeting it's helpful to pray for the new member, that she'd be fruitful in the life of the church, and that the church would bear much fruit in her life.

It's a privilege to conduct membership interviews. It can feel wearisome when a lot of people want to join and my schedule (and those of our other elders) is tight. But it's important to the church's health that we carefully examine people before they become members, and it's a joy to hear candidates' testimonies of God's grace and to consider together how God might bless them through the church.

McKinley, Mike. "How to Conduct an Effective Membership Interview." TGC. September 9, 2012. Accessed January 8, 2016. http://www.thegospelcoalition.org/article/how-to-conduct-an-effective-membership-interview.

# ENDNOTES

1   "SBA Office of Advocacy, Frequently Asked Questions." Small Business Administration. March 1, 2014. Accessed January 8, 2016. https://www.sba.gov/sites/default/files/FAQ_March_2014_0.pdf.

2   Stetzer, Ed, and Phillip Connor. "How Many Church Plants Really Survive--And Why?" North American Mission Board. 2007. Accessed January 8, 2016. http://www.namb.net/namb1cb2col.aspx?id=8590001104.

3   Merriam-Webster. Accessed January 8, 2016. http://www.merriam-webster.com/dictionary/threshold. (Entry 3b)

4   Spurgeon, C. H. *Lectures to My Students: Complete & Unabridged.* New ed. Grand Rapids, Mich.: Zondervan Pub. House, 1954. 26-27.

5   Thayer, Joseph Henry, and Carl Ludwig Wilibald Grimm. "ὀρέγω: Strongs G3713." In *Thayer's Greek-English Lexicon of the New Testament: Coded with Strong's Concordance Numbers.* Sixth Printing. ed. Peabody, Mass.: Hendrickson, 2003.

6   *Ibid.* "πιθυμέω: Strongs G1937."

7   Piper, John. *Brothers, We Are Not Professionals: A Plea to Pastors for Radical Ministry.* Nashville, Tenn.: Broadman & Holman, 2002. 1.

8   Spurgeon, *Lectures.* 35.

9   "Learning a New Skill Is Easier Said Than Done." Gordon Training International. 2011. Accessed January 8, 2016. http://www.gordontraining.com/free-workplace-articles/learning-a-new-skill-is-easier-said-than-done/.

10  Henry, Matthew. "Complete Commentary on James 4". "Matthew Henry Complete Commentary on the Whole Bible". 1706. Accessed January 8, 2016. http://www.studylight.org/commentaries/mhm/view.cgi?bk=58&ch=4.

11  *Ibid.*

12  *Ibid.*

13  Chesterton, G. K. *What's Wrong in the World*. Christian Classics Ethereal Library. 1910. 114. Accessed January 8, 2016. http://www.ccel.org/ccel/chesterton/whatwrong.pdf.

14  Quoted by Pearcey, Nancy. *Total Truth: Liberating Christianity from Its Cultural Captivity*. Wheaton, Ill.: Crossway Books, 2004. 18.

15  Quoted by *Ibid*. 5.

16  Lewis, C. S. *The Collected Letters of C.S. Lewis, Volume 3: Narnia, Cambridge and Joy 1950-1963*, edited by Walter Hooper. San Francisco, California: Harper Collins, 2007. 766.

17  Stott, John R. W. *Between Two Worlds: The Challenge of Preaching Today*. Grand Rapids, Mich.: W.B. Eerdmans Pub., 1994. 292.

18  McKinley, Mike. *Am I Really a Christian? The Most Important Question You're Not Asking*. Wheaton, IL: Crossway, 2011.

19  DeYoung, Kevin, and Ted Kluck. "Church: Love It, Don't Leave It - OnFaith." OnFaith. July 1, 2009. Accessed January 8, 2016. http://www.faithstreet.com/onfaith/2009/07/01/church-love-it-dont-leave-it/123.

20  Dever, Mark Edward. *A Display of God's Glory: Basics of Church Structure Deacons, Elders, Congregationalism & Membership*. New England: Center for Church Reform, 2001. 5.

21  "The Waterer Watered -- C. H. Spurgeon." Bible Bulletin Board. Accessed January 8, 2016. http://www.biblebb.com/files/spurgeon/0626.htm.

22  Thayer. "μαθητής: Strongs G3101."

23  Bruskas, Dave. "Churches Planting Churches Biblically." ChurchLeaderscom. November 15, 2010. Accessed January 8, 2016. http://www.churchleaders.com/outreach-missions/outreach-missions-blogs/146052-churches-planting-churches-biblically.html.

24  C. Peter Wagner, *Church Planting for a Greater Harvest*. Ventura, California: Regal Books, 1990. 11.

25  Thayer. "κκλησία: Strongs G1577."

26    Spurgeon, "The Waterer Watered"

27    "Simple Church - Why?" Simple Church - Why? Accessed January 13, 2016. http://www.simplechurchathome.com/Why.html.

28    Olson, David T. *The American Church in Crisis: Groundbreaking Research Based on a National Database of over 200,000 Churches.* Grand Rapids, Mich.: Zondervan, 2008. 16.

29    Stetzer, Ed, and Phillip Connor. "Church Plant Survivability and Health Study 2007." North American Mission Board. 2007. Accessed January 8, 2016.

30    Rainer, Thom. "13 Issues for Churches in 2013." ChurchLeaderscom. January 15, 2013. Accessed January 8, 2016. http://www.churchleaders.com/pastors/pastor-articles/164787-thom-rainer-13-issues-churches-2013.html.

31    "The World Factbook: United States." Central Intelligence Agency. Accessed January 8, 2016. https://www.cia.gov/library/publications/the-world-factbook/geos/us.html.

32    Keller, Timothy, and J. Allen Thompson. *Church Planter Manual.* New York: Redeemer Presbyterian Church, 2002. 30.

33    Keller, Timothy, "Why Plant Churches?" Redeemer City to City, 2009. Accessed January 8, 2016. http://www.rockcreekfellowship.org/wp-content/uploads/2012/12/Why_Plant_Churches.pdf

# when the signals come home

Jordan E. Franklin

ISBN: 978-0-9861876-9-8
Library of Congress Control Number: 2020948418

Cover and book design: Alyse Knorr
Cover image by Zac Ong on Unsplash
*when the signals come home* is set in Minion Variable Concept.


Switchback Books
Kate Partridge and Alyse Knorr, Editors
editors@switchbackbooks.com
www.switchbackbooks.com

*For Dad,*
*who instilled in me a love of words, creation, storytelling, and Prince*

# Track List

## Inheritance

To raconteur tongue,
       solar flare temper,
Mom's cheekbones,
       Pop's weak eyes,
to knuckle-busted hands,
       arachnid fingers,
Bible names,
       terracotta curves,
to plantations taken,
       vows broken,
a potential future: green-
       legged and stalling
       until the surgeon's saw,
to musical ears,
       a fine reed of mouth,
solitary mothers,
       separations, restraining orders,
to holes:
grandfather-shaped,
and fathers who
       fantasized absence,
plastic spoons,
       tall folks,
to soldiers, sailors
in violent jungles, .
roseless spring days,
       nights above melodic
       crack vial crunches,
to Bed Stuy,
       gunshots beyond school fences,
grandmother midwives,
       Ellis Island,
to Atlantic graveyard,
       blackened sea floor,
bad hearts,
       troubled brains

to titles, never-ending christenings,
  mistakes both breathing
  and not,
to accepting blame,
love under gaslight,
child-shaped collateral,
  juvenile bullseye,
to never ending right:
  a daughter, a poem.

**i.**     **"maybe i'm just like/**
                **my Father**

                     —"When Doves Cry" by Prince and
                                     the Revolution

# Find the River

*After Talking Heads*

### 1.

Back in the day when Civil Rights was in vogue, Bedford-Stuyvesant boy back when it was *do or die*, a river of silver roamed in my father's mouth, dragged and sharpened over whetstone recruitment at the chime of eighteen. A man in Nicaragua far from home: serrated and leaking from butchered astronomy and Bed-Stuy, *always Bed-Stuy that eats its young like the East New Yorks and the Brownsvilles* (lies we startle trust-funders and yuppies with but still they stay and things change). My father, right-handed, but always trading steel with the left, ambidextrous-knuckles quicker than the drop of bass, the eighties left him without a unit, a knife and the melted river swaying to life between his lips.

### 2.

My mother trapped hummingbirds in her stomach which fluttered when she laughed. Brooklyn-girl, single-mothered, house full of uncles, aunts, and cousins who chased a whiff of the American Dream in war-ill Korea. House full of Spanish, English, *a village, a village*, my mother heavy with love and a cut-out where her old man should be. Had my older brother at twenty-three, beautiful and screaming so many promises, the night black and simmering with stars ready to open their kitchen windows and shout librettos. Mom, college-fresh, a taxing, government woman.

### 3.

Brooklyn Hospital in the nineties, my parents and brother waiting as I'm cut from Mom, all Lorca-green and a month late into the new, weary space. My name fell from her lips then—the story of my name: Jesus swaddled in a river's mouth, *descending* as John the Baptist watched.

**J,**

the first letter
of my name, coiled
to lead the current
of sounds as Mom
opened the Good Book
to find my name there.

A reed with a curled end,
an axolotl with its joyful
tail tip uplifted.
Cosmonaut of language,
it buoys above
the horizon—
the David Bowie
of the lexicon.
Sometimes,
J masquerades
as *H* when Spanish
makes a home
from Grandma's lips.

I's moon, romanced
from his gravitational pull,
and given its own
space, stars, name,
This letter overwhelms the mouth
as Mom makes
a hymn of my name,
her trills a litter
of bells—satellites
for the waiting ear.

## Graffiti Love Letters: Skewered Abecedarian

Someone's bound to be a
king in *Kings*
loose-lipped grins at the bootleg
man. Shops are all
neon
hand
grenades devastating the sidewalk
open or closed. Jehovahs and
panhandlers peddle similar gods and there's no time for
quiet when metal handles metal.

Someone told me that under all this stone,
there's a dream. The only things
under all this stone are more steel, folks, and screeching. I watch the
vexed cop
with the beach glass eyes, some newspaper like
Xenias boa-knuckled in his triggerhand. Always speeding, his rubber
yammers over roads with no appreciation for the
school
zone.

**Saturdays with the Koi**
*For Jonathan*

I can still taste the cocoa bread clouds
in my mouth, the warm braille imprinted
on my tongue courtesy of Christie's.
Yours is plump with beef patty,
the bag clutched in your hand
like an upside-down balloon.

We are cartographers of hands
these Saturdays. We chart every callus
and line as Dad holds ours, twin rolls
of footsteps on either side of his own.
We watch the koi create
swift circles under the pond's skin.

There's not a ripple to be seen
as they bully the turtles
in flashes of color—robbing
them of the bits of bread we pour
onto the water's face.

## Recipe

The first dish I tried to make was scrambled eggs
with cheese, sprinkled spices. Dad raised them against
a sea of pearled grits, an island of butter at the center.
I built chicken parm on top of Dad's old recipe

With cheese, sprinkled spices. Dad tried to raise us against
Mom's cooking but her recipes held fast to us.
I built chicken parm on top of Dad's memory.
On my birthday, he brought home lobsters from Chinatown

but Mom's recipes held fast.
Beef was the domain of Mom.
Dad brought his lobsters from Chinatown as
her stews sang inside her crock pot.

Beef was the domain of Mom,
boiled in its juices. Potatoes bobbed
above the water, singing inside the crock pot.
Dad hummed as he cut my ice cream cake.

Stewed in our juices, our heads bobbed
between homes. Dad's army knife opened cans,
and hummed, my ice cream cake cut
as our taste buds floated between plates.

Between homes, Dad's army knife opened cans
and memories. In his freezer, meat rotted
as we floated between their plates.
The first dish I failed to make was scrambled eggs.

## One Father's Day

Dad broke
open and cried at our small church

as if the pastor's sermon on forgiving
one's father removed him

from the concrete
he built around himself.

Holding my younger brother and I still
under each arm, the only movement came

from his body rocking
in the pew, cracked

by his loud sobs.
Dad's head bowed over us

his tears raining upon our bodies.
He never spoke a word of his prayer to us.

I never knew he could cry—
never knew he could find a place

with us where he could weep
so freely and I wondered if this

instead was the boy my father was
before he fitted the cracks in himself

with cement—before he decided stone
was a better alternative to soil.

## July-August Interlude

Three damaged vertebrae. Tetraplegia.

They repair Dad's spine with screws and plates. His diabetes, instigator of his dizzy spell and fall, is monitored and tended with various drugs. Everything's cool for a few days until Dad gets feverish. The head doctor declares the prior surgery is the cause. They cut him open once, then twice, when the bedsores make homes in his backside and feet.

They move him to Mount Sinai and it's a few more months of surgeries, visits and illnesses. Everyone decides that the best option is to give me Power of Attorney and, after months of paying his rent, we get rid of his place only after weeks of cleaning out the place of everything that *is* him.

It's September when he lands in the VA hospital tucked far out in Kingsbridge and I add another hour to my commute. When I land a city job in December, my Saturdays now belong completely to his failing body.

## Take Five
*For Tiffany*

I have nearly forgotten what waiting is like
outside of a hospital:
My sister-in-law destroys us at cards—
shuffles like Vegas is her second home
and I feel like she only invites us over to lose.
My older brother hits the table at another loss,
demands to play again
as their black puppy sneaks teeth
in his kiss under the dining room table.
The air conditioner chills both stories of the house
while Summer rails at their front door.
I dance with my nephew to Jain in the kitchen
with moves I stole from Joe Cocker.
Mom stews chicken on the stove
and the house welcomes its taste.

**Some songs I'm listening to on the way to Dad, Day #**

"Born under Punches (the Heat Goes On)" by Talking Heads
"Take the A Train" by Duke Ellington
"Astral Weeks" by Van Morrison
"Starfish and Coffee" by Prince
"Buggin' Out" by A Tribe Called Quest
"Home Is Where the Hatred Is" by Gil Scott-Heron

**Take the 4 Train (Solitary Freestyle)**

*Grey Skies over the Bronx:*

Could be morning.

Could be the water cooled
on used glass.

Could be
the window.

Could be
a minnow dribbling
over some fool's chin.

Could be
us.

Could be
shadows
stealing dopamine.

Could be
the rain.

Could
be Mingus wringing
Bebop from clouds.

Could be the sun.

Could be this new-
found hole in our
heart valves.

Could be snow.

Could be Eurydice
blue from a snake's
kiss.

Could be denial.

Could be
this head
closing its doors.

Could be compulsion.
Could be
this clot
thick
in the back
of our throats.

Could be this day.

Could be
the way Dad asks
why God left
him this way.

Could be me.

Could be
the way that old train
of an answer
skips
the station
of my mouth.

# Center Mass

*Jugular. Femoral. Carotid.*
*Ten to fifteen minutes.*
Under the Nicaraguan heat,
Dad became the man's shadow.

*As close to the heart as you can.*
The knife slips through ribs
and into a lung.

*Twist the knife,*
Dad's mantra as he recalls the man's face,
the roses bubbling at his lips.
Everything stills for the rust.

*Begin again.*
Words steal Dad from his gurney.

*A little too high.*
South Carolina—another green—
the stench of pecans tease the iron.
This time, a familiar man lies
on the floor of this story.

*Children are meant to be seen, not heard.*
By twenty-one, a blade in Dad's hands
was just another finger.

*Not seen. Not heard.*
Family secrets are a special kind of violence:
kinder, quieter.

*Begin again.*
A knife is awkward in my hands.
Dad's hunting knife, his machetes
I hold.

## Map of Maladies

2011: kidney stones. A two-inch tube's
planted in Mom—its bleeding can wait

for my hands and gauze
to trap the red. She can wait

on her side, voice fogged in unease, me
a step below tears as I work. I can wait

under the loneliness of our bathroom light
to rinse her blood off my fingers. Grief can wait

for another year when the living room
gives way to her news of *cancer.* Tears can wait

over her body, heavy with new tubes, smeared
in anesthesia and pain. The cancer can wait

until chemotherapy wipes everything clean. I count
her hairs lost to the tub's drain. She can wait

to shave the rest as realization drags itself
under the light. *Beautiful,* the word can wait

on my tongue until she returns
to life before me again. I can wait

for the fast forward to 2014, Dad's now
wheelchair-bound, diabetic. We can wait

for his bedsores, surgeries, hospitals circulating
him between them like clots in his blood. He can wait

until 2015 for the hopelessness, for his *J, Baby,*
*let me go. Heaven is a broken vein and it can't wait.*

## Triggerfinger

Ten years old sees me gripping
a handgun fat with
BBs sweat-polished
in the summer glow, my
feet shoulder-width apart,
their bare soles played like harps
by grass—yards away
sits a small target, its concentric
circles complacent, its colors
like every front porch flag
in Carolina. The nearby rail-
road cars shake the garden. Smokestack lightning muddies
the vibrating air—I take
the breaths my target can't
and pull.

The bullet is a fraction
off its sticker heart—
His finger inspects,
shows me the wound.
A pleased hum from him
harmonizes with the sizzling air.

The bullseye doesn't breathe,
but under his gaze, proud,
my finger lax on the heated
trigger, part of me wishes
for a pulse.

## Driving with Joshua

we were Brooklyn before the millennium,
                                    the day to day

quarrel of siblings parted by a decade
                                    Day to day,


there is our Brooklyn: its hospitals that cast us

out like dice, its people in our every birthmark,

                                    day to day

in this city heat that not even your AC can dismantle, traffic

restless like K in the backseat. We watch how the day today


makes an uneasy cut into night, your headlights dispute

with the stars as Miguel sings on the radio
                                    This day today

we debate which hero would win: "*Spiderman. Always Spiderman,*"

you quip as we turn onto Kings Highway
                                    This day today,

its air frank—Linden Blvd made easy prey to Summer

With you, I enjoy this small break now from
                                    the day to day

## The Hospital

Dad's on the death row
of the mind, strapped
under the last rites,
the minutes silent
as they search for a vein.
This glass between us
is thicker than before—
I see him clearer now,
and me in smudge
like I was
and always am.

The VA hospital's air
is poor and piss-heavy.
I lulled him from the ledge
last night with cracked tongue
and saltwater song.

Only a foot returned.

This flag of thorns
is heavy over my heart—
my tongue in splinters
when I see him.
He, oblivious,
and me always pleading
for a pardon
that never comes.

## When I Wake up to More Grief
*After Emily Dickinson*

Hope is the thing with feathers that I clip
and leave in a jar—
I don't bother to kill it—
I want it nowhere near me—

I don't want to hear its chirps
to be held or to let it into my room—
I want it to drown in that jar I painted black—
shut away deep in the closet—

that old Schrodinger's hope—
Every day it comes back, unscrews the lid—
Hope wiggles its toes and walks into my room—
I catch it before it can try its wings in the air—

Hope is the thing with feathers that cries—
It fills the dark air with its beggar songs and mess—
Oh, Hope, I can kill it, but I won't—
I want it nowhere near me—

## March Interlude

Dad's baritone is under fathoms of saltwater creating a surreal harmony with mine.

The printer bleats off in a corner of the office as I speak and plead but Dad's always been a stubborn one, same as me. He wants to waste away, thinks it's better for everyone if he does so but I can't let him go. I always was selfish and no amount of lost Saturdays or fatigue will change that.

Later that night, Mom will tell me that it isn't my choice. I carry those words as I tell Pop to wait until April—that if nothing has changed, that if no improvement has been made by the next hospital conference, then I will let him go. The tear tracks are dried by then and my voice has lost most of its depth from earlier.

We both harmonize a heavy fatigue.

On Visiting Students Day two days later, I'm on the Hampton jitney headed to Southampton, the roads surrounded by white. I will seldom remember a single face of my potential cohort or word spoken and I will not really care. All I'll remember is feeling like I'm up to my neck in chilled water, unmoving as Dad's words repeat in my head:

*Just let me go.*

**Waiting for Dinner at Warren Street**

Dad's in the kitchen
singing into a spoon's head.

In a boombox are the Mary Jane Girls
stacked above the stove's heat,

Brooklyn outside the window
in a night that redacts the Sun.

The bridge, green-lit
and dressed to the nines

in stars, straddles
the horizon.

There are many pictures
like this in my head:

of a man and his music held
in the warm, orange eye

of our brownstone. Dad
sings over dinner plates,

his triumphant cry as the station
switches to Slave,

then Prince. This
is the Dad I'm not sure

I've ever had, these pictures,
their frames cracked like a radio

that can still serenade me
once a day.

ii.       **"i'm not saying what i did/
was alright"**

—"Across 110th Street" by Bobby Womack

**some songs /i'm listening/ to on the way to Dad's, day #**

"Smokestack Lightning" by Howlin' Wolf
"All I Do" by Stevie Wonder
"All Falls Down" by Kanye West
the *Purple Rain* soundtrack by Prince and the Revolution
"Lazarus" by David Bowie

## how to read my poems/

don't say *spider*/
say someone sews
in the trees

instead of *happy*/
say Spring wakes
in your chest

not *excited*/
say woodwinds sing
in your cheekbones

don't say *hurt*/
say bee stings race
over your body

instead of *grief*/
say someone rebuilt
your heart wrong

not *crazy*/
say someone else works
the stick shift upstairs

don't say *daughter*/
say almighty screw-up
not easy

instead of *sorry*/
say I want to see
you again

whatever you do
do *not* say *spider*/
say someone sews
in the trees

27

**Storytelling**
*After Johnny Cash*

I left my head
at strange altars,

swallowed the slugs
rusting in Dad's right hand,

leapt through rings of fire
and pulled stories out

like teeth.
I promised to stop

telling these tales
but they gather like thorns

in my throat. When my mouth
opens, they cut its roof

as I sing.

## Rain

*After Tina Chang*

I didn't spring from a tower of marble. The
spoon fixed in my hand was Sterling plastic. When the world
spun *en pointe* amongst the stars, I stood still until the next chorus began
on my block. I want to say this understanding of everything started inside my father. In
that ruby-christened cavern, I listened to his blood sing—heard an
echo of what rumbled and waited for me outside of that dark—the explosion
of sense and color when the axe opened the gates of
his skull. I want to say the fever
that wracked my father then was the beginning of my wisdom and
that I heard it—heard it as clear and easy as the rain
hit the windows.

## The Color Game: Bounce

Bounce
back to a nine-year-old me. Back to those days
spent with Dad and my little brother
in the park. Dad taught us to ricochet a
rubber handball off the court walls
and we failed, but laughed, the afternoons spent
listening to its blue
body crash against concrete.

Bounce
back to last decade. I went to a new high school—
the one that walked like a Crip. Our book
bags must be nothing but blue
despite my younger brother's cry for red,
his favorite color back then.
This blue's the shield we wore
to get back home.

Bounce
back to the days when the other kids
said I talked "white"
and nearly chucked Prince from the classroom's
CD player. His Royal Badness, his Purple
Majesty's an anomaly to them same as me.

Bounce
back to a college-aged me, wandering
Brooklyn with my older cousin and friend
to the subway and no matter how "white"
the other kids said my talk was, I am still
christened "nigger" by the pale
homeless man, my dollar some
color other than green
to him.

# That Other America Between Clarendon and Avenue D

There were three bodies to a bed some nights,
seldom fewer than two and no one
stirred, not even for thunder
or storm past the window blinds.
Two beds side by side in that room
with the single closet and white walls,
the wooden dresser a roof
to dust bunnies on the brown carpet.
Like sardines, the people there lived
and knew nothing better
than roaches provoked to flight,
leaking roof and rodent carcass
in living room cushions. A home
even as the grandmother complained
of invisible men past the windows
and became unable to leave
the bed. You should've heard her gibberish,
her sparrow's eye, her screams of the man
watching her as she's loaded
into a van and to a place greener
than her *Panama*
and greener than her legs
failing: *some home.*

## Dad's Hands

Which on his Fridays held ours
during walks from the video store
as he told us tales of Bobby Bootygas
who could leap huge walls
with a single fart

Curious hands which brought home
rocks and owl pellets to dissect
in our living room—plucked
mice bones and mapped
the grooves in each stone

Hands which siphoned power
from our apartment's hallway light
when ours went dark—splashed us
with water and pelted us with balled socks
through our laughter during the blackout game

Hands which followed
a new recipe each weekend
and guided me as I first made
scrambled eggs or canned salmon
on the stove

Hands which gripped a PlayStation controller
to progress through *Resident Evil 4*
and *Dynasty Warriors*—
tearing through zombies
and imperial soldiers

Hands which taught me to jab
with enough power to interrupt
the signals to an attacker's brain
and follow up with a right cross
that made floors rise

Hands which boosted the volume
on old radios when Evelyn Champagne King
or Cyndi Lauper purred
from the speakers as we duetted
over the washing machine

Hands that took to a butter knife
and a machete with ease—
formed the letters of our names
in music boxes crafted
for us from wood.

Gentle hands which held me
in old photos from the hospital
as my tiny, new body
remained unaware of the world
opening around me

Hands which lost to tetraplegia,
unable to complete crosswords
or hold mine during visits—
hands now sunken in, useless
except in photos and my memory.

# Losing Signals

*"The more you talk, the less people listen."*
—Meg White

i...///    wanted you    ~~to stop~~
listening    i...///    wanted
to talk    until
my tongue    dried
in its mine    shaft    i...///    am less    of
a    woman
and more    of a    canary
my song    rattling
against    the black    fog    i...///
let in
~~my head~~    sometimes.

I...///    ~~don't~~ expect    to be  believed

i...///    expect    to Cassandra
my way    into another
~~wrecked~~ home
where    roaches
will  make    a chapel
~~of me~~
no one
taught me    ~~to lie~~
right
and    i...///    swore off
~~the   Bible~~
several mouths    ago.

With    each  page
i...///know    you will
hear    ~~less.~~

## Bullseye

A bar in Southampton

I didn't question how
the only Black things
for miles were me,
the sky and the patches
on the dartboard.
As expected,
my aim was poor
but my teachers were good.

Within a week or two,
I nicked my first

Bullseye.

There is a power
in nicking the heart
of things—

levels in video games,
poems, people—
I need to know
the damage I do,
so when I say
my final words
to Dad and hear
his bite muzzled
by the door to his room,
a bitterness grazes
my heart.

**iii.**     **"thought you died alone/**
                       **a long, long time ago"**

—"The Man Who Sold the World" by David Bowie

**/some/ songs**          **/on the way/**          **to Dad, Day #?**

"Lovesong" by the Cure
"Moneygrabber" by Fitz and the Tantrums
"American Pie" by Don McClean
"Swimming Pools (Drank)" by Kendrick Lamar
"Hey Joe" by Jimi Hendrix
"Little Wing" by Jimi Hendrix

## Garden Interlude I

April is rose season.

It is a fact Pop instills in you from young. Whether you're six or eight or ten, it doesn't matter. When Spring comes, it is always off to the Brooklyn Botanical Gardens. In this huge section, you find them and they sit under the sun like a big Rivera mural—a blend of reds and pinks and yellows—a burst of color in every step and you tear your hands away from Pop to absorb everything. When you adjust your eyes to the vibrant mosaic, you see hummingbirds. They hover in place, their wings like the Flash as he vibrates his molecules through solid matter.

**Dive**

*After Kendrick Lamar*

Backstroke's for Carolina
where your old man broke
bloodlines with shaking toe—
Carolina where his daddy
drowned sense, ruled
home with knuckles and
gun, who made him practice
kissing with a cooling barrel,
whom your dad escaped
in jungles with Army knife
and rebel smoke.
Gramps with his whiskied
noose swings
in a chromosome.
When alcohol lurks
in a room, you close
your throat for Gramps
is in a cell somewhere,
always thirsty.

## grandpa's poem

Baby, I'm Cack as they come, blood hotter than a sunrise or hot sauce on catfish. Been Cack since my granddaddy and his folks took back that plantation, knuckle by knuckle, and I'd tell that story whenever whiskey threatened my lips or I hear that old forehead scar of mine sing its love song for the rock that cracker drove into it.

I never wanted to be a father. I prayed and prayed, but your grandma pushed out four boys. I took one look at them little black mugs and knew I had to beat men into them. As for your granny, she was alright—too much lip though. A nurse in her suit that ran so white against the blues and yellows I sang into her bones.

And your daddy?

Big mouth like his momma.

Big enough to holster my gun into that night. Told your granny I was a backdoor man and why this corn stalk of a boy think he could talk like a man? I wish I could say I learned to keep my hands clean as a father, but I've never been one for lyin'. The bottle made me dance as well as sing. I danced all over my house—worked my hands and feet into every surface I touched.

I've always been an entertainer. Could send that one-eyed-Sammy-Davis nigger packin' with his rats and yet your grandma ups and leaves me.

I want to tell you the distance was enough to stop me, but whiskey got a kick like a drum and even when old cancer took my tongue from my mouth, I still sing, and sing, and sing

# Garden Interlude II

There's a section of the garden adorned in Japanese aesthetic and architecture. In the middle of all the small shrines and temples is a pond filled with turtles and koi. From his bag, Dad retrieves a loaf of bread. Before you feed them, he makes you take off the crusts so they won't choke. You break off piece after piece and toss them in, amused as they buoy the surface before being devoured by the opportunistic water dwellers.

The koi are always too fast. By the time the turtles get the floaters in their sights, the koi pluck it from the pond's face with all the charm of a taxi. Always trigger happy, the koi see no ally in their quest and will fight for their meager Wonderbread even against their own brethren. You always pity the turtles so you change tactics. You start to take a bread piece and drop it on one's head as they near. The yeast rain is only a minor nuisance as they readily eat the offerings.

The koi are all rainbow tail flashes as they see it and torpedo to the spot. However, the turtle gets the meal.

**Dancing with Myself**

Pop's
    a                       music  man,
Prince-ly disciple,
                    radio  patriarch
with    heavy hands
                  and lips
                  to sing
                  Rick James
                  or Jeffrey Osborne.

Music surrounds him,
even those times
he'd make you
        tremble
                  like tunes
           in a    piano's mouth,
his living room
a mess
of straight      spines and
                  silence
and the only
moves
are your eyes
                  rubberhosing
in your head.
The orange lights    hum
                  a warm motif
overhead
as Pop

weighs belts
in the backroom,
leather            jitterbugging
in his palms.

You could only be

threatened       in     song.

2017 now
and Pop's
limbs have
atrophied

            atonal,

      their

morphine

      metronome,

tetraplegic

      time signature,

bedsore

      beats.

Pop's
in a hospital
courting
diabetic

      bebop,

your strange history
caught in the      hum

     of his

chair's motor,
his hands no longer

      a scale

for leather.

Even weakened,
Pop's still

     got a

cruel      solo

Don't      dance.

**ex-wife's kid**

noun

1. How you and your brothers were introduced to your father's acquaintances.
   *"hi, oh these are my ex-wife's kids"*

2. Your nickname/title for over 18 years, from the ages of 5-23.
   *synonyms: mistake, not-my-problem, weekend child, child support, first-born*

3. A hint that your father still has issues about the separation.
   *See Also: conditional love,*

4. A term accepted by a little kid.
   *synonyms: self-blame*

5. The bile you smother in your stomach every time you are with your old man.
   *See Also: makes you want to put your skin through a cheese grater*

6. One of the first things that leave your mouth when you come clean to your mom at twenty-eight.

Origin of ex-wife's kid

    Single father, first came into existence ca. 1995
    Became obsolete ca. 2013
    Reintroduced into the lexicon ca. 2018

**Antonyms**

1. Wanted child

## ~~Your Grandson~~

spent his early years
as ~~my~~ "nephew" and "Muskrat"
when we played ~~together~~ watched

Paw Patrol from the deepest comforters
I'd calm him with punk lullabies
placing his name into songs

by the Clash and the Cure
grinned as his teeth poked from his gums
watched as he outgrew clothes and

the Ninja Turtles from his highchair
I held his hand as we crossed streets
and chased the ice cream truck

when Summer hit his block
he ~~still~~ lights up when I sing
"Daydream Believer" since ~~many~~ nights

ended under its bars

You've never met him or heard
his voice none of his pictures sat
on the dressers ~~of your many homes~~

~~your pride~~ refused the phone
and you never miscounted sheep
over it          You lost

~~the right to~~ him the day
you turned my older brother's name
into a curse

if it makes you feel ~~better~~
he never asks ~~about you~~

## Garden Interlude III

The massive willow tree is one of your last stops in the garden. Shielded from the sun and the outside world by tassels of leaves, the three of us sit in its strong branches. The older you get, the closer you stay to the earth, each year adding a notch to the agoraphobia butterflying in your gut. Even on the lowest branch, you're an acrobat as agile as Nightwing flipping across Gotham rooftops.

songs, day #

"Somebody Loves You Baby" by Patti LaBelle
"Songbird" by Fleetwood Mac
"Landslide" by Fleetwood Mac
"Somebody That I Used to Know" by Gotye
"Losing My Religion" by R.E.M
"the Great Beyond" by R.E.M

to **dad**'s

**Black Girl's Rondo**

~~Or the Other Side of Writing~~

Or           where they make you           trade faces
with the only other ~~Black~~           writers for miles
and their tongues slip into their names
                    ~~when they see you~~

Or      where old Southerners           say the word *"colored"*
and nod ~~to you~~
                    the only ~~Black~~ face           in the classroom

Or           where it's assumed           Dad
is in prison           and not the hospital           you mentioned
~~time and           time~~           again

Or           where professors advise you
*"to learn ~~the pastimes           of the rich~~"*

Or           where everyone's           been to
Cancun                    or           Italy
or      Dizzy's Tunisia
and all you can afford           are ~~subway~~ rides
to the                    Bronx
to keep Dad                    ~~alive~~

Or           where you're called out
for being one of two           ~~Black~~           funded students
by your Asian peer
~~count the *hyphenated Americans*~~
~~on one hand here~~

Or           where not even cheese cubes
and wine are enough           to forget
another           ~~Black~~ body
was downed by police

49

Or              where you're told
you don't write       ~~"Black"~~
~~or "Black~~          enough"

Or            where you're reminded
that ~~before you are a poet~~
      ~~an artist~~
          ~~a woman~~
you are Black:
~~that albatross~~     here to stay

**just visiting**

Crows know themselves
        in mirrors    fingers    gone
sleep in bed
        sore   eyes   throat
        new      neck/
plate    empty   bed        sky   *let/*
clouds shout    name        above  *let me/*
sleep  /heart/  fails    step
    back      next hospital    will be better
blue cross /  saved   night/
      stand
    back         /burning/
*four*     *always four*   see/four   chart
face  with        flat mouth
    fever/   cook
like white sauce        in head/
      ache
phone    doctor  your pillows       trap/
      tears
limbs won't work   social worker  window
      close
call  lost     /home/      sun/
light  X-ray   chipped  /spine/  book
lost  memory  /lost/  money  night of
    salt/water
    no sleep
fight       gone are the days of
    your /father/
    Crows *see* themselves in mirrors
four   C four  fall  rise
    fall   rise     fall

                                    can't
                    three     discs      /years/
visit

            visit

                    /visit/

                            visit/or

            visits

                            /visited/

Baby                        call

                                let me

                                            /go/

## That Other America Between Clarendon and Avenue D, Reprised
*On the fourteenth Anniversary of Grandma's death*

There were six of you on the second floor
of the second house on that block:
your mother, two brothers,
grandmother, great aunt
and you. You knew no greater warmth
than Grandma's bedside,
knew no fear of storms or loneliness.
One day, you saw Grandma exit
her skull, heard old hymns pass
her lips like the blue soprano
of birds. Dementia made its home
there when the doors shut.
Diabetes turned her green
from the floorboards upward.
You were eleven when her legs
failed and then you were no longer
on the second floor
in the second house,
Clarendon: a life closed off to you
like the doors of the nursing home van
that hauled her away and its years
before you can say the word:
*home*

**The Color Game, Take 2**

You watch the birds
at Pop's nursing home:
plumed tapestries
of greens, rubies, and
grays, most of them stomached
in golds that ebb
into rich violets. They flutter
and preen in this prism
of plastic, their wooden huts
suspended under artificial light.
Occasionally a bird will flit
onto one of the side doors
and peck but nothing budges.
They train beaded eyes
on you and you wonder
how you appear
to them, your appearances
like clockwork outside
their dwelling every Friday.
Maybe you seem to them
the one confined in strange
acts, trapped in this love robed
in as many colors as their throats.

## Garden Interlude IV

You're fifteen with acne and the thousand-yard stare meant only for high school. When you return to the garden, younger brother and father in tow, there are no roses and the willow tree no longer permits daredevils in its branches. You can't feed turtles or koi anymore because some asshat's too lazy to remove the crusts had made a few unfortunate, gilled souls belly up.

You chalk it up to global warming and the economy but there's something else. Fifteen and you're too big for hand holding.

It's the last time you ever go.

## Father-Daughter Dance in Six Stages

### Stage 1.
By October,
they wanted three toes.
They ignored
the ossified shard
like an angry thorn
in Dad's hip.

### Stage 2.
*"Call a lawyer. I can at least leave you some money before I go."*

*"Let me go."*

*"I'll never get to walk you down the aisle."*

### Stage 3.
You say, "I love you."

You say, "See you, Pop."

You bring him everything
he wants:
food, books, supplies
and he takes
and takes.

When he talks of suicide,
you distract him
with movies
and jokes.

You are a consistent visitor
same as pain,
surgeries,
and complications.

This June,
you'd have carried on this tradition
for three years.

**Stage 4.**
With a jolt to the spine,
they promised the return
of his hands.
How many times can
they work the clay
before he breaks
down?

**Stage 5.**
*"Fuck him,"*

He says about your absent
brother after one absence
too many.

One counter-bastard argument
later and all you see
in this evening's wheelchair
is a six-foot middle finger
propped with screws.

**Stage 6.**
It's June
and you don't make it
to your three-year anniversary
before the fighting starts
and his heart toughens
at the sight of you.

Even from a wheelchair,
Dad can threaten you—
can tear at you
until you're a kid again.

*"Say the word,*
*and we'll dance."*

Here is your father—
a bruised clay,
middle fingered-
incarnate, nesting
doll of thorns.
You are not the one
to let him go.

### The Nikola Tesla of Compulsion
*After Jeffrey McDaniel*

You can't write poems.

Some days, Dad admits you're "his kid" to strangers/ Some days, you believe if you think hard enough about him, he will stride out of an ear and onto his own two feet again/ Some days, you are the apple of his eye: sweet, but defective/ Some days, you eat raspberries to keep the taste of these words off your tongue/

You can't write poems about—

Some days, you forget his hands don't work/ Some days, you're almost worth something/ Some days, you envy your brothers for stepping out of his life/ Some days, his words flit on repeat in your head: *"I would've been a doctor if it wasn't for you," "I tried not to be my father, and I failed"/*

You can't write poems about Mom/

Some days, you remember his hugs, the warmth of his hands/ Some days, you regret becoming a poet/ Some days, you don't want to waste prayers on him/ Some days, not to speak of him is to drown your larynx in raspberries/

You can't write poems about Mom because—

Some days, he'll wish you were his son/ Some days, he'll wish he left/ Some days, he'll take you to the gardens, other days to the Auto Show/ Some days, you're his favorite and he'll tell you so/ Some days, he'll say *"fuck your brothers"*/ Some days, you're used to his threats/

You can't write poems about Mom because she—

Some days, he'll ask you for a gun/ Some days, you realize he was dead long before you entered the world/ Some days, writing helps/ Some days, there's a grave between syllables/ Some days, if you turn your headphones up enough, you can breathe past the raspberries in your mouth/

You can't write poems about Mom because she loves—

Some days, he laughs and the world brightens/ Some days he's not Dad on the phone/ Some days, you have a plan for if his hands come for your brothers again/ Some days, second person isn't confession/

You can't write poems about Mom because she loves you—

Some days, you feel like you're the Nikola Tesla of Compulsion—as if you designed yourself to coil and convulse every time you dared to write or speak ill of Dad/

Some days, the raspberries are fresh.

## Garden Interlude V

In the Bronx in February 2017, it is every word you associate with Winter: *frigid, quiet, cruel.*

There's a cemetery across the street from Dad's nursing home and your favorite way to pass it is across the street in near sub-zero temperatures so that when you make the human error of shivering, you can blame it on the wind chill and not your twenty-six-year-old mind traipsing over the bitter irony of it all.

That your father—your athletic, strong, huge old man—is a tetraplegic and from a fall of all things and there's a cemetery a block long covered in snow just a street away from your bundled, head-phoned form. Whenever you chance a glance down that path in your head, you focus on the melodic morphine beating away in your earlobes.

Today's a Muse day, after all: *Stockholm Syndrome.*

But, the glance inside becomes a stare, then finally footprints through your mind and, for a beat, you wonder when your Pop has last seen roses or even sunlight since moving here. You shift the pizza box between hands. Although simple, it is a minor solution to the cravings and whims he gave you before this visit.

It's hot over your gloved hand and the delicious fusion of the chill in your coat, the warmth bleeding into the glove and the luscious "Stockholm Syndrome" is enough to erase the map upstairs.

Snow is absence: an absence of color, of warmth, of ground and sidewalks. You don't remember the last time you saw koi or a rose but they're out there somewhere and so is April.

**Father's Day**

Today you are
without your father,
smothered in this spot-
light of song.
You barter your service,
a daughter's waiting ears
and receive his teeth,
aired suicide notes.
He says, *"Say the word
and we'll dance."*

Everything is your fault here.
Dad charts the ledger
like failed stars
in the skyline—
twenty-seven years' worth.
He's in a God mood
this evening, throned,
unable to offer
knees or folded hands.
It reminds you
of church, of why
you don't pray,
of how you always lose
under the eye
of almighty fathers—
and how can you tell
so many dads apart?

*By the aches*, you think.
*By the size of the absences
they sing in you.*

## Acknowledgments

Thanks to the following journals for publishing these pieces:

| | |
|---|---|
| *acorn & iris* | "Rain" |
| *Cagibi* | "Take the 4 Train (Solitary Freestyle) |
| *Eastern Iowa Review* | "Garden Interlude I" |
| | "Garden Interlude II" |
| | "Garden Interlude III" |
| | "Garden Interlude IV" |
| *Easy Paradise* | "Graffiti Love Letters" |
| *Guesthouse* | "Find the River" |
| *Lumina Journal* | "Losing Signals" |
| *Memoir Mixtapes* | "Garden Interlude V" |
| *Nightjar Review* | "Dive" |
| *[PANK] Magazine* | "Dancing With Myself" |
| *Pinky Finger Press* | "Saturdays with the Koi" |
| *The Southampton Review* | "Triggerfinger" |
| *Sporklet* | "ex-wife's kids" |
| *Tilde Journal* | "That Other America Reprised" |
| *Tinderbox Poetry Journal* | "Inheritance" |

# Liner Notes: Thanks and Shout Outs!

Thank you Kate, Alyse, and Switchback Books for giving my book a loving home!

Thank you to Brooklyn College, Stony Brook Southampton, Sarah Lawrence Summer Seminar for Writers, Cave Canem, Provincetown Fine Arts Work Center, The Home School Claremont, Brooklyn Poets, Poets House, Unterberg Poetry Center, and 92Y.

Thank you to Prageeta Sharma, Jeffrey McDaniel, Lou Ann Walker, Susan Scarf Merrell, Roger Rosenblatt, Emily Gilbert, Roger Reeves, Tim Seibles, Major Jackson, Nick Flynn, Jason Koo, Patricia Spears Jones, Sara Jane Stoner, Kelly Ginger, Star Black, Diane Seuss, Nathan McClain, Robert Pinsky, Derrick Brown, Constantine Jones, Tina Chang, Rowan Ricardo Phillips, Kwame Dawes, and Mahogany L. Browne for the workshops and support!

To Thomas Lux: one of my biggest supporters and mentors—a brilliant, luminous soul who put me on the path to this book—I hope you can see what your guidance has sparked, wherever you are!

To Matthew Burgess: my first mentor and guide who taught me to embrace both the big and small words I willed onto the page and into the world, love you Professir!

To Julie Sheehan: who threw her hat in the ring and got me fellowshipped-up at Stony Brook Southampton—who supported the madness that shaped this book!

To Natalie Diaz: you read my book when it was just a sliver of a thesis. Thank you for paving the way for this!

To Shira Erlichman, who heard the music I played in these poems and understood, love you and thanks!

Alexis, Alana, Sana, Siri, Stephanie, Alex, and Marie: thanks for expanding my Lil' Universe!

Natalya, Jody, and Denise: thanks for reading and critiquing my mischief! Love you ladies!

Erica, Helene, Margaret, Rooney, and Sophia: thanks for the impromptu workshops!

Big shout out to Gwynn-Friendly, Jesse Katz, Vic, Jon Riccio; Ed, Nicole, Roxanna, and the Kearns Army who always believed in me and my words! Big love to the Suffragette City Zine crew, Jamie Frey and the Whiskey Coke Crew, Sophie, Afua, Nicole, Lucinda, Cameron, Will, and my peers!

To R, thank you for helping me with Dad!

Finally, the biggest love to my family:

Jon, Josh, Tiff, K, this book is as much yours as it is mine!

Auntie Meg, Auntie Ann, Tyler, Uncle Gerard, Uncle Tony, and the rest: thanks for your support and love!

Mom: you supported me and watched as poetry evolved from a hobby to a life path. You saw me through these years and the tears they brought with them. Words aren't enough and they never will be.

Jordan E. Franklin is a Black poet from Brooklyn, NY. An alumna of Brooklyn College, she earned her MFA from Stony Brook Southampton, where she served as a Turner Fellow. Her work has appeared in *The Southampton Review, Breadcrumbs, easy paradise, Tinderbox Poetry Journal, Frontier Poetry Journal*, and elsewhere. Her first chapbook, *boys in the electric age*, is forthcoming from Tolsun Books in summer 2021.